IMAGES
of America

FOREST HILL CEMETERY

On the Cover: Forest Hill was founded in 1870. Separate sections make up the 50 acres of land. The area pictured is known as Briar Hill, set across from the cemetery's Arch Bridge. This photograph is from the book *Scranton, Illustrated, Published in Twelve Parts*, from H.R. Page and Co. in 1890. (Courtesy of the Albright Memorial Library.)

IMAGES
of America

FOREST HILL CEMETERY

Margo L. Azzarelli and Marnie Azzarelli

ARCADIA
PUBLISHING

ISBN 978-1-4671-2835-3

Published by Arcadia Publishing
Charleston, South Carolina

Printed in the United States of America

Library of Congress Control Number: 2017952990

For all general information, please contact Arcadia Publishing:
Telephone 843-853-2070
Fax 843-853-0044
E-mail sales@arcadiapublishing.com
For customer service and orders:
Toll-Free 1-888-313-2665

Visit us on the Internet at www.arcadiapublishing.com

To Norma Reese, a woman whose selfless mission in life is the preservation of history

Contents

Acknowledgments 6
Introduction 7
1. Breaking Ground 9
2. Old Soldiers Never Die 19
3. The Sung and Unsung 47
4. Cemetery Ephemera and Memorabilia 73
5. Always Remembered 85
6. Organizations 115

ACKNOWLEDGMENTS

Thank you first and foremost to Norma Reese; without her endless knowledge and help, this book would not have been possible, and thanks also goes to the Forest Hill Cemetery Association.

We would also like to thank our editor, Angel Hisnanick, for all her help and encouragement. We are grateful to the families of the residents buried in the Forest Hill Cemetery for sharing their stories with us.

Last but not least, thank you to our family members, Dominick, Donna, and Christine, and to our four-legged family members, Bella, Callie, Agent Scully, and Phoebe Snow, for all their love and wet-nosed kisses.

INTRODUCTION

The boast of Heraldry, the pomp of Power,
And all that Beauty, all that Wealth e'er gave,
Await, alike, th' inevitable hour;
The paths of Glory lead but to the Grave.

—Gray's Elegy

Early in 1870, George Sanderson, Elisha Phinney, William Breck, and J.A. Robertson, with J. Gardner Sanderson and George S. Kingsbury, purchased 50 acres of land from the Pennsylvania Coal Company, which now comprises the Forest Hill Cemetery. During those days, the only public burial place in the city of Scranton was the Pine Brook Cemetery, which had become overcrowded and unfit for future burials.

The following quote from the original trustees clarifies their reasoning for the founding of this beautiful cemetery:

> The great necessity for a cemetery, to meet a want which has been sorely felt by the citizens of Scranton, has been for several years earnestly expressed by occasional demonstrations in public meetings, called for the purpose of maturing some plan to secure to the public an appropriate and honored resting place for the dead. The failure of these attempts here, is but the repetition of a similar struggle experienced by most communities similarly situated; and this to, notwithstanding the hallowed associations cherished for those of our relations and friends taken from us by death and the sympathy expressed in all intelligent and Christian communities in the affliction which death entails.
>
> The hindrances in this community to the founding of a cemetery, which should be both eminently appropriate and creditable, have not been from want of disposition, interest or appreciation, but rather in the difficulty of securing suitable and convenient grounds, in the development of a plan likely to be successful in securing unity of action, and the tendency, generally prevalent to the postpone till the messenger of death crosses our threshold. The Pine Brook Burying Ground has answered its purpose; but its present demands of all, having in mind the improvement and future maintenance of the cemetery, in which all, the single grave owner and the largest lot owner, share alike.

An act of incorporation had been granted, constituting a company by the name of the Forest Hill Cemetery Association of Scranton to hold and manage the property. The cemetery would later become part of Dunmore, Pennsylvania. The affairs of the cemetery association would be managed by a board of not less than five trustees, and elections were held annually. The act of incorporation also authorized the land acquired by the association to be disposed of and used exclusively and forever for the burial of the dead.

According to the original trustees, few cemeteries during this time period enclosed a greater area of land than Forest Hill. At first, the trustees thought it would have been wiser to include less ground, but to do so might hinder enlarging it in the future. They also took into account that additional land might not be available to purchase, if needed at another time. With pride, the trustees undertook the work of founding the cemetery for the community, because it was an evident necessity that some ample and decent provisions should be made for burying the dead at once. The failure of repeated attempts to locate a cemetery and the increasing urgency for one appealed strongly to the community, whether successful or not, would now entirely depend on that same community.

The association had been liberal in the expenditure of their means, in order to have the cemetery ready for burial at the earliest date. The purchase of lots from citizens would complete all their work. The trustees earnestly and respectfully called upon the public to aid them in their work. It would require additional money to make all the improvements upon the ground, necessary to meet public expectations, especially to beautify it, and this could only be done if members of the community came forward early on and purchased lots. The acres, where Forest Hill was founded, were mainly covered in woods and included Meadow Brook, which ran through it. Driving avenues were laid out, stone bridges were built across the brook, and the rest of the cemetery was developed into differently named sections. By 1899, there had been 934 lot holders, 1,439 single plot holders, and 4,416 internments.

It has always been the aim of succeeding trustees to carry out and exemplify the ideals of the founders, and whether they have succeeded in their task can best be judged by a visit to the cemetery.

If you did happen to take a walk through the cemetery, which is right next to Dunmore High School's athletic field, behind the former Scranton School for the Deaf and right down the road from Marywood University, you would see a cemetery that more resembles a national park instead of a place for eternal rest. It is no wonder how the cemetery got its name, as there are over four dozen different kinds of trees and shrubs, plus bushes that produce blackberries, raspberries, blueberries, strawberries, and grapes. There are also over six dozen kinds of wildflowers and numerous ferns, fungi, moss, and lichen that cover the grounds. Next to the flora, the fauna is also in great variety at the cemetery. Dozens of butterflies, moths, grasshoppers, bees, beetles, and various other insects call Forest Hill their home. Over 30 different kinds of birds fly through and sometimes roost at the cemetery, along with 20 different kinds of animals, from toads to deer to the occasional dog walking alongside its owner. Since the first plans of development were set in place, the dirt driving avenues were paved, and the Meadow Brook is no longer an active stream, but many members of the community still walk through or pay their respects in a cemetery known for its peaceful serenity. While it is still a place to inter ones who have passed on, Forest Hill is almost always teeming with life.

As stated before, the cemetery was developed into different sections with names like "Pine Hill," "Briar Hill," "The Circle," "The Odd Fellows," and "The Hill." These sections are then split into divisions A through M. An entire map of the cemetery shows all of these section names, plus the names of each road and every lot in the caretaker's office, which is situated near the entrance of the cemetery and is next to the building called the Lodge. This Lodge was built in 1872 and was occupied by five care-taking families. The original office for the cemetery was located in George Sanderson's bank and law office. During the early-20th century, the office was built next to the Lodge, both of which are still standing and in use today. All of the burial records of every person interred in the cemetery are kept in a safe that was originally in Sanderson's bank. The desk, which sits in the middle of the office, also belonged to Sanderson's bank.

Today, the cemetery has lived up to its early expectations through its beauty and depth of colorful history held behind its gates. With over 18,000 residents from about 39 states (including Washington, DC) and 34 countries, Forest Hill Cemetery has become what the original founders hoped it would be: a cherished institution of the community.

One

Breaking Ground

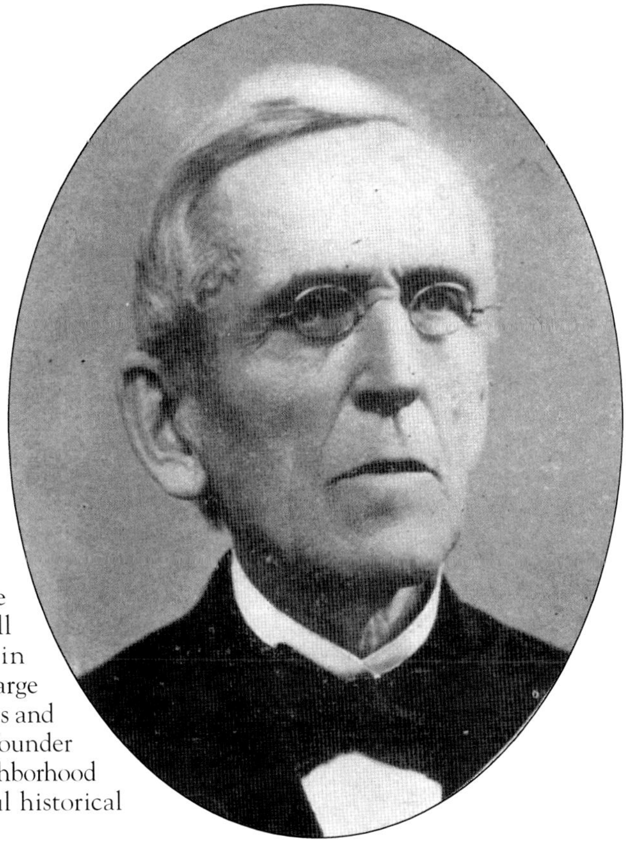

George Sanderson was one of the original six founders of Forest Hill Cemetery. Sanderson arrived in Scranton in 1854; he purchased a large tract of land where he opened streets and laid out lots. He is known as the founder and developer of Green Ridge, a neighborhood in Scranton noted for its beautiful historical mansions. (Author's collection.)

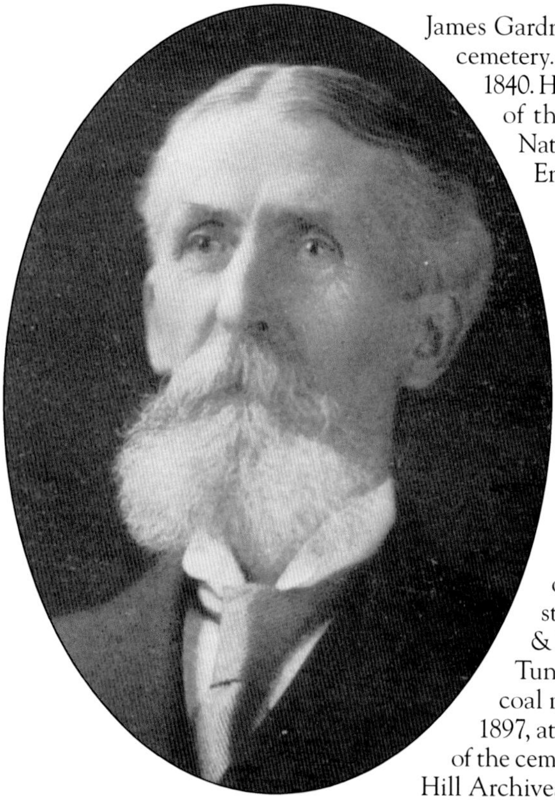

James Gardner Sanderson was another founder of the cemetery. He was born in Towanda, Pennsylvania, in 1840. He worked as a civil engineer and was a member of the American Society of Civil Engineers, National Geographic Society, and the Scranton Engineers' Club. (Author's collection.)

Another of the cemetery's founders is Elisha Phinney. In 1856, he came to Scranton and opened a wholesale flour and feed business on Franklin Avenue. He was one of the first stockholders of the Delaware, Lackawanna & Western Railroad. He built the Factoryville Tunnel and, later in life, dabbled a bit in the coal mining business. Phinney died on June 20, 1897, at the age of 82. Pictured is his original share of the cemetery with his signature. (Courtesy of Forest Hill Archives.)

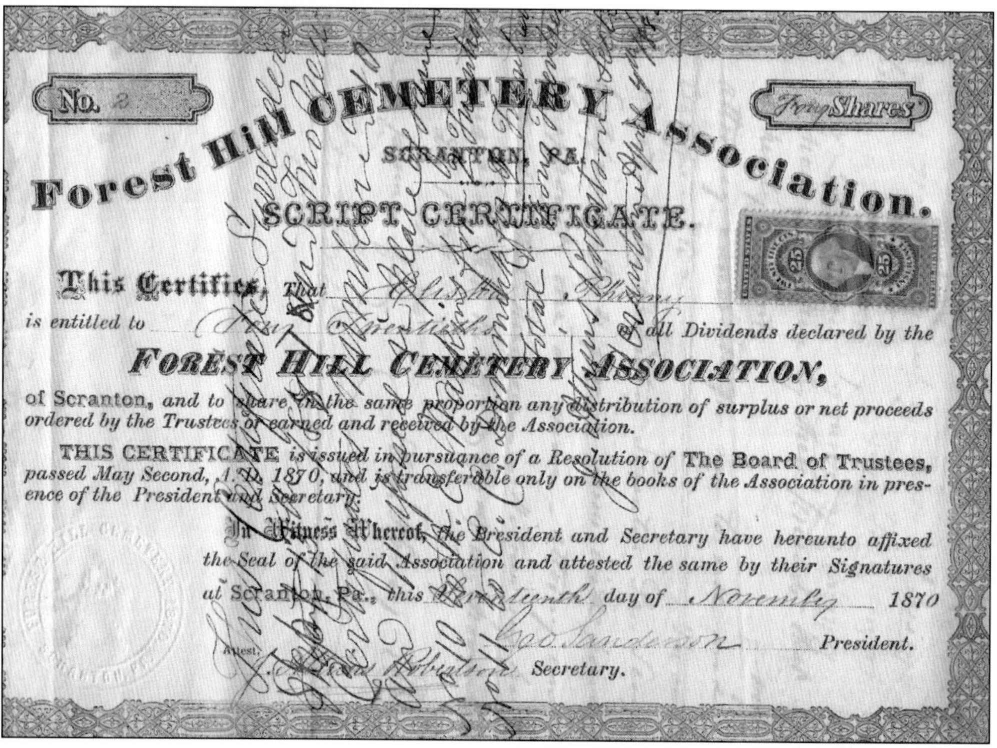

No. 2

Four Shares

Forest Hill CEMETERY Association.

SCRANTON, PA.

SCRIPT CERTIFICATE.

This Certifies, That Elisha Phinney is entitled to Four Twentieths of all Dividends declared by the

FOREST HILL CEMETERY ASSOCIATION,

of Scranton, and to share in the same proportion any distribution of surplus or net proceeds ordered by the Trustees or earned and received by the Association.

THIS CERTIFICATE is issued in pursuance of a Resolution of The Board of Trustees, passed May Second, A.D. 1870, and is transferable only on the books of the Association in presence of the President and Secretary.

In Witness Whereof, the President and Secretary have hereunto affixed the Seal of the said Association and attested the same by their Signatures at Scranton, Pa., this [illegible]teenth day of November 1870

Geo. Sanderson President.

Attest: [illegible] Robertson Secretary.

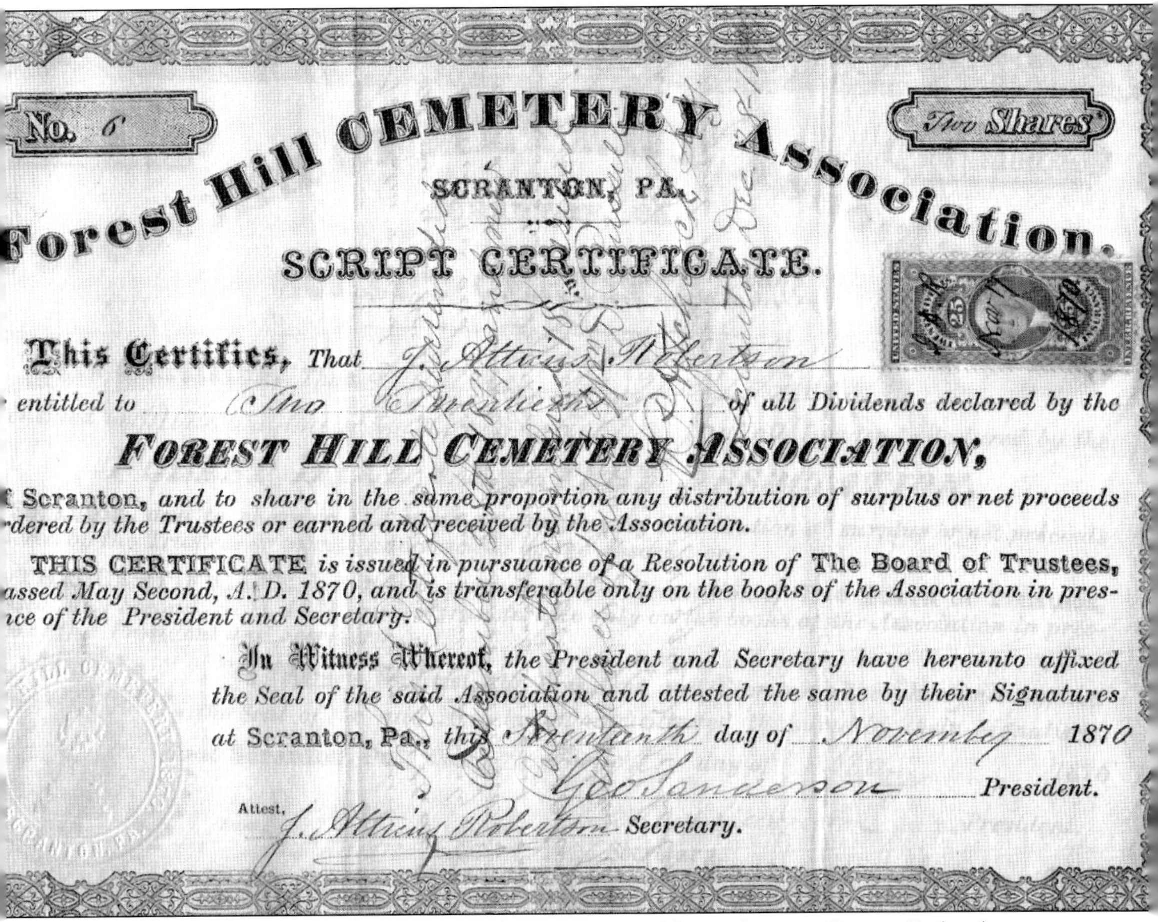
No. 6

Two Shares

Forest Hill CEMETERY Association.

SCRANTON, PA.

SCRIPT CERTIFICATE.

This Certifies, That J. Atticus Robertson

entitled to Two Twentieths of all Dividends declared by the

FOREST HILL CEMETERY ASSOCIATION,

Scranton, and to share in the same proportion any distribution of surplus or net proceeds
dered by the Trustees or earned and received by the Association.

THIS CERTIFICATE is issued in pursuance of a Resolution of The Board of Trustees,
assed May Second, A. D. 1870, and is transferable only on the books of the Association in pres-
ice of the President and Secretary.

In Witness Whereof, the President and Secretary have hereunto affixed the Seal of the said Association and attested the same by their Signatures at Scranton, Pa., this Seventeenth day of November 1870

Geo Sanderson President.

Attest, J. Atticus Robertson Secretary.

J. Atticus Robinson was a civil and consulting engineer. He was born in Greece. Before he came to Scranton, he had been working with Frederick Law Olmsted on the development of Central Park in New York City. This is the original share certificate issued in Robinson's name. (Courtesy of Forest Hill Archives.)

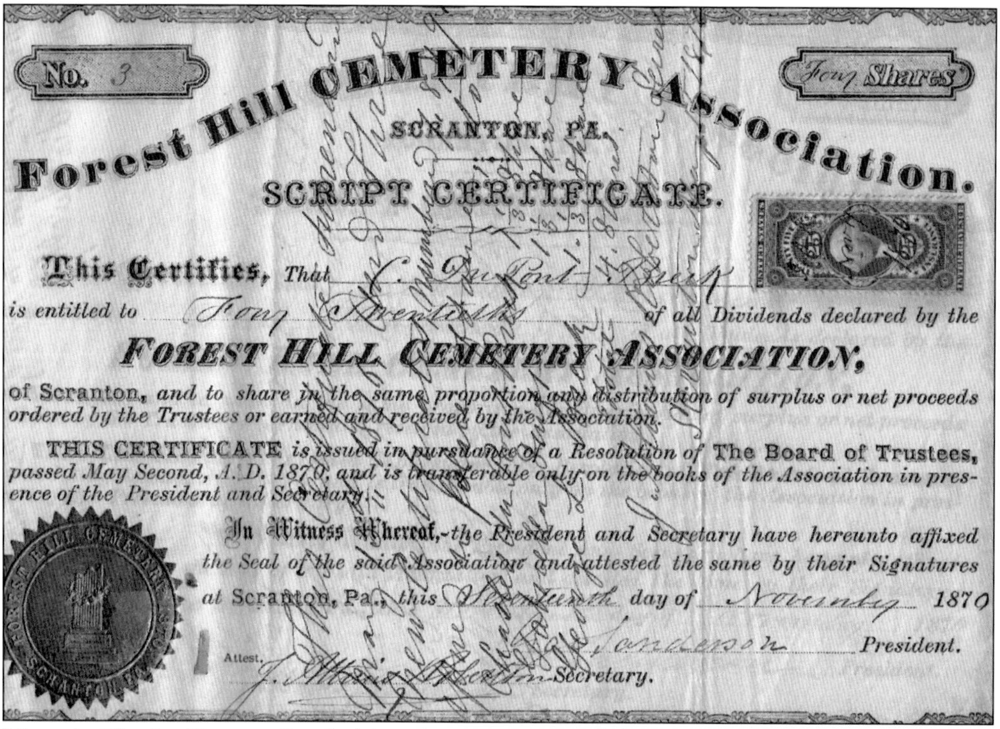

Though Charles Dupont Breck (above) was not one of the original founders, he took over immediately upon his father's death, shortly after the cemetery's incorporation. William Breck is the only founder who is not buried in Forest Hill. George S. Kingsbury's (below) interest in developing a new much-needed cemetery led him to becoming involved with the founding of Forest Hill. Kingsbury was born in Towanda, Pennsylvania; he relocated to Scranton in 1853 and showed interest in the banking house of George Sanderson and Company. He was quickly made partner. "G.S.," as he was called by his friends, never married. He made his home at the Hotel Jermyn and was considered a man of many striking characteristics. He rose the same time every day and did everything with regularity. A creature of habit, G.S. Kingsbury remained a bachelor until his death on March 30, 1903, of Bright's disease, a chronic inflammation of the kidneys. (Both, courtesy of Forest Hill Archives.)

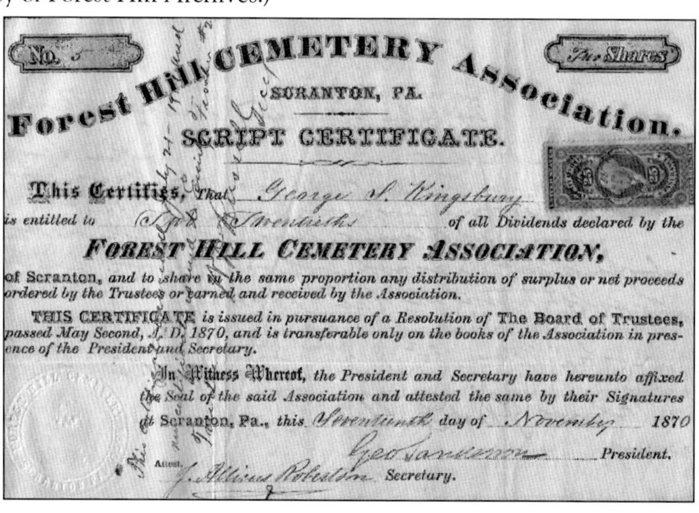

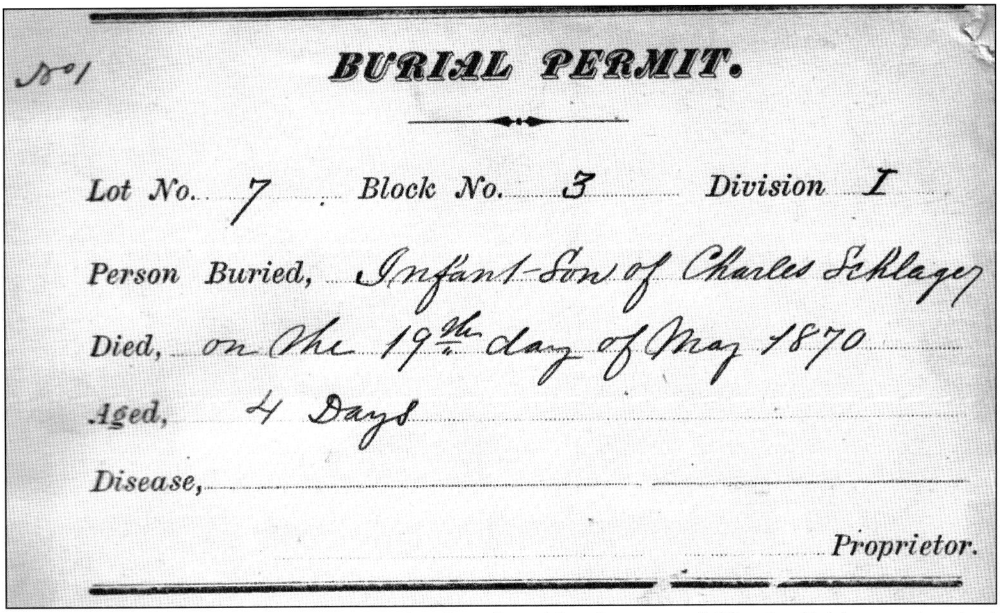

No 1

BURIAL PERMIT.

Lot No. 7 Block No. 3 Division I

Person Buried, Infant Son of Charles Schlager

Died, on the 19th day of May 1870

Aged, 4 Days

Disease,

Proprietor.

The first burial in Forest Hill was for the four-day old infant son of Charles Schlager, who died on May 19, 1870. The burial permit pictured states that the child was laid to rest in Lot No. 7, Block No. 7, Division I. (Courtesy of Forest Hill Archives.)

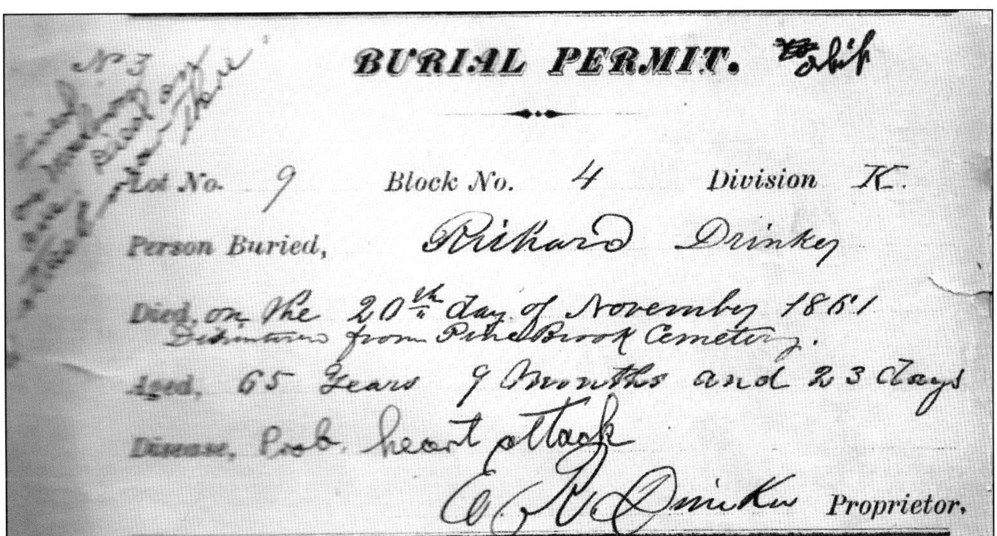

No 3

BURIAL PERMIT.

Lot No. 9 Block No. 4 Division K.

Person Buried, Richard Drinker

Died, on the 20th day of November 1861
Disinterred from Pine Brook Cemetery.

Aged, 65 Years 9 Months and 23 Days

Disease, Prob. heart attack

Proprietor.

Richard Drinker was 65 years old when he passed on November 20, 1861, of a probable heart attack. He was a resident of Dunmore. His was the first reburial from the Pine Brook Cemetery to Forest Hill. (Courtesy of Forest Hill Archives.)

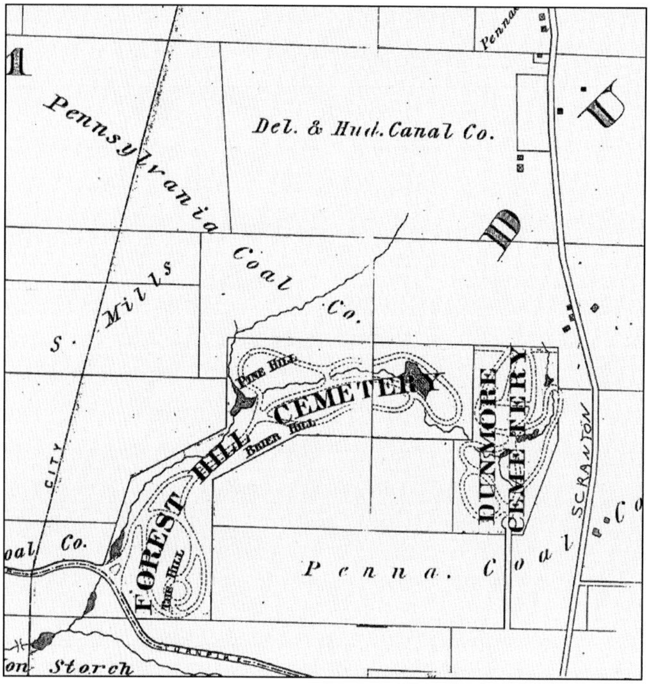

The map of Forest Hill shows that the land was once owned by the Pennsylvania Coal Company. As seen from the layout, Forest Hill borders two other cemeteries: the Dunmore Cemetery and the Jewish Cemetery. (Courtesy of Forest Hill Archives.)

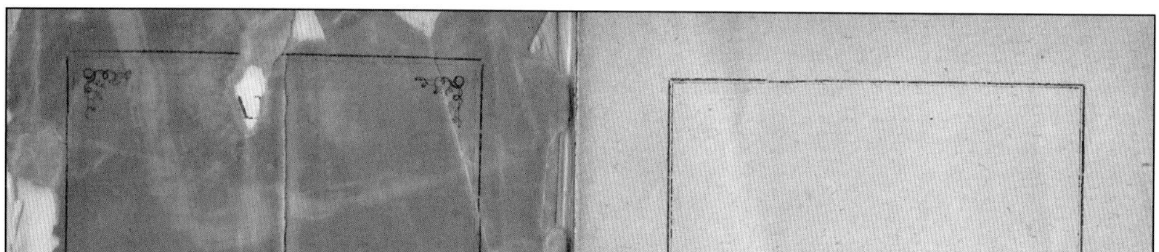

This photograph shows the booklet that contains the original charter, bylaws, rules, and regulations of Forest Hill when it was incorporated in April 1870. The booklet was printed in both English and German because many people of German origin are buried in Forest Hill. The archives contain both versions. (Courtesy of Forest Hill Archives.)

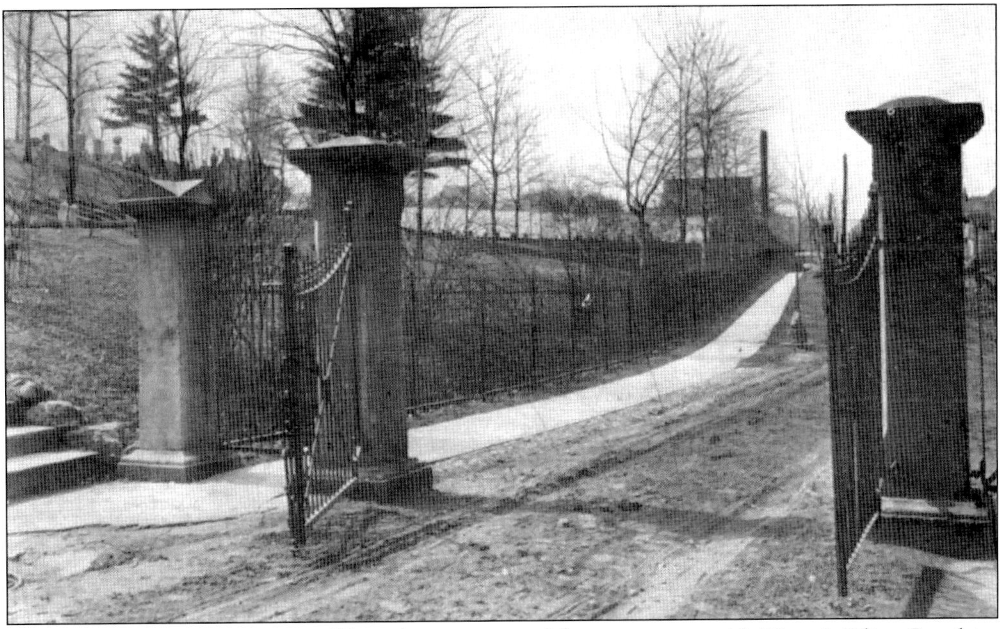

The gates leading into Forest Hill have been preserved for many years with Dixon's Silica-Graphite Paint. The entrance to the cemetery displays its rustic beauty. The original trustees felt there was a great need for a cemetery by the citizens of Scranton and surrounding areas. At the time, the only public burial place in the Electric City was the old Pine Brook Cemetery, which had become crowded and unfit for use. (Both, courtesy of Forest Hill Archives.)

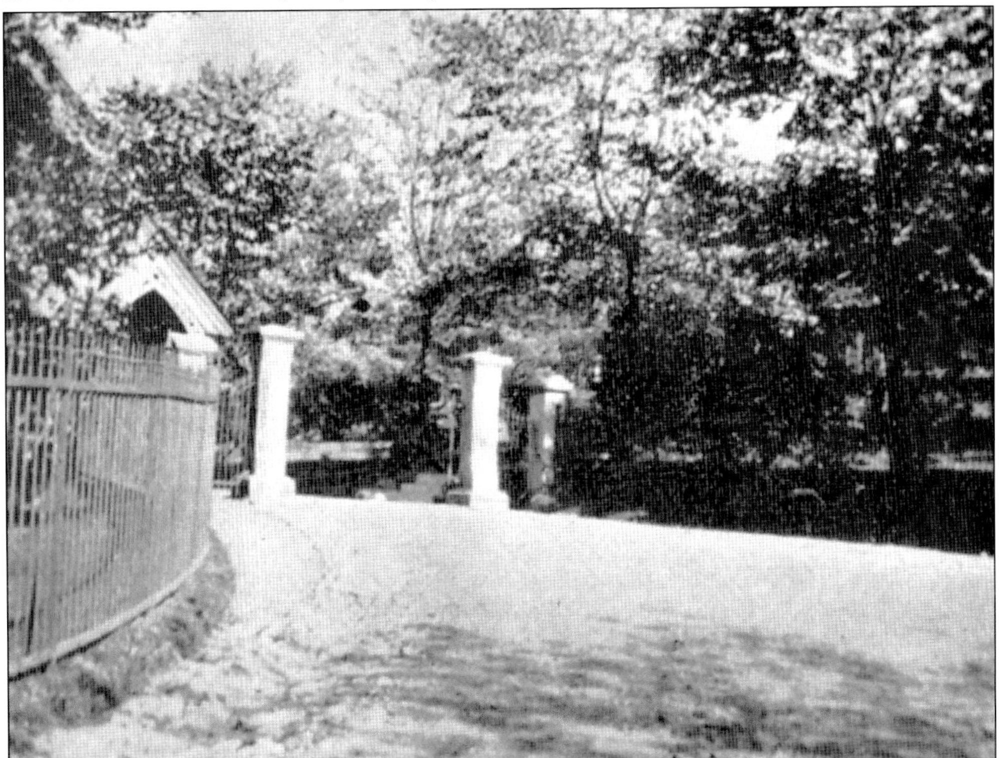

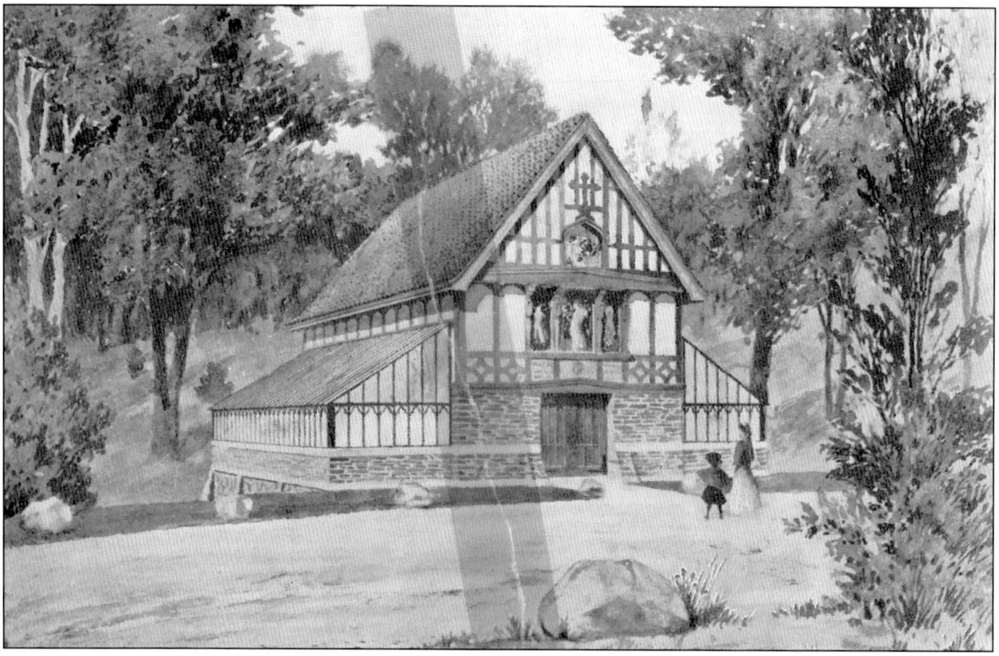

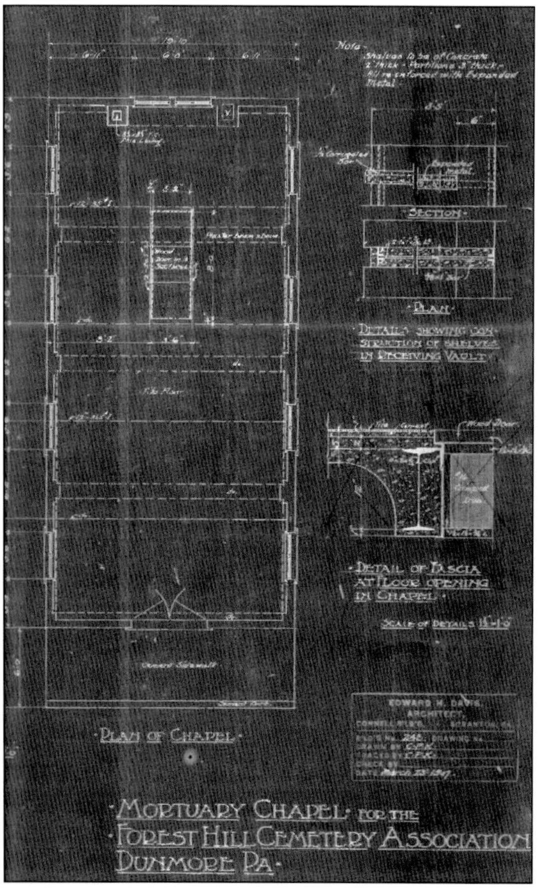

The original plan for the chapel is shown above. Edward H. Davis, who is buried in the cemetery, was the architect. The building was built in 1907; it was made of concrete block and steel rods, a first of its kind. In the basement are catacombs that, for various reasons, such as poor weather or until the family bought a lot, held the bodies until they would be buried. There is also a trap floor in the chapel used to lower the bodies into the basement. Pictured left are the original blueprints of the chapel and receiving vault. (Both, courtesy of Forest Hill Archives.)

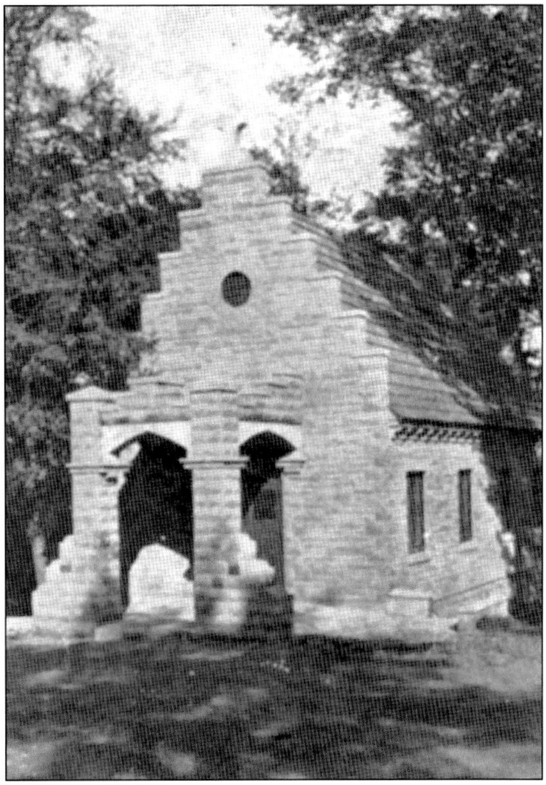

The pamphlet of the rules and regulations for the chapel and receiving vault were at one time given to everyone who purchased a lot in the cemetery. Pictured are the chapel and receiving vault. (Both, courtesy of Forest Hill Archives.)

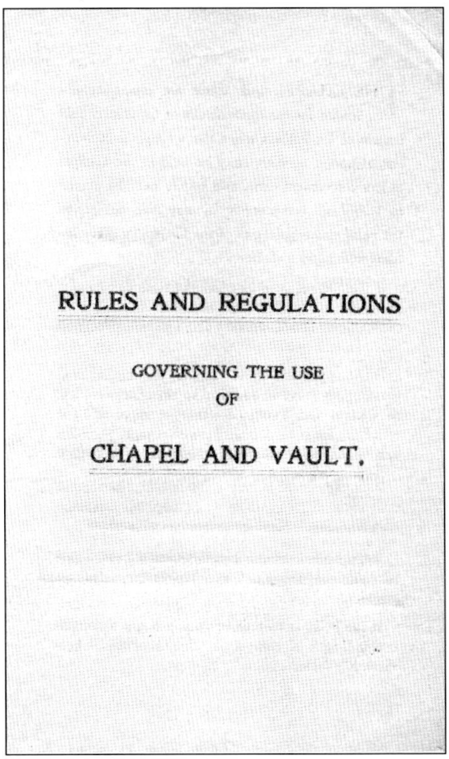

RULES AND REGULATIONS

GOVERNING THE USE
OF

CHAPEL AND VAULT.

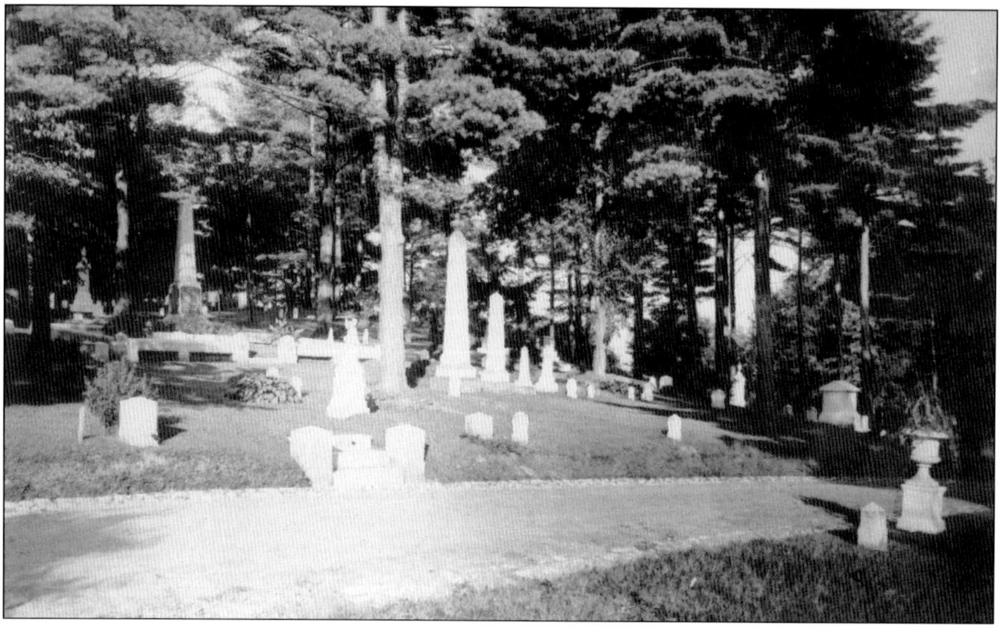

The different sections of Forest Hill include Pine Hill, Briar Hill, Upper Brook Side, and the Grand Army of the Republic, where the Civil War soldiers are buried. The Pine Hill section of the cemetery is among the oldest. Many of the area's pioneers, the same men and women who in life had helped make the city flourish, are buried beneath its soil. (Both, courtesy of Forest Hill Archives.)

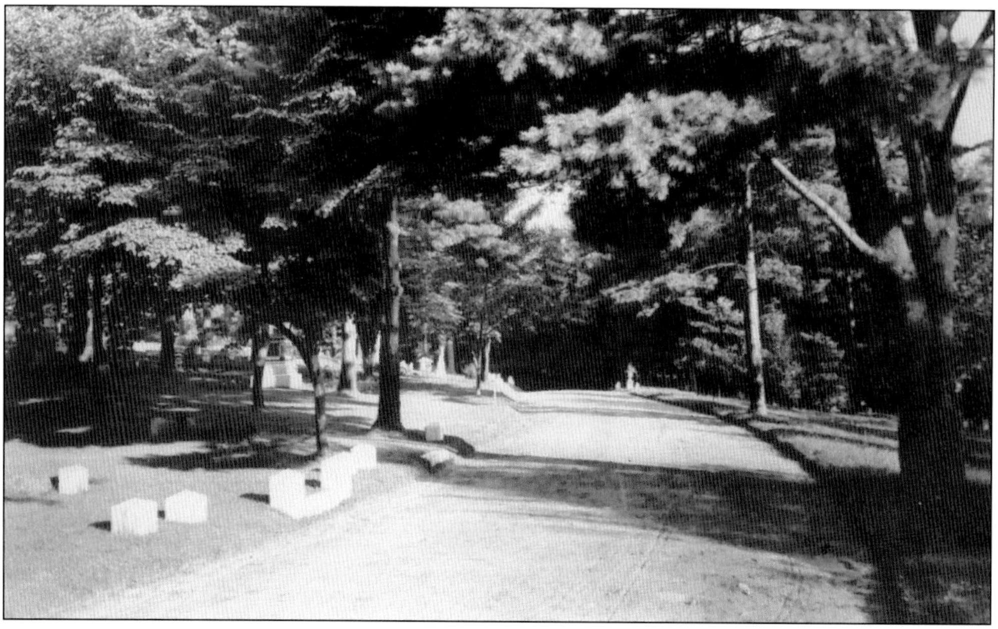

Two

Old Soldiers Never Die

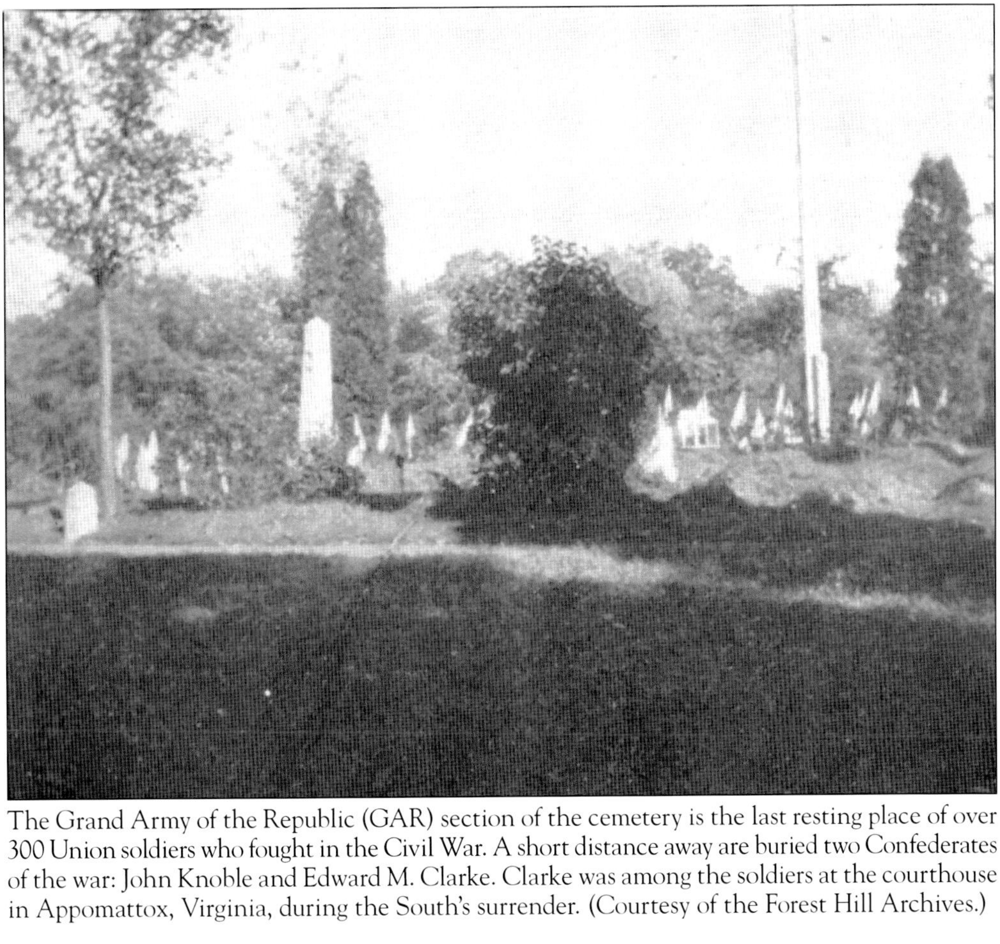

The Grand Army of the Republic (GAR) section of the cemetery is the last resting place of over 300 Union soldiers who fought in the Civil War. A short distance away are buried two Confederates of the war: John Knoble and Edward M. Clarke. Clarke was among the soldiers at the courthouse in Appomattox, Virginia, during the South's surrender. (Courtesy of the Forest Hill Archives.)

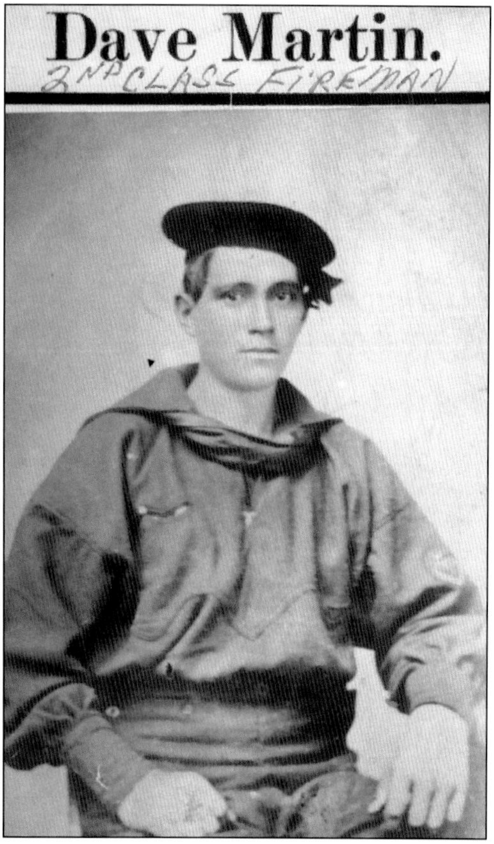

David Martin Sr. was born in Dundee, Scotland on September 19, 1840. He was a 2nd class fireman in the US Navy during the Civil War from December of 1861 to December of 1864. Martin was a machinist who lived in Scranton until he passed away from a stroke in August of 1906. At left is David Martin's enlistment picture, and below is a picture of him later in life. (Both, courtesy of Joe Long.)

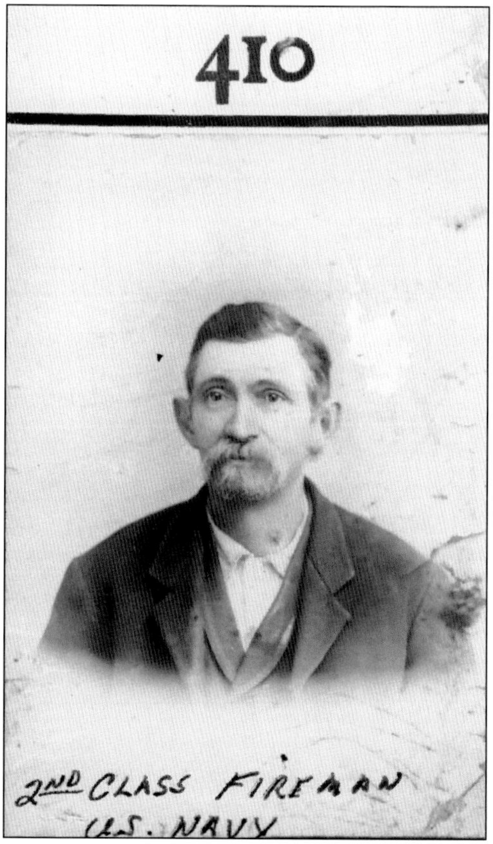

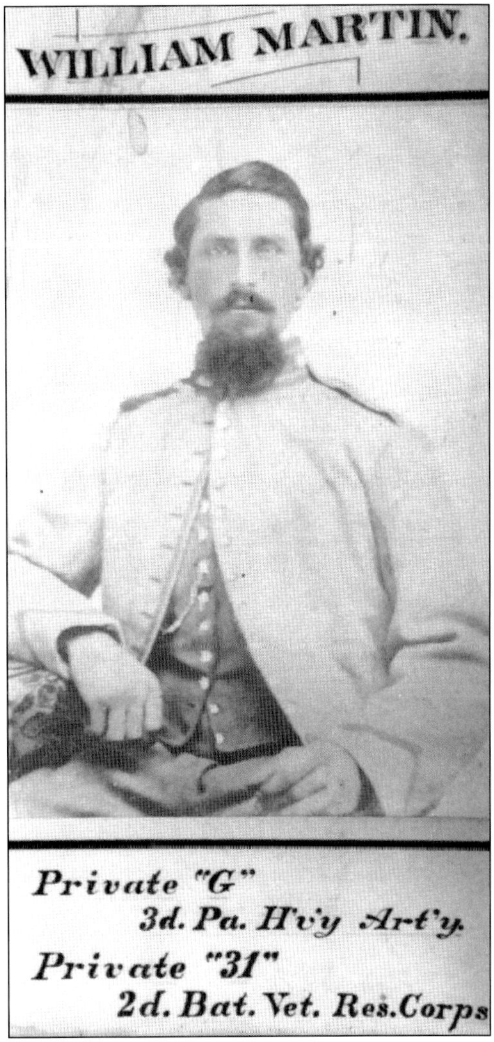

William Martin was born on June 14, 1834, in Yorkshire, England. He served as a private in Battery G of the 152nd, 3rd Pennsylvania Heavy Artillery during the Civil War. He started his service in November 1862 but was transferred to the 2nd Battery Veterans Reserve Corps. 31st P Regiment in 1864. His service ended on November 7, 1865. For the rest of his life, Martin was a church sexton and gardener in Norwood, Ohio. He was also a charter member of GAR Post No. 139 in 1879. He passed on when he was 82 years old in 1916. At right is William Martin's enlistment picture, and below is a picture of him later in life. (Both, courtesy of Joe Long.)

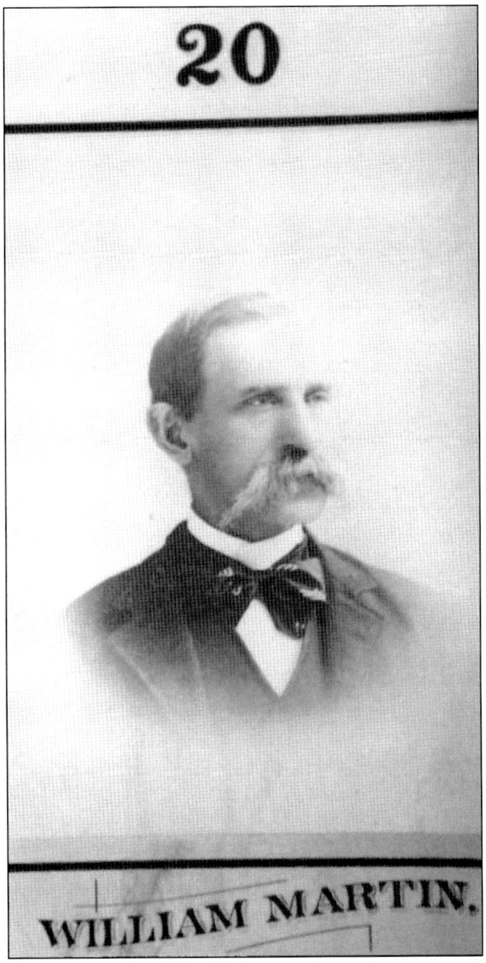

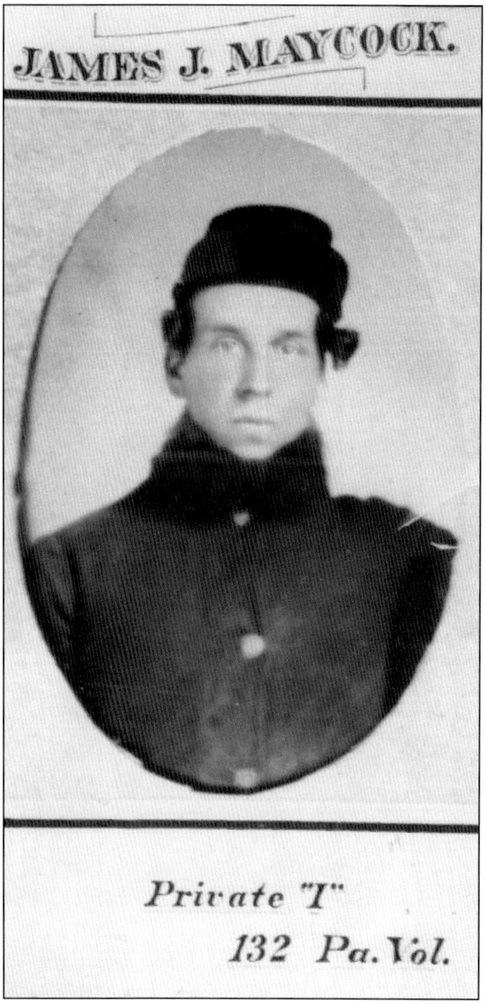

James Maycock was born in Coventry, England. Before he came to America, he served as a soldier and sailor during the Crimean War. He served as a private in Company I, 132nd Pennsylvania Volunteer "Railroad Guards" during the Civil War from August 1862 to May 1863. During the Battle of Antietam, he suffered a gunshot wound to his face, which resulted in part of his jaw being blown away. After the war, "Jem" Maycock became a superintendent of the Delaware, Lackawanna & Western Railroad (DL&W) Wrecking Department. He was also a charter member and the junior vice commander of Lt. Ezra S. Griffin Post, No. 139 GAR. When he died from an abscess caused from a fall in 1884, members of Col. Monies Post and Ezra Griffin Post attended his funeral. At left is James Maycock's enlistment picture, and below is a picture of him later in life. (Both, courtesy of Joe Long.)

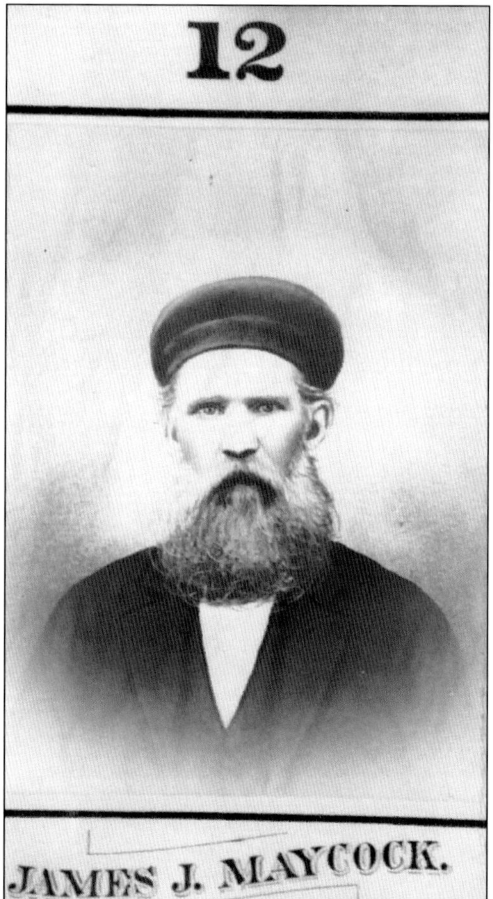

Jackson Merryweather was born into slavery on the Fauquier estate in Fauquier County, Virginia, in 1848. Merryweather was probably living in Scranton when he enlisted as a private in Company C of the 24th US Colored Troops during the Civil War. He served until 1865 and then returned to Scranton to open his own barbershop on Wyoming Avenue, which he ran until his death from nephritis in 1909. GAR Post No. 139 attended his funeral at Forest Hill Cemetery with Smith B. Mott, Halsey Lathrope, F.C. Rozelle, D.J. Newman, James Connolly, and J.E. Newman as pallbearers. (Courtesy of Joe Long.)

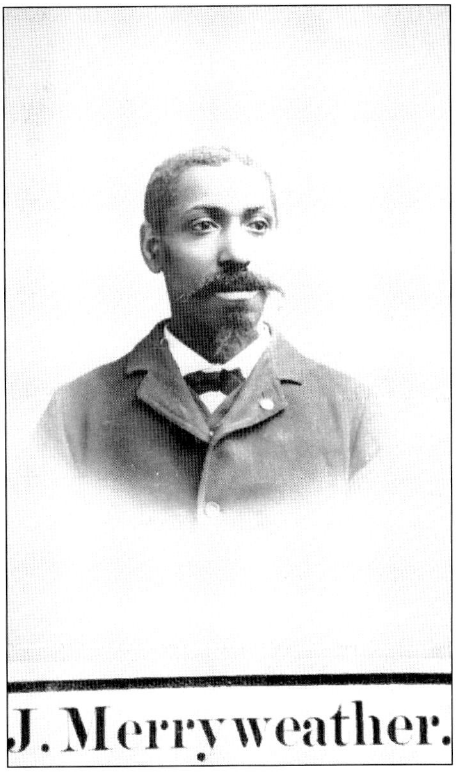

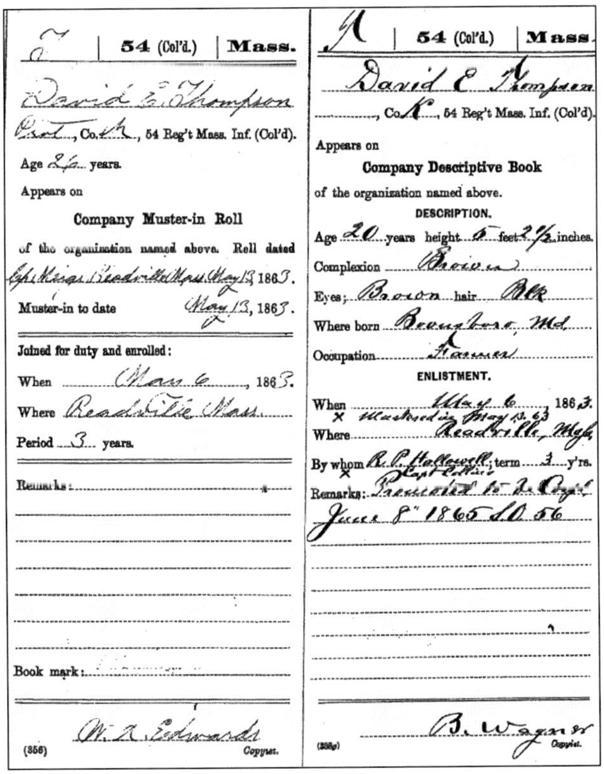

T | 54 (Col'd.) | Mass.

David E. Thompson

Pvt., Co. K, 54 Reg't Mass. Inf. (Col'd).

Age 26 years.

Appears on

Company Muster-in Roll

of the organization named above. Roll dated

Camp Meigs Readville Mass May 13, 1863.

Muster-in to date May 13, 1863.

Joined for duty and enrolled:

When May 6, 1863.

Where Readville Mass.

Period 3 years.

Remarks:

Book mark:

W. A. Edwards
(356) Copyist.

K | 54 (Col'd.) | Mass.

David E. Thompson

Co. K, 54 Reg't Mass. Inf. (Col'd).

Appears on

Company Descriptive Book

of the organization named above.

DESCRIPTION.

Age 20 years height 5 feet 2½ inches.

Complexion Brown

Eyes; Brown hair Blk

Where born Boonsboro, Md

Occupation Farmer

ENLISTMENT.

When May 6, 1863.

× Mustered in May 13, 63

Where Readville, Mass

By whom R. P. Hallowell; term 3 y'rs.

× Capt Collins

Remarks: Promoted to 1st Sergt June 8" 1865 S.O. 56

B. Wagner
(358) Copyist.

Born in 1843, David Thompson enlisted as a private in Company K 54th Massachusetts Infantry in 1863 when, due to the Emancipation Proclamation, African American men were allowed to participate in the war. The 54th Massachusetts is known as the first official African American regiment during the Civil War. Originally led by Robert Gould Shaw, the regiment composed of over 1,000 men from different Union states. Fathers and sons flocked to enlist together, and even two sons of famed abolitionist Frederick Douglass joined. The 1989 movie *Glory* recounted the story of the 54th Massachusetts, including the battle at Fort Wagner, where 600 soldiers of the regiment, including Shaw, were killed. Thompson survived the battle and returned to Scranton, where he lived for the rest of his life. (Courtesy of Joe Long.)

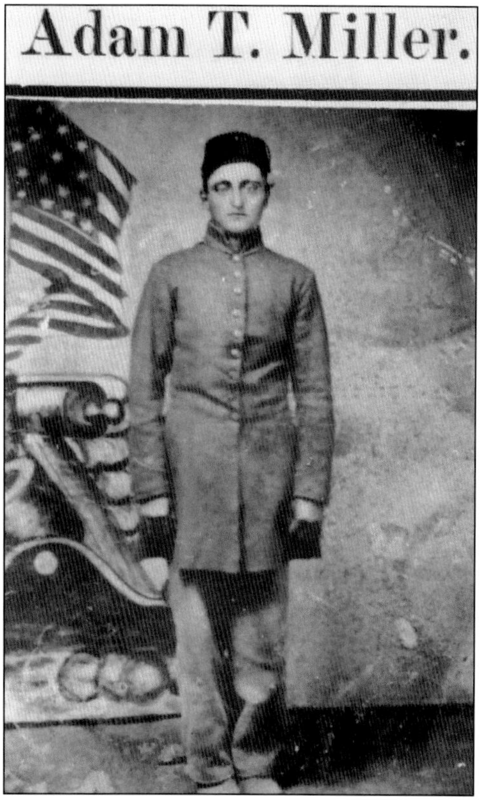

Adam Miller was born in St. Charles/ Milstadt, St. Clair County, Illinois, in either May 1846 or October 1847. He was enlisted into the Civil War as a private for Company K, 149th Illinois. He died from a stroke in 1917. (Courtesy of Joe Long.)

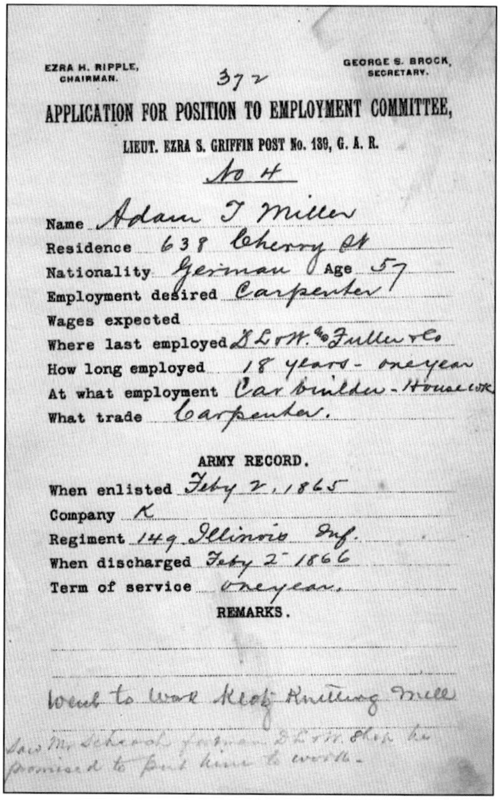

EZRA H. RIPPLE, CHAIRMAN. 372 GEORGE S. BROCK, SECRETARY.

APPLICATION FOR POSITION TO EMPLOYMENT COMMITTEE,

LIEUT. EZRA S. GRIFFIN POST No. 139, G. A. R.

No 4

Name Adam T Miller
Residence 638 Cherry St
Nationality German Age 57
Employment desired Carpenter
Wages expected
Where last employed D L & W. & Fuller & Co
How long employed 18 years - one year
At what employment Car builder - House work
What trade Carpenter.

ARMY RECORD.

When enlisted Feby 2, 1865
Company K
Regiment 149 Illinois Inf.
When discharged Feby 2 1866
Term of service one year.

REMARKS.

Went to work Kleotz Knitting Mill
Saw Mr Schroch foreman D L & W. Shop he promised to put him to work.

Pictured is Miller's application for the employment committee at the Ezra S. Griffin Post No. 139, GAR. He wanted to be employed as a carpenter as he worked for 18 years building cars for the DL&W Railroad. (Courtesy of Joe Long.)

Charles Graham was born in 1843 and served as a private in Company C, 67th Pennsylvania Volunteer Infantry. He served from February 1864 to June 1865. In 1909, he passed away from a cerebral hemorrhage. At right is Charles Graham's enlistment picture, and below is a picture of him later in life. (Courtesy of Joe Long.)

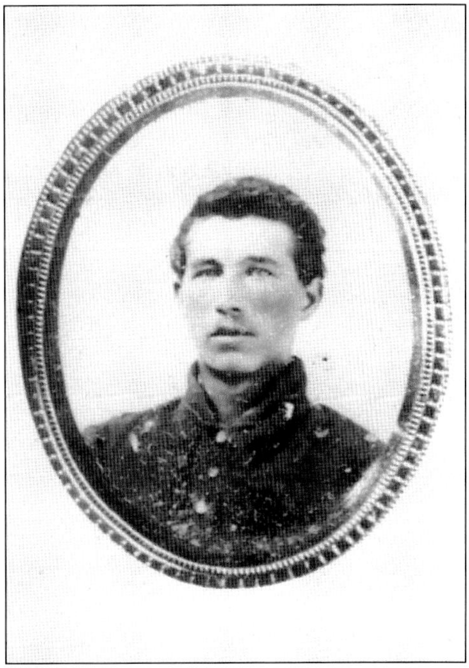

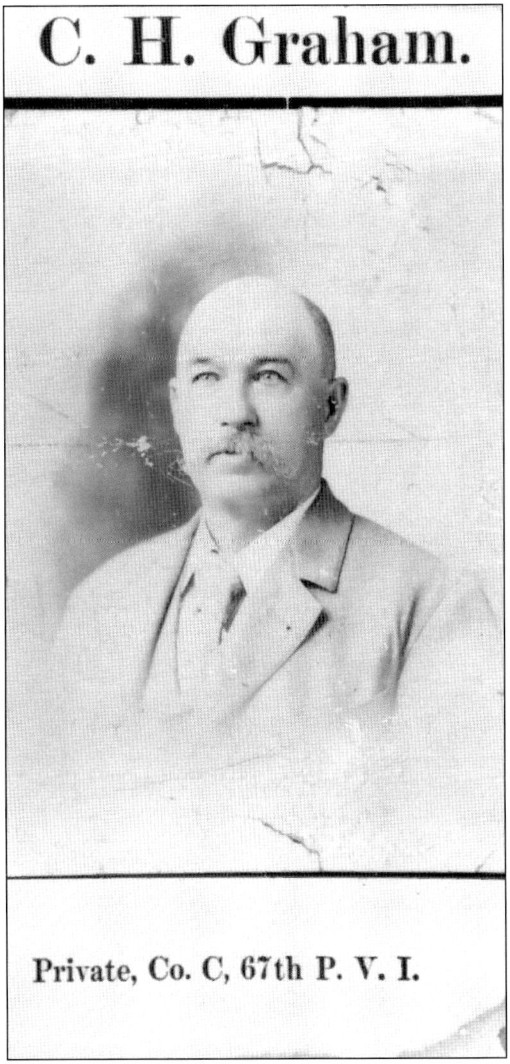

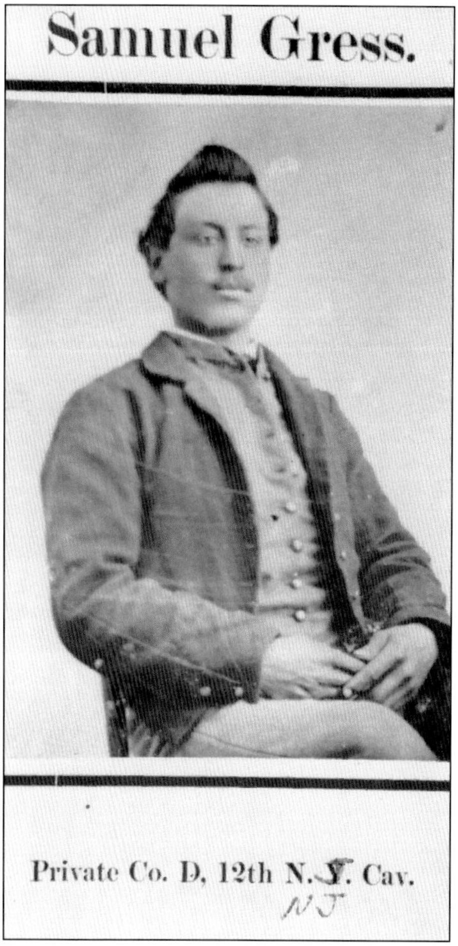

Samuel Gress was born on December 14, 1839, in Wilkes-Barre, Pennsylvania. He enlisted as a private in Company D, 12th New Jersey Calvary in November 1862. He served through the Civil War until July 1865. Gress worked as a blacksmith and lived on Jackson Street until his death on October 11, 1910, from Bright's disease, which now refers to acute or chronic nephritis. Pictured at left is Samuel Gress at his time of enlistment, and below is a picture of him later in life. (Both, courtesy of Joe Long.)

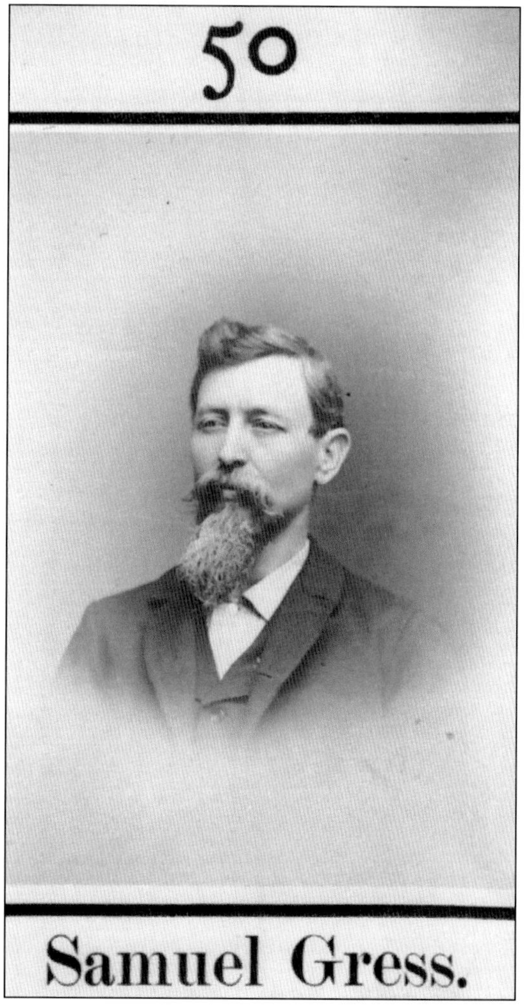

Thomas Griffith was born on January 24, 1841, in Schuylkill County, Pennsylvania. He was a miner in Scranton and enlisted into the Civil War on April 22, 1861, as a private in Company A 6th Pennsylvania Reserve Regiment (35th Pennsylvania Volunteer Infantry). At the age 68, he passed away from dropsy, otherwise known as edema due to congestive heart failure. At right is his enlistment picture, and below is a picture of him later in life. (Both, courtesy of Joe Long.)

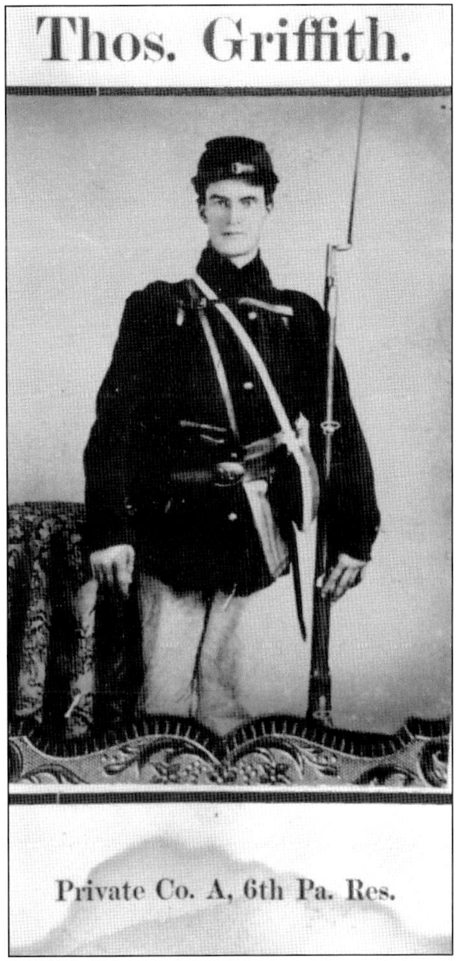

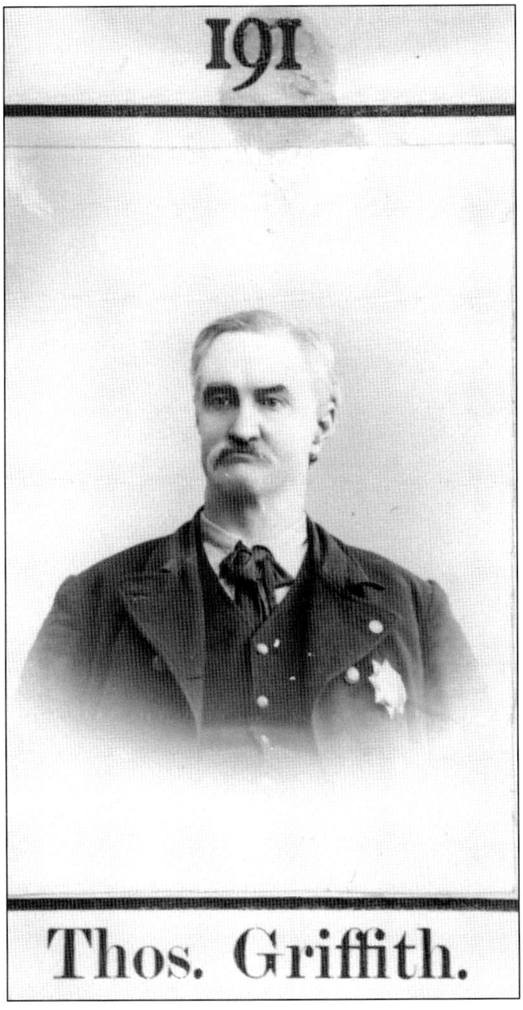

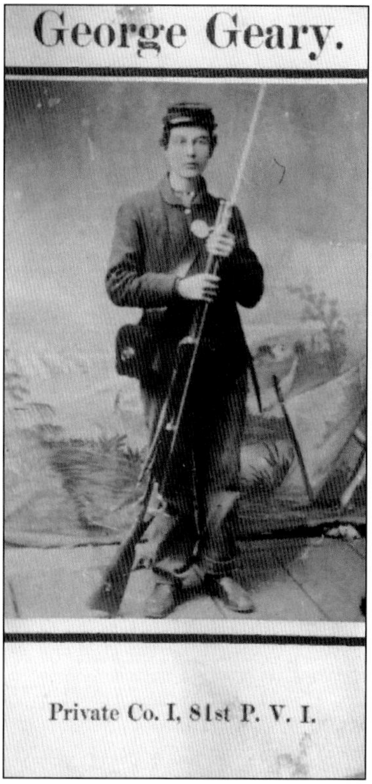

George Geary was only 15 when he enlisted to fight in the Civil War. The enlistment age, at the time, was set at 18, but many young men like Geary lied about their age. He first became a private in an independent cavalry called the "Luzerne Rangers." After that enlistment period was up, Geary kept trying to reenlist until he was taken on as a private in Company I for the 81st Pennsylvania Volunteer Infantry in 1864. In 1865, he was shot in the arm and partly deafened by explosions. He recuperated but would be hearing impaired for the rest of his life. After the war, Geary was very active in the Griffin Post No. 139 of the GAR. He actually suffered from the stroke that would end his life in the library of the GAR on March 18, 1921. At left is Geary's enlistment picture, and below is a picture of him later in life. (Both, courtesy of Joe Long.)

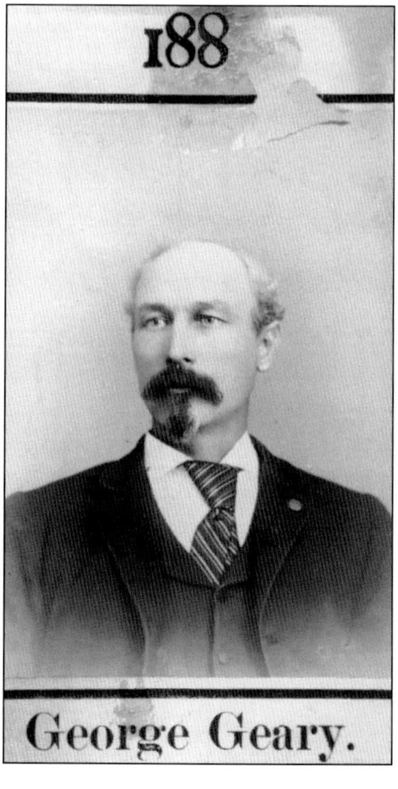

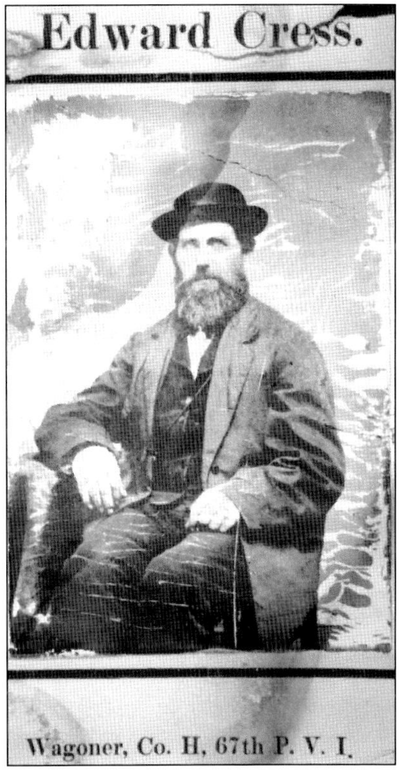

Edward Cress was born in Monroe County in 1820. During the Civil War, he was a wagoner in Company H, 67th Pennsylvania Infantry in 1862, and then a wagoner for Company H, Veteran Volunteers from 1864 until the end of the war in 1865. He worked as a flagman for the rest of his life until he died at the age of 84 in 1905. At right is a picture of Edward Cress at his time of enlistment, and below is a picture of him later in life. (Both, courtesy of Joe Long.)

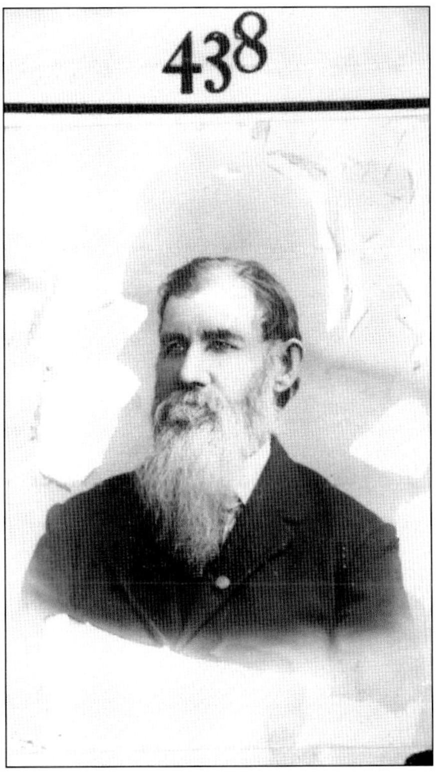

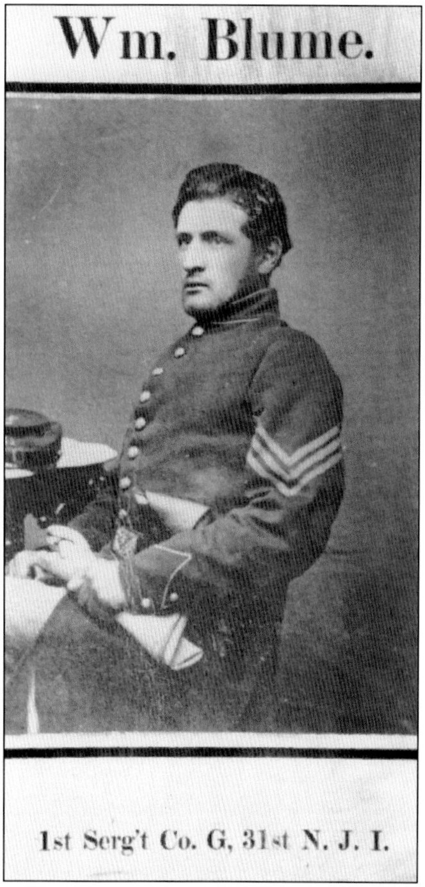

William Blume was born in Baden-Baden (or Heidelberg) Germany on April 6, 1838. During the Civil War, he was a wagoner for Company H, 67th Pennsylvania Volunteer Infantry. Blume continued his passion well after the Civil War when he opened William Blume & Son, Manufacturers of Carriages and Wagons in 1891. The factory produced light and heavy wagons and carriages, usually made to order, and was equipped with a 20-horse-powered steam engine and 35 skilled workers. The factory was located in Scranton and provided wagons and carriages locally and statewide. A special feature of the business at that time was that they also repaired broken wagons and carriages. Blume died from chronic nephritis in Scranton, Pennsylvania, on December 12, 1908. At left is Blume's enlistment picture, and below is a picture of him later in life. (Both, courtesy of Joe Long.)

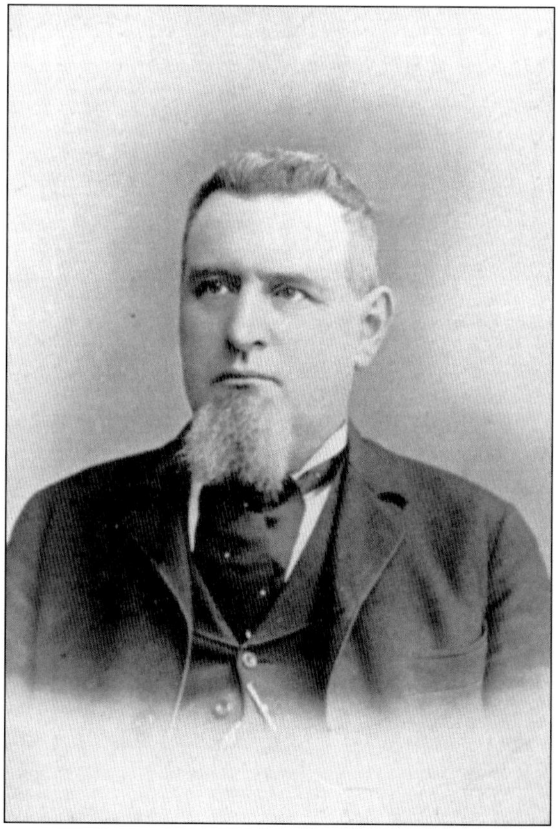

William F. Albro enlisted for the war one day after his 24th birthday on May 21, 1861. He was first mustered in as a private for Company F, 28th regiment, New York volunteer infantry. Albro was one of the few privates who had the privilege of speaking with Pres. Abraham Lincoln, which he considered the greatest honor of his life. He was soon mustered out of service and reenlisted in February 1862 and was assigned to the 105th New York regiment, Company E. He participated in the battle of Cedar Mountain, Rappahannock River and Junction, Second Bull Run, Antietam, Gettysburg, and Fredericksburg. He was discharged on February 14, 1864, but immediately reenlisted in Capt. Charles Mink's battery for a three-year period, and he was at Appomattox Court House at the climax of the war. At right is a photograph of William Albro, and below is a handwritten note from Albro recounting what was left on the battlefield after Gettysburg, including how many Union and rebel soldiers were wounded. (Both, courtesy of Joe Long.)

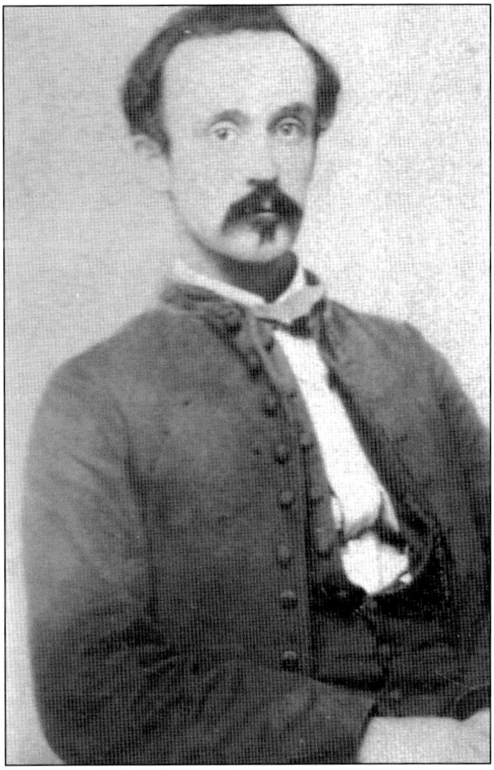

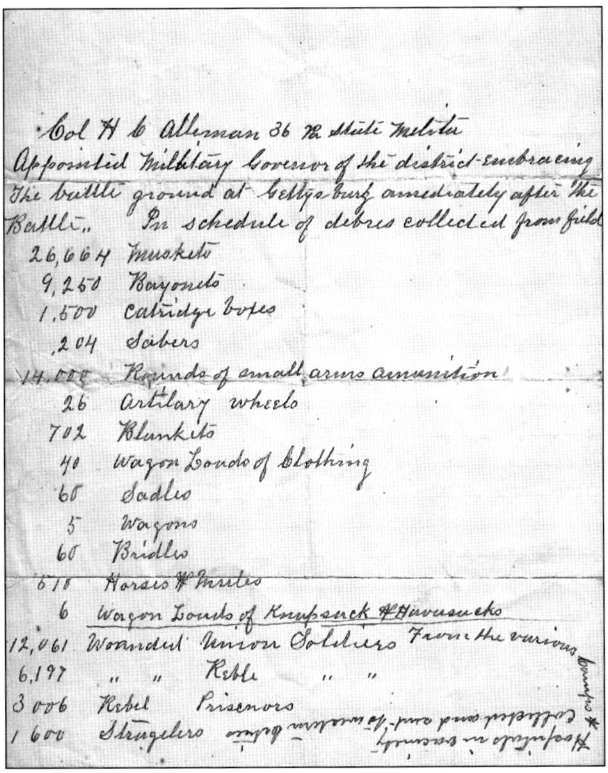

Col H C Alleman 36 Pa State Militia
Appointed Military Governor of the district embracing
The battle ground at Gettysburg immediately after the
Battle.. In schedule of debris collected from field

26,664 Muskets
9,250 Bayonets
1,500 Catridge boxes
204 Sabers
14,000 Rounds of small arms ammunition
26 Artilary wheels
702 Blankets
40 Wagon Loads of Clothing
60 Sadles
5 Wagons
60 Bridles
610 Horses & Mules
6 Wagon Loads of Knapsack & Haversacks
12,061 Wounded Union Soldiers From the various
6,197 " " Rebel " "
3006 Rebel Prisenors
1600 Strugglers

* Hospitals in vicinity collected and out of woodland before corps

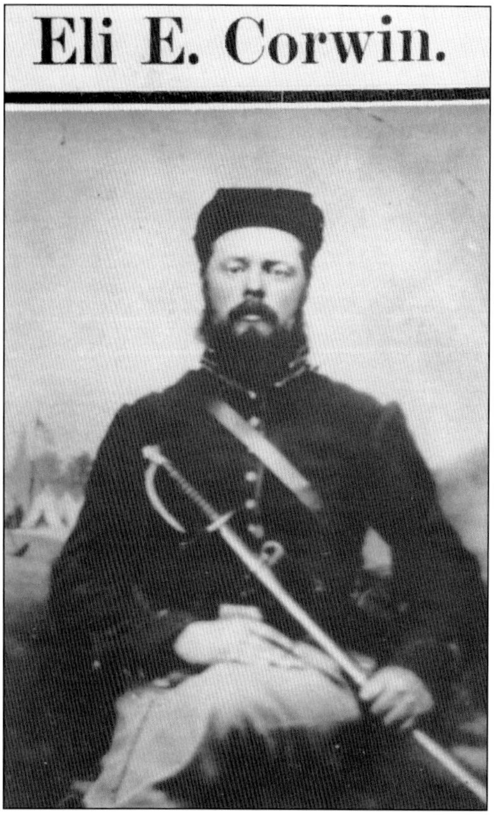

Eli E. Corwin was born in Susquehanna County, Pennsylvania, in 1834. During the Civil War, he was a private in Company B, 162nd, 17th Pennsylvania Cavalry. He served from September 21, 1862, to January 27, 1863. He was released from service with a surgeon's certificate for disability. For the rest of his life, Corwin was a carpenter specializing in cabinetmaking. (Courtesy of Joe Long.)

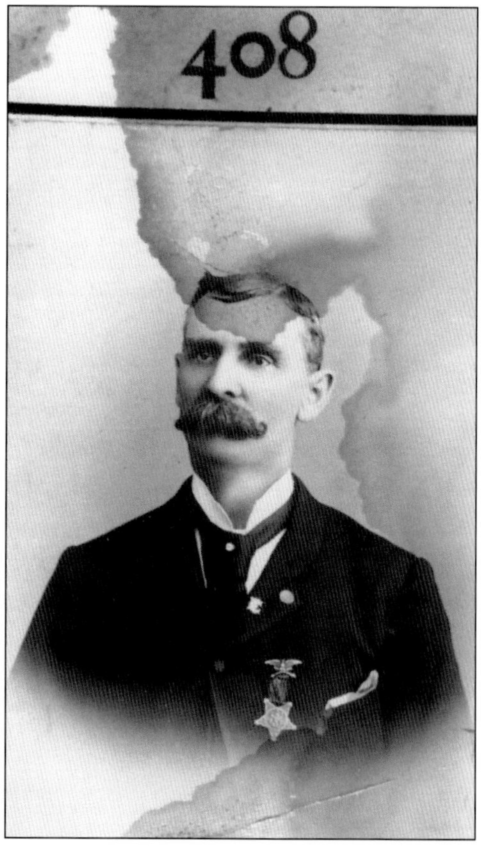

George A. Carr was born on August 19, 1845, in Lenox, Pennsylvania. He was mustered into the service on September 2, 1864, where he was a corporal in Company H of Captain Redfield's 137th New York Infantry. He was active in the war until June 9, 1865. After the war, he worked as a Lackawanna Railroad engineer. (Courtesy of Joe Long.)

James K. Brady was born in Laurence, Pennsylvania, on March 30, 1845. He was a private in Company H, 14th New York Heavy Artillery. He fought in the Civil War from February 3, 1865, to June 25, 1865. He worked as a carpenter and died in Scranton on November 4, 1925. (Courtesy of Joe Long.)

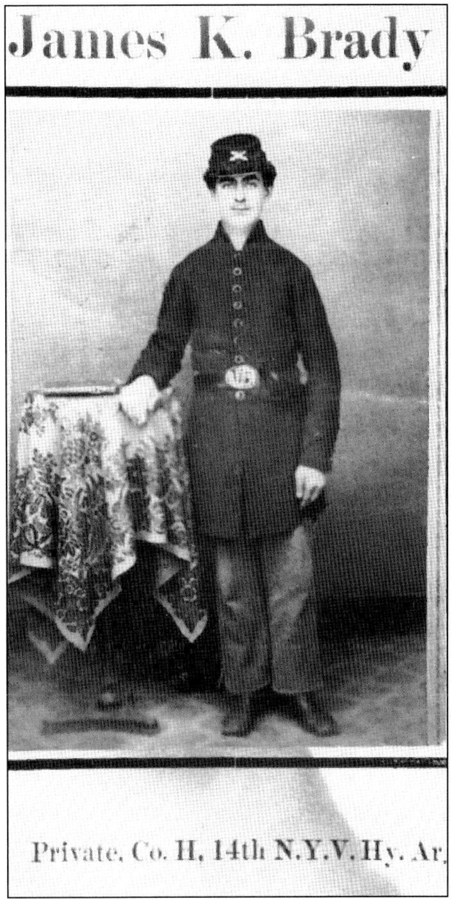

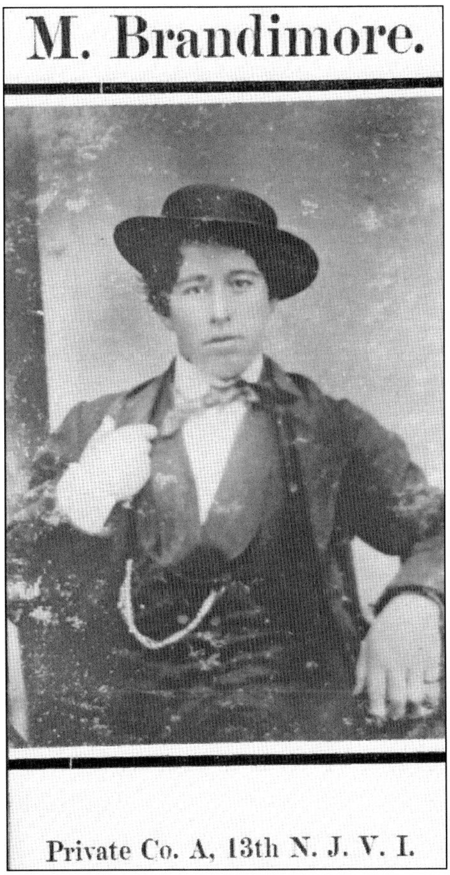

Marlow Brandimore was born in Ellenville, New York, on November 8, 1843. He rose from the rank of private to corporal in Company A, 13th New Jersey Regiment during the Civil War. He was in active service from March 17, 1864, until July 17, 1865, and was a part of Sherman's March to the Sea, otherwise known as the Savannah Campaign. This march was led by Gen. William Tecumseh Sherman to capture the port of Savannah in Georgia. The march started on November 15, 1864, and ended on December 21, 1864, when the port was successfully captured by the Union army. (Courtesy of Joe Long.)

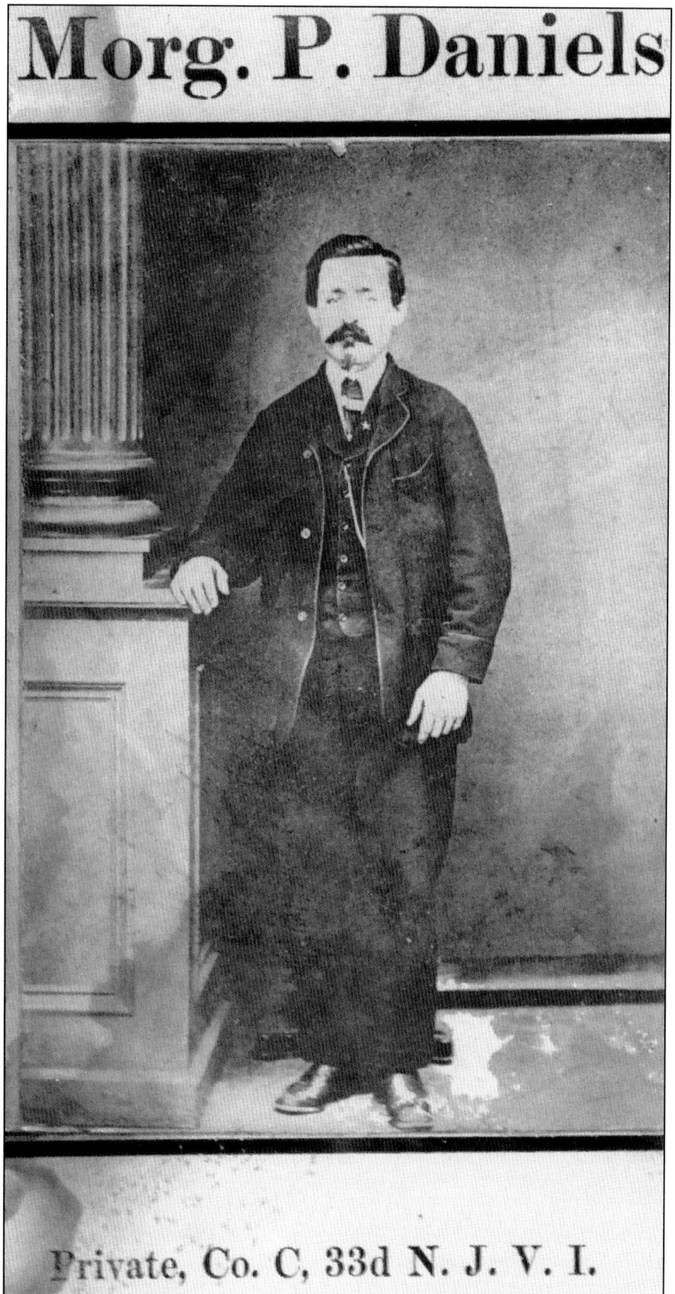

Morgan P. Daniels was born on March 18, 1843, in Beaver Meadow, Pennsylvania. Before joining the service, he worked as a coal miner in Scranton, Pennsylvania. He entered into active service on September 3, 1864, and was a part of the Army of the Cumberland; he then served in Company C, 33rd New Jersey Regiment. Like Marlow Brandimore, Daniels also marched with General Sherman during the capture of the Port of Savannah. He wrote a letter soon after the capture, relating how there was looting for a short period in Savannah by Union soldiers until the generals showed up and that many of the slaves he encountered were celebrating the Union victory in Savannah. (Courtesy of Joe Long.)

David J. Davis was born in Merthyr Tydfil, Wales, on April 16, 1825. He enlisted as a private in Company C, 185th New York Infantry on September 4, 1864, and was active in the service until May 13, 1865. He joined the Griffin Post No. 139 GAR on December 10, 1880. After he died from a stroke in 1894, a total of 60 members of Post No. 139 attended his funeral under the command of Capt. E.L. Haas. Some men from the post were also pallbearers. At right is a picture of David J. Davis during his time of enlistment, and below is a picture of him later in life. (Both, courtesy of Joe Long.)

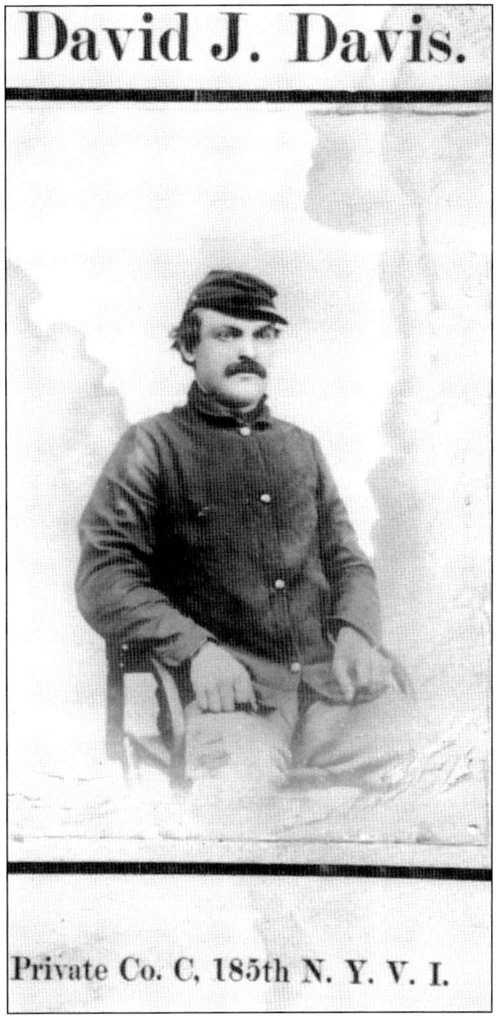

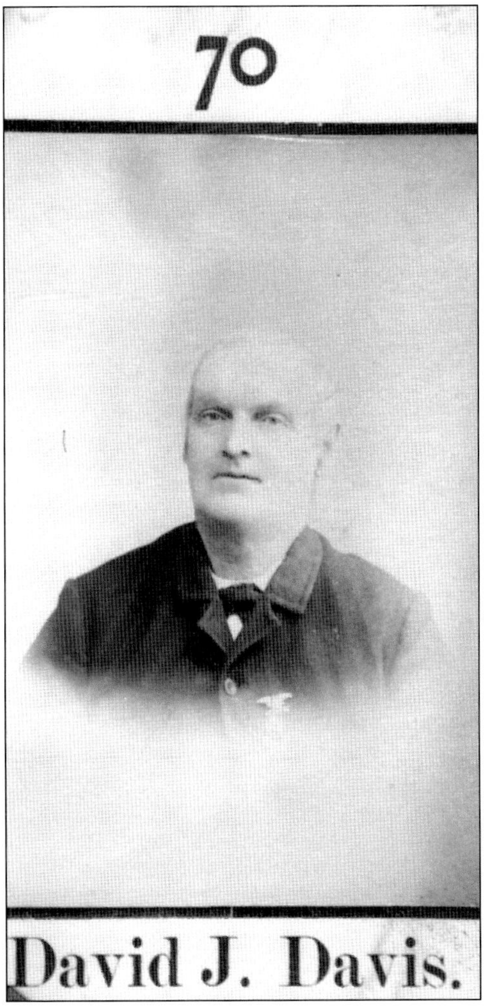

William S. Decker was born in North Abington, Pennsylvania, in May 1835. He was a quartermaster sergeant for Company K, 11th Pennsylvania Cavalry from August 13, 1861, to May 2, 1863, when he was released with a surgeon's certificate for disability. Decker worked as a druggist in Scranton until his death in 1885, which was due to pneumonia caused by Typhoid fever. He was only 50 years old. (Courtesy of Joe Long.)

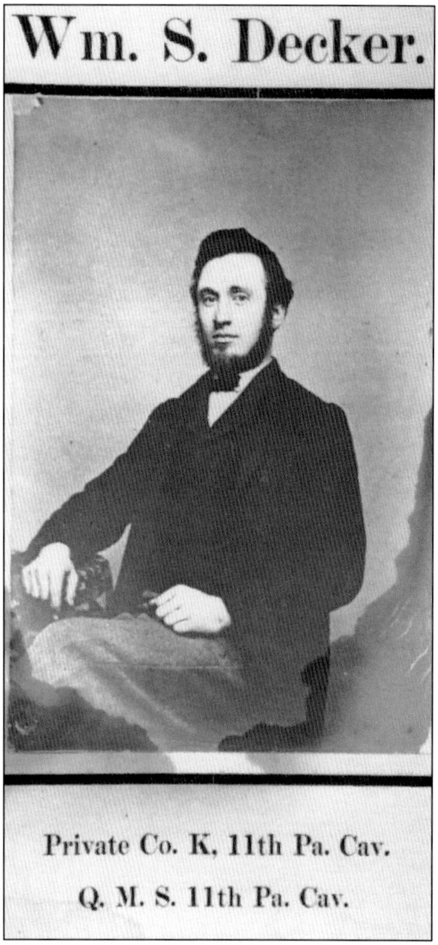

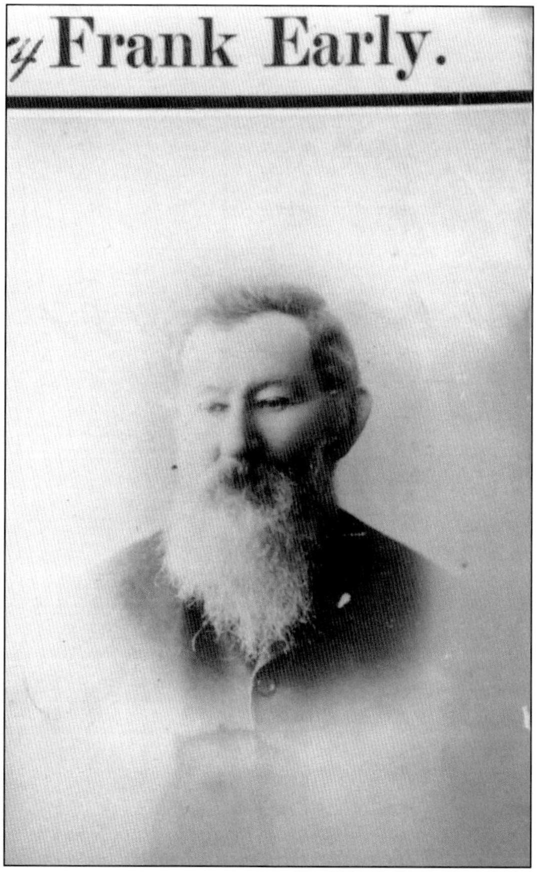

Frank Early (or Earley) was born in Germany on January 26, 1820. During the Civil War, he was a first sergeant for Company I, 52nd Pennsylvania Infantry. He was in active service from August 22, 1861 to July 12, 1865, fighting for the Union army for almost the entirety of the war between the North and the South. Early worked as a laborer in Scranton and died from a stroke on March 5, 1897. (Courtesy of Joe Long.)

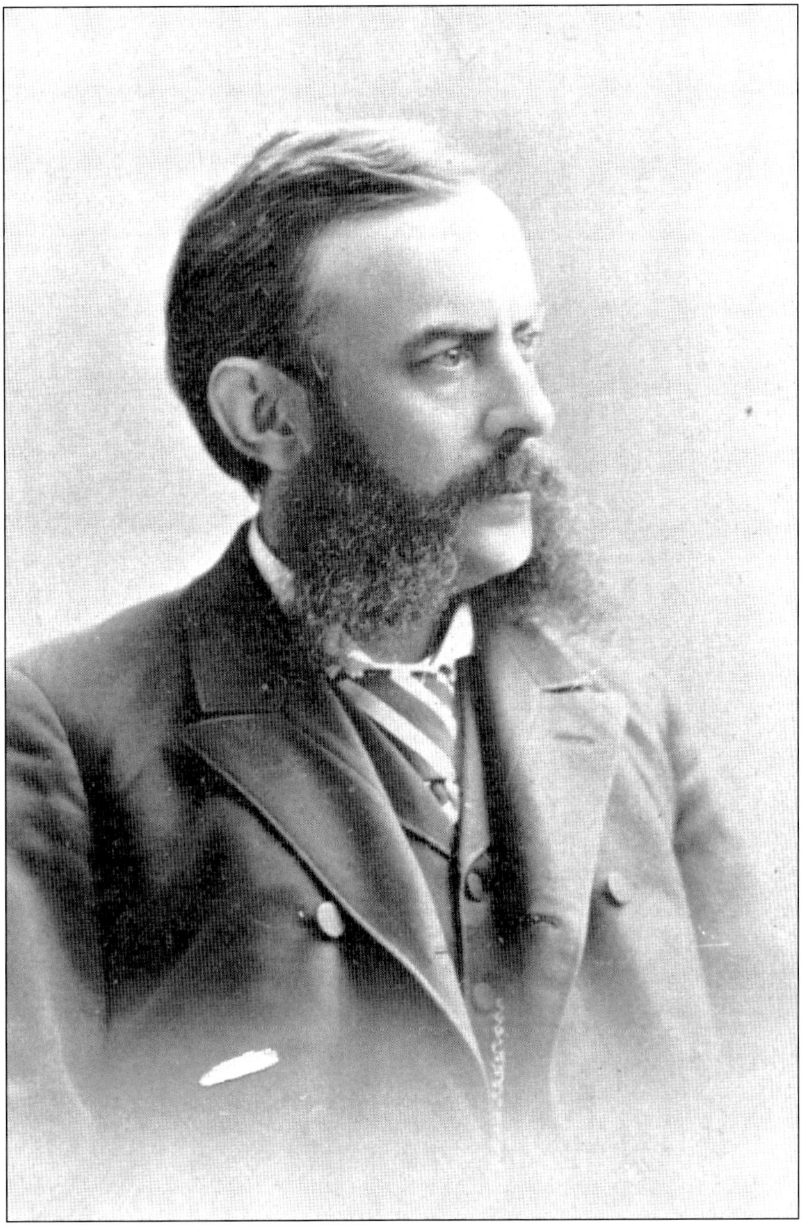

Dr. John Emmett O'Brien was the youngest telegrapher to serve during the Civil War. He entered the Military Telegraph Corps in January 1862, just three months after his 13th birthday. Prior to that, he had worked by sound on the railroad since the age of nine, deeming him the youngest telegrapher in the world. Dr. O'Brien served with the Army of the Potomac. He was a cipher operator for Gen. John Schofield in the last campaign and was the last field operator retained at the War Department at the close of the war. Through his years of service, he met Generals Grant, Meade, McClellan, Seward, Butler, and Sherman. He had also been in the company of President Lincoln. After his time in the service, O'Brien became a doctor and was one of the first surgeons of Lackawanna Hospital. He has contributed to medical and general literature in journals of worldwide circulation, which also included the text he penned about his service in the Civil War, titled, "Telegraphing in Battle." (Courtesy of Joe Long.)

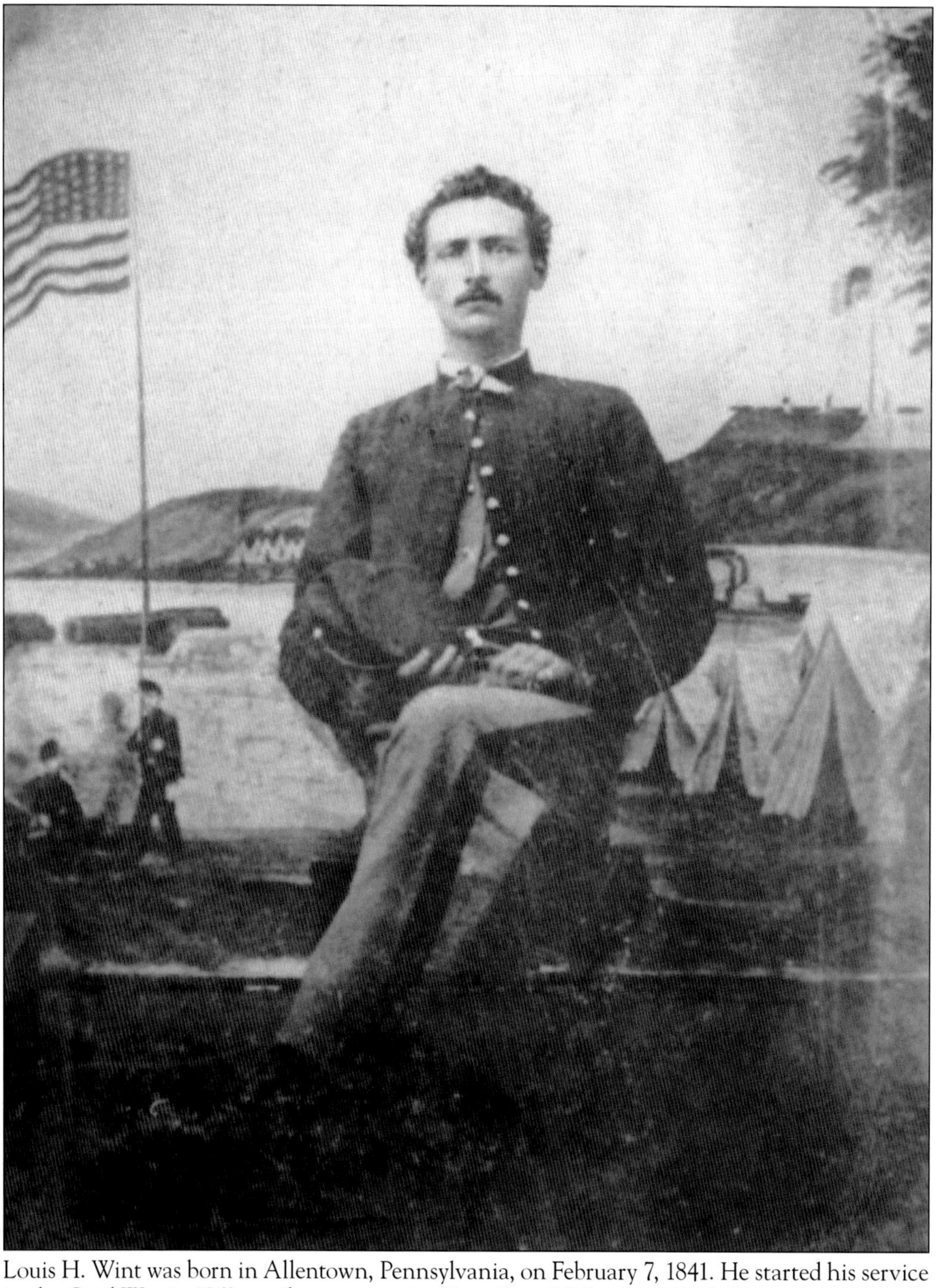

Louis H. Wint was born in Allentown, Pennsylvania, on February 7, 1841. He started his service in the Civil War in 1862 as a first sergeant in Capt. David Schooley's 112th Pennsylvania Heavy Artillery. He later became an orderly sergeant for Battery M, Pennsylvania Heavy Artillery after he was severely wounded from a shot through one of his limbs. He spent several months at Point of Rocks, Fortress Monroe to recuperate. During that time, he had his friends carry him to the polls so he could vote for Abraham Lincoln in 1864. After the war, he was a councilman in Scranton. He died in March 25, 1914, due to a chronic weakening of his heart. (Courtesy of Joe Long.)

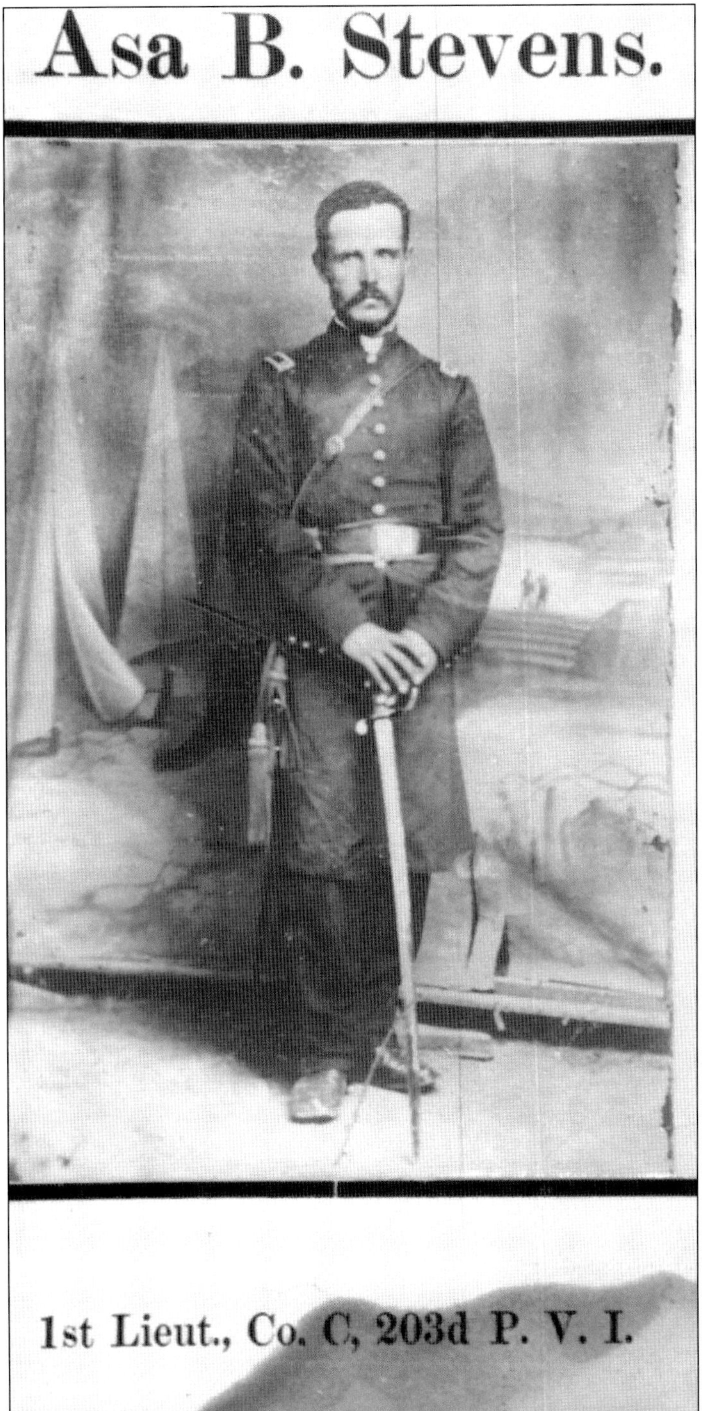

Asa B. Stevens, pictured in his enlistment photograph here, was born in Windsor, Broome County, New York on September 21, 1834. He was mustered in as a private to the first lieutenant in Company C, 203rd Pennsylvania Regiment. He served from September 21, 1864, to May 13, 1865, during the Civil War.

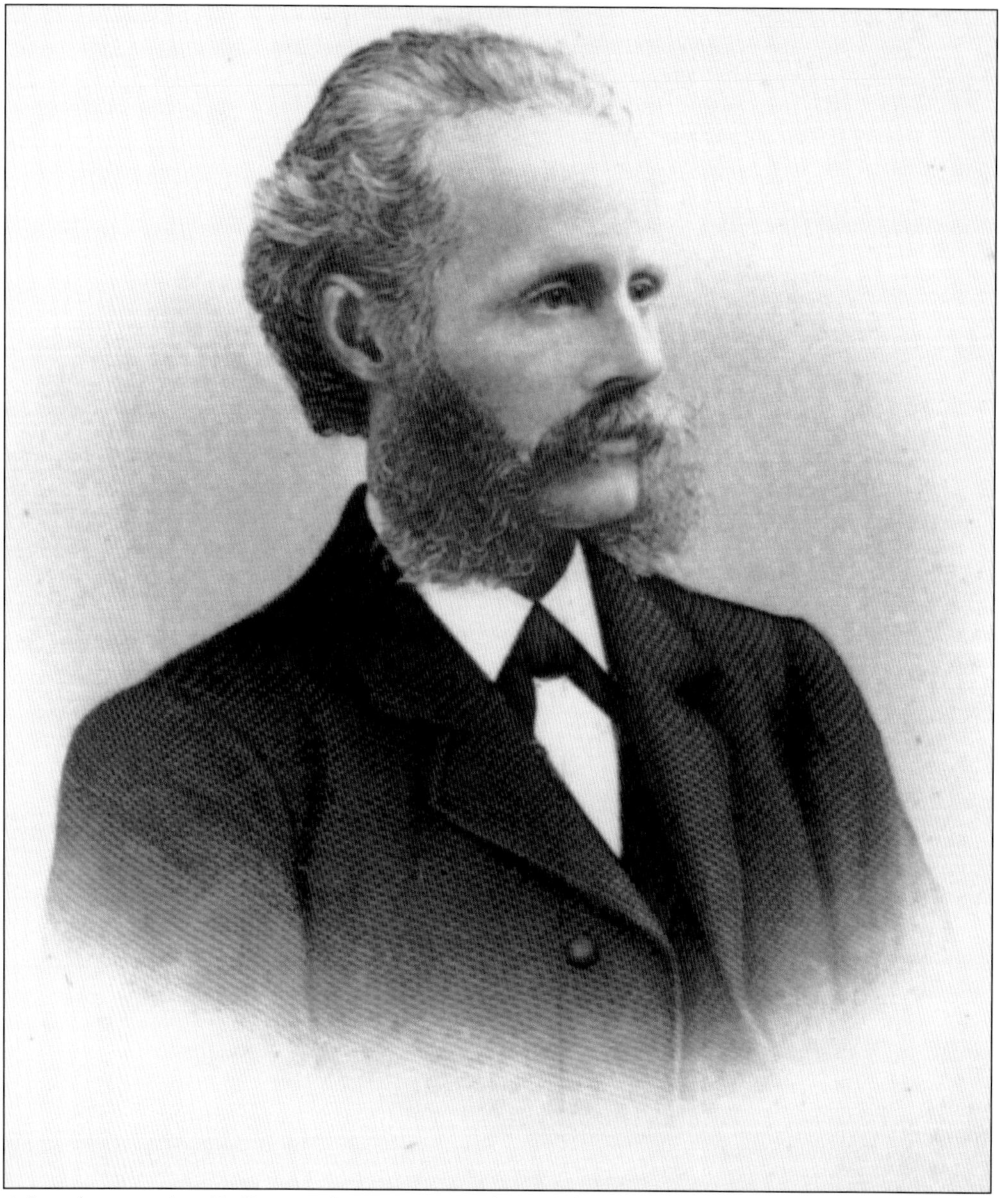

After the war, Asa B. Stevens became a member of the first select council and the board of commissioners when Scranton became a city in 1866. He also became the first sheriff of Lackawanna County in 1878 and was a burgess for the borough of Hyde Park. He was known for being active in the GAR and became commander of Griffin Post No. 139. (Courtesy of Joe Long.)

John Westpfahl was born in Mecklenberg, Germany, on April 9, 1836. He came to America in 1850 and upon his arrival found employment in a blacksmith shop. During the Civil War, he enlisted for nine months in Company K of the 132nd Pennsylvania Volunteers and was mustered out with an honorable discharge at the term of his enlistment. Westpfahl returned to his work of following the forge in the blacksmith shop. (Courtesy of Joe Long.)

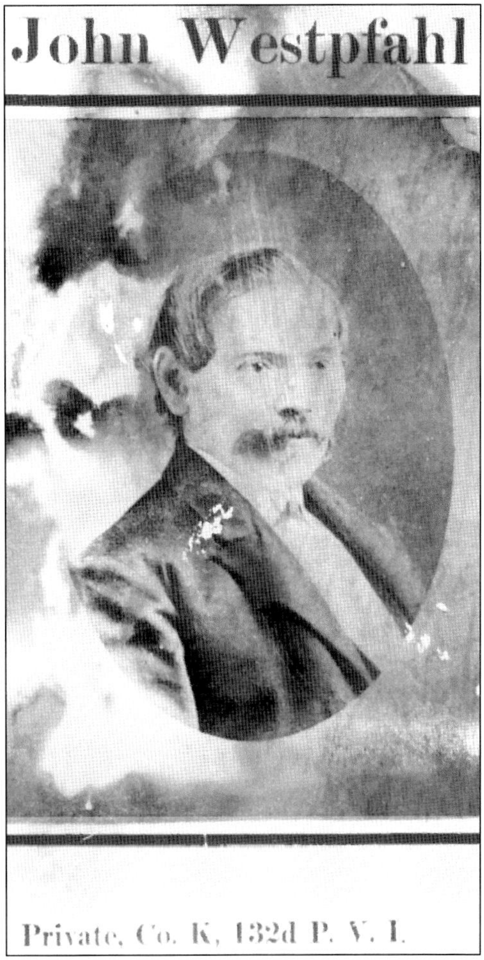

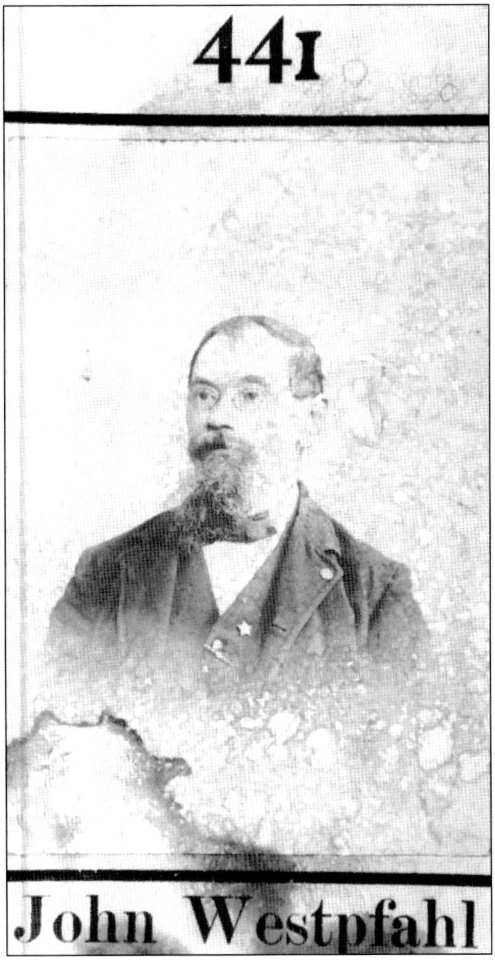

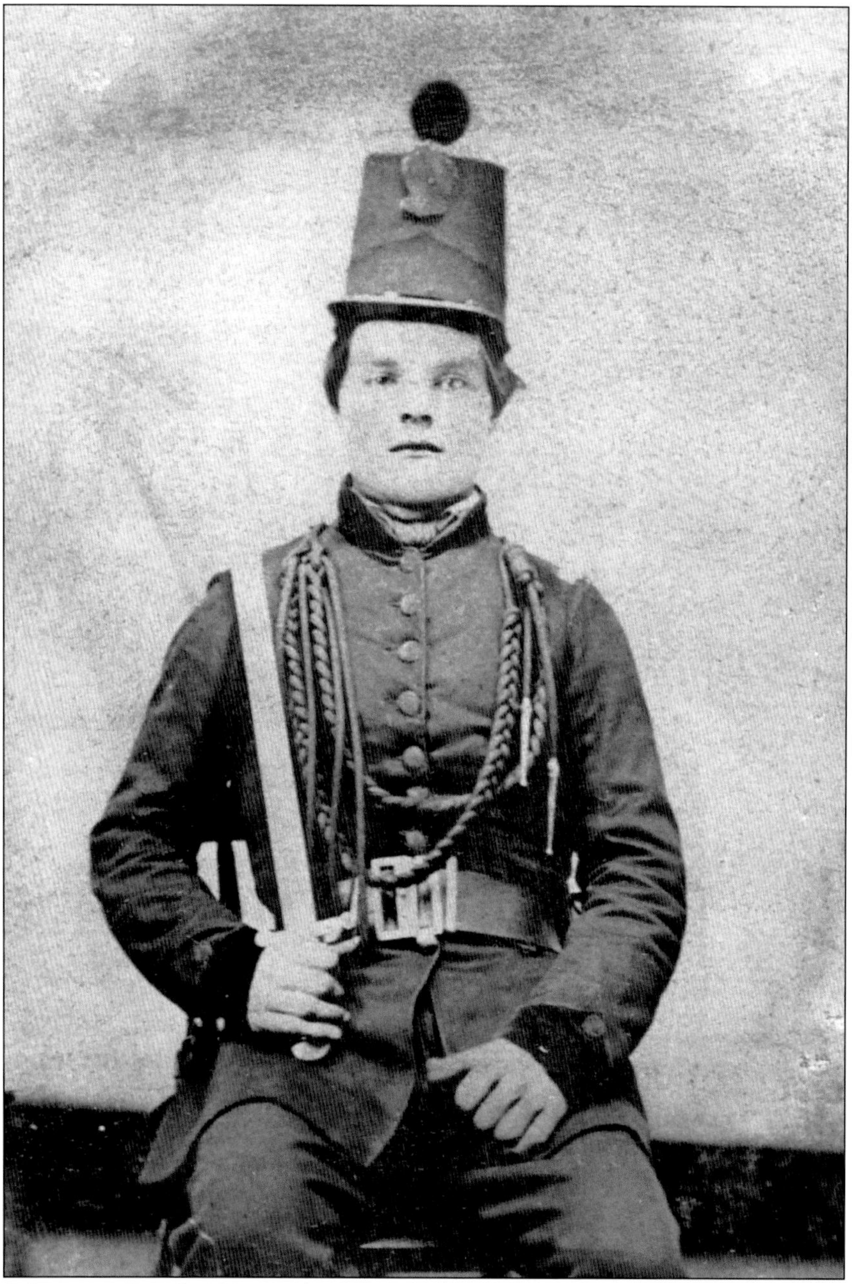

Philip Schweitzer Sr. of 1030 North Irving Avenue was a member of the 9th Pennsylvania Cavalry Band, which had the distinct honor of playing at the funeral of Pres. Abraham Lincoln. Schweitzer also had the distinction of being the oldest resident of East Scranton. Originally, he was from East Prussia, where he was born in 1840. He and his parents immigrated to the United States when Philip was 16. Just five years later, at the age of 21, he answered Lincoln's first call for volunteers and became a member of the 9th Pennsylvania Cavalry, which he served with throughout the entire war. In 1927, the year Schweitzer passed away, there were very few survivors left of that famous cavalry band that played "Taps" at the funeral of the martyred president. (Courtesy of Joe Long.)

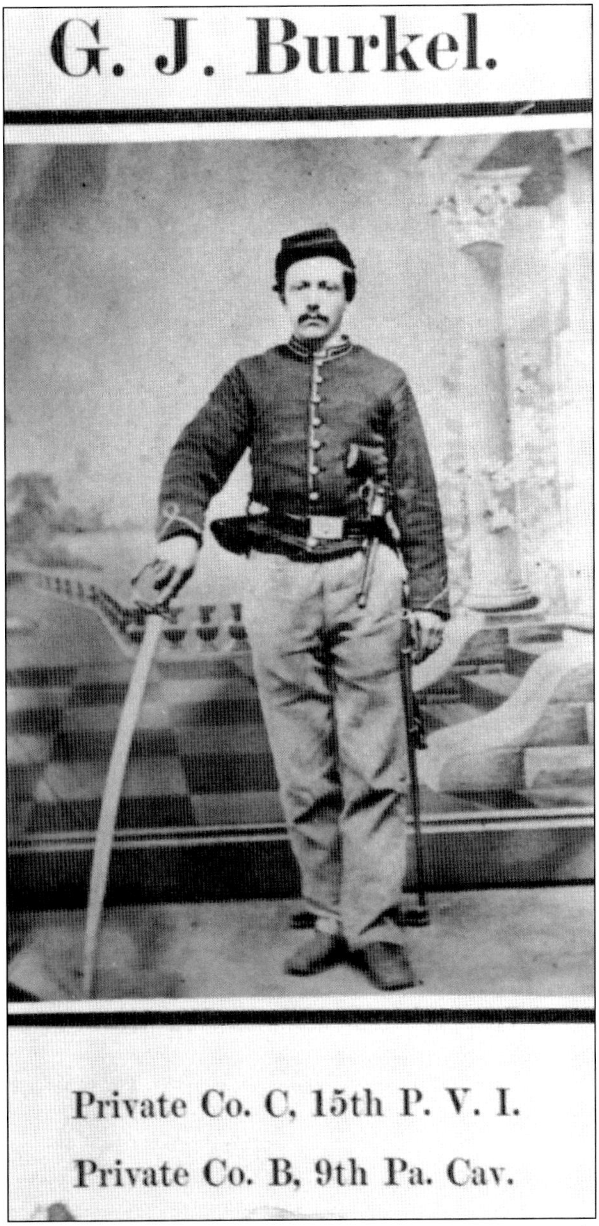

George J. Burkel was born on October 4, 1838, in Germany. He came to America in 1849 and settled in New York City for a short time before making Scranton his permanent home. When volunteers were called in 1861, Burkel enlisted for three months in Company C, 15th Pennsylvania Volunteers. At the end of his term, he left the company and then reenlisted for a period of three years, being honorably discharged at Missy Creek, Tennessee, in December 1863. Again, he reenlisted, and this time, he was assigned to the Cavalry of the 92nd Pennsylvania Regiment and subsequently transferred to the artillery of that regiment. On the day peace was declared, Burkel was with a portion of Sherman's command at Morrisville, Tennessee, where it was opposed by General Johnson's men. He was in charge of a field piece and kept firing it for several minutes after his commanding officer had been notified that peace had been declared. Because of this, it is claimed that George Burkel fired the last gun of the Civil War. (Courtesy of Joe Long.)

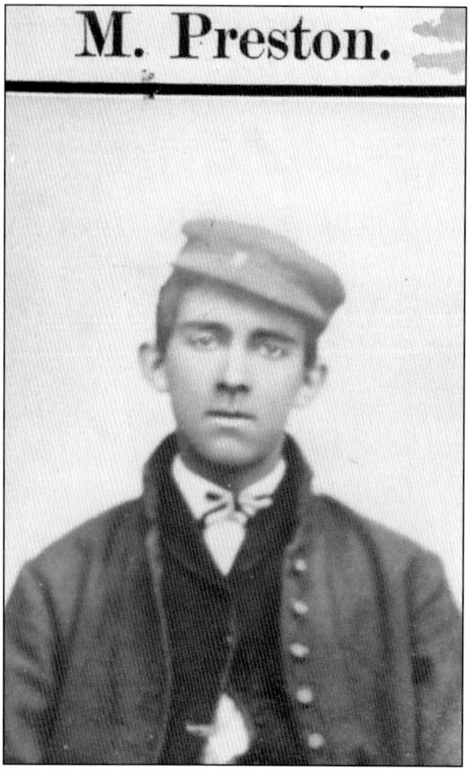

Marshall Preston was known for his humor and writing talent. He worked for Horace Greeley at Greeley's *New York Tribune*; was the foreman and superintendent of the *Scranton Republican*; was one of the founders of Scranton's first Sunday paper, the *Sunday Free Press*, which was also only the second Sunday paper to exist in the United States; worked briefly at the *Scranton Times*; and was the editor of the first edition of the *Bugle Call*. Through all of his journalistic accomplishments, Preston also served as a private of the 2nd Ohio Independent Battery during the Civil War. At left is his enlistment picture, and below is a picture of Preston later in life, standing with his granddaughter. (Both, courtesy of Joe Long.)

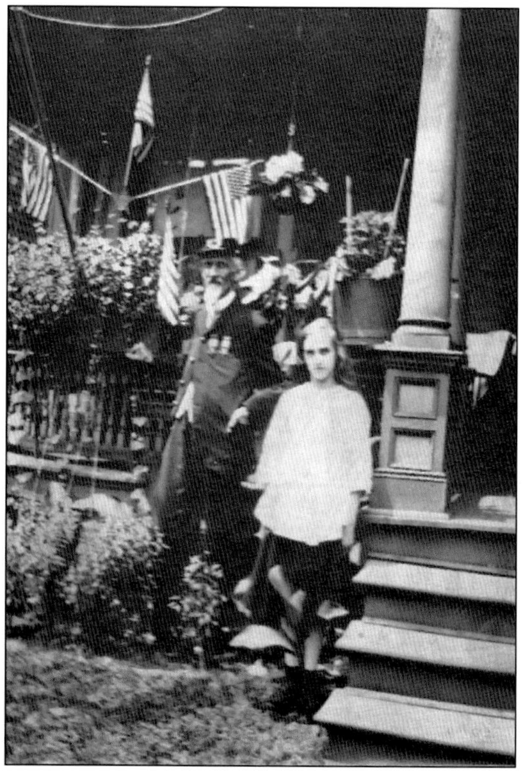

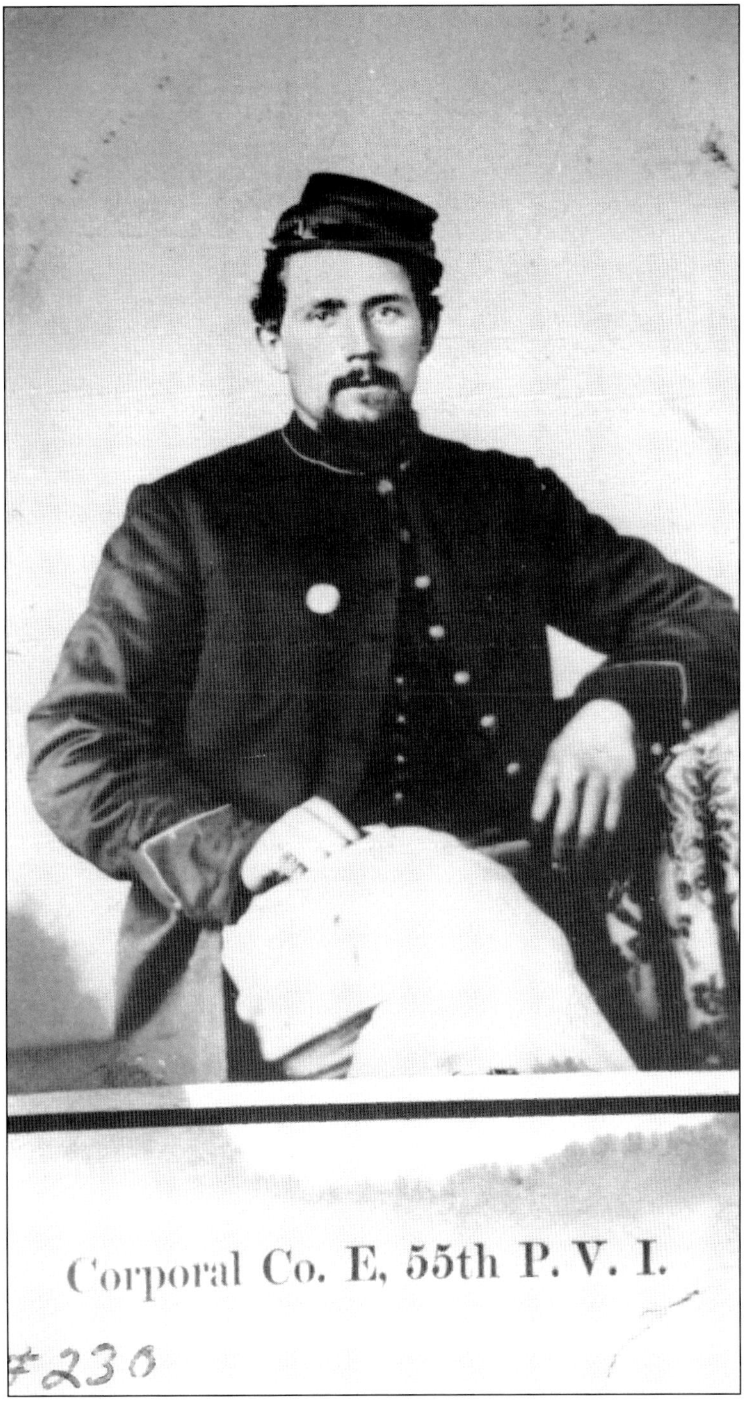

Frank W. Zimmerman rose from a private to a corporal during his time of service in the Civil War. Born in Schuylkill County, Pennsylvania, on June 10, 1843, Zimmerman was enlisted into Company E, 55th Pennsylvania Regiment in 1864. He was wounded in action on March 31, 1865, when a rifle ball passed entirely through his body during a battle at Hatcher's Run. He would recover and serve his country until August 30, 1865. (Courtesy of Joe Long.)

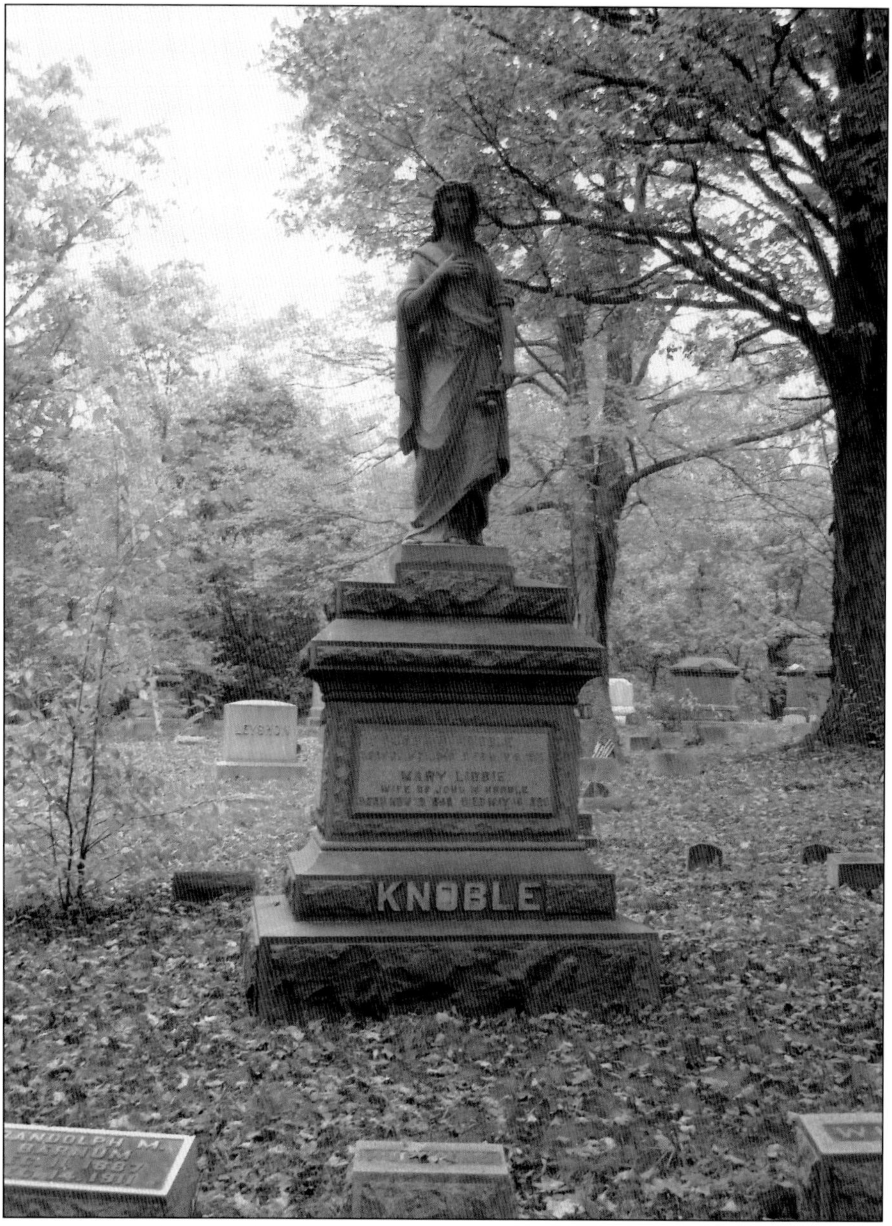

There are two Confederate soldiers buried in Forest Hill. The first is John Knoble (whose tombstone is pictured here), who was born in Switzerland. He later immigrated to New Jersey, and he and his brother became carriage makers. Before the war, he moved down to Georgia and enlisted into the Confederate army when the fighting started. His brother, who still lived in the North, fought for the Union side during the war. The other Confederate soldier buried in Forest Hill is Edward M. Clarke. Clarke was born to a fine family in Northampton, Massachusetts, in 1834. For a time in his life, he drifted southward from Massachusetts until he reached Columbus, Georgia, where he stayed for 12 years. During part of his time there, the Civil War was raging, and Clarke fought with Company F, 17th Georgia Regiment. He was also at Appomattox and took part in the tearing down of the rebel flag at Fort Sumter on February 17, 1865. The Union flag was then raised some five days later on February 22. (Author's collection.)

Three

The Sung and Unsung

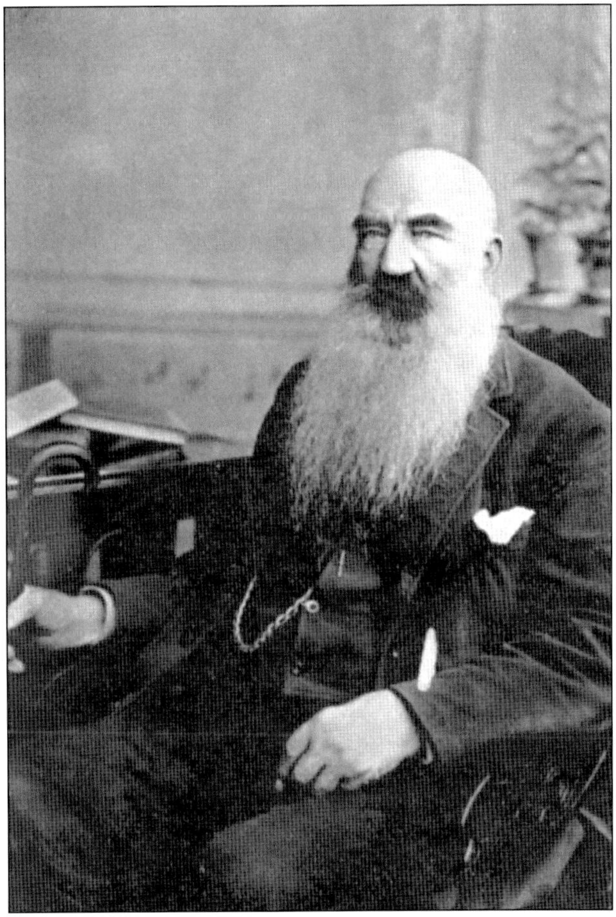

The Tripp family in America is descended from John Tripp, who sailed from London in 1635. Isaac Tripp I brought his family to the Lackawanna Valley in 1771. Pictured is the fourth generation of the family. Ira Tripp took an active interest in the city; he was a director of numerous banks, founder of the Scranton Trust Company and president of the North Branch of the Lackawanna Railroad Company. (Courtesy of Forest Hill Archives.)

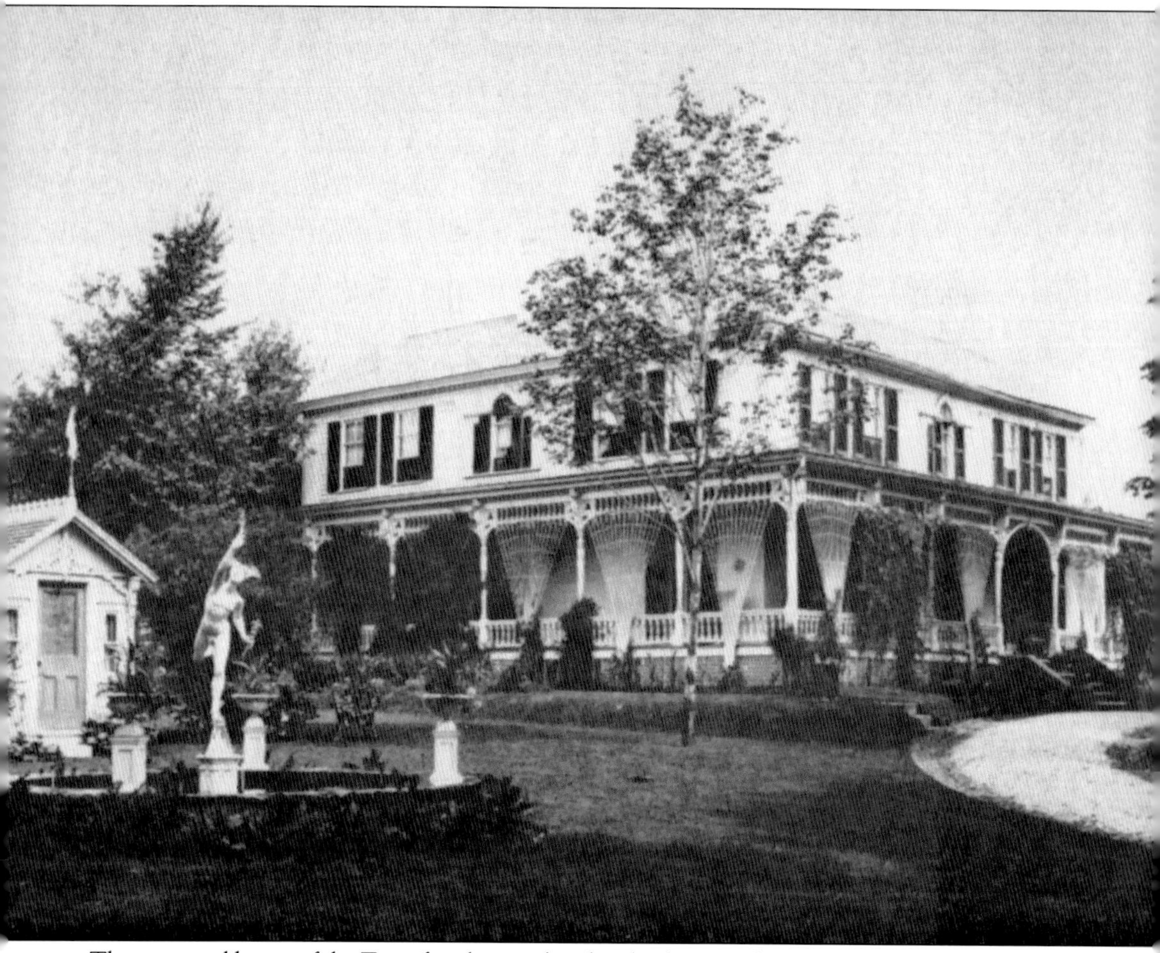

The ancestral home of the Tripp family is said to date back to revolutionary times when it began as a log cabin built by Isaac Tripp I. Several years later, Tripp I, with his son Isaac Tripp II, expanded the building to a sizable L-shaped structure. Isaac Tripp III took over his father's house in 1807, and it was he who engaged builders from Connecticut to remodel and enlarge the structure. The house has been described by the National Heritage Corporation as "an expression of the city's history." The Tripp family monument is among one of the largest in Forest Hill. Many generations are laid to rest there. (Courtesy of Forest Hill Archives.)

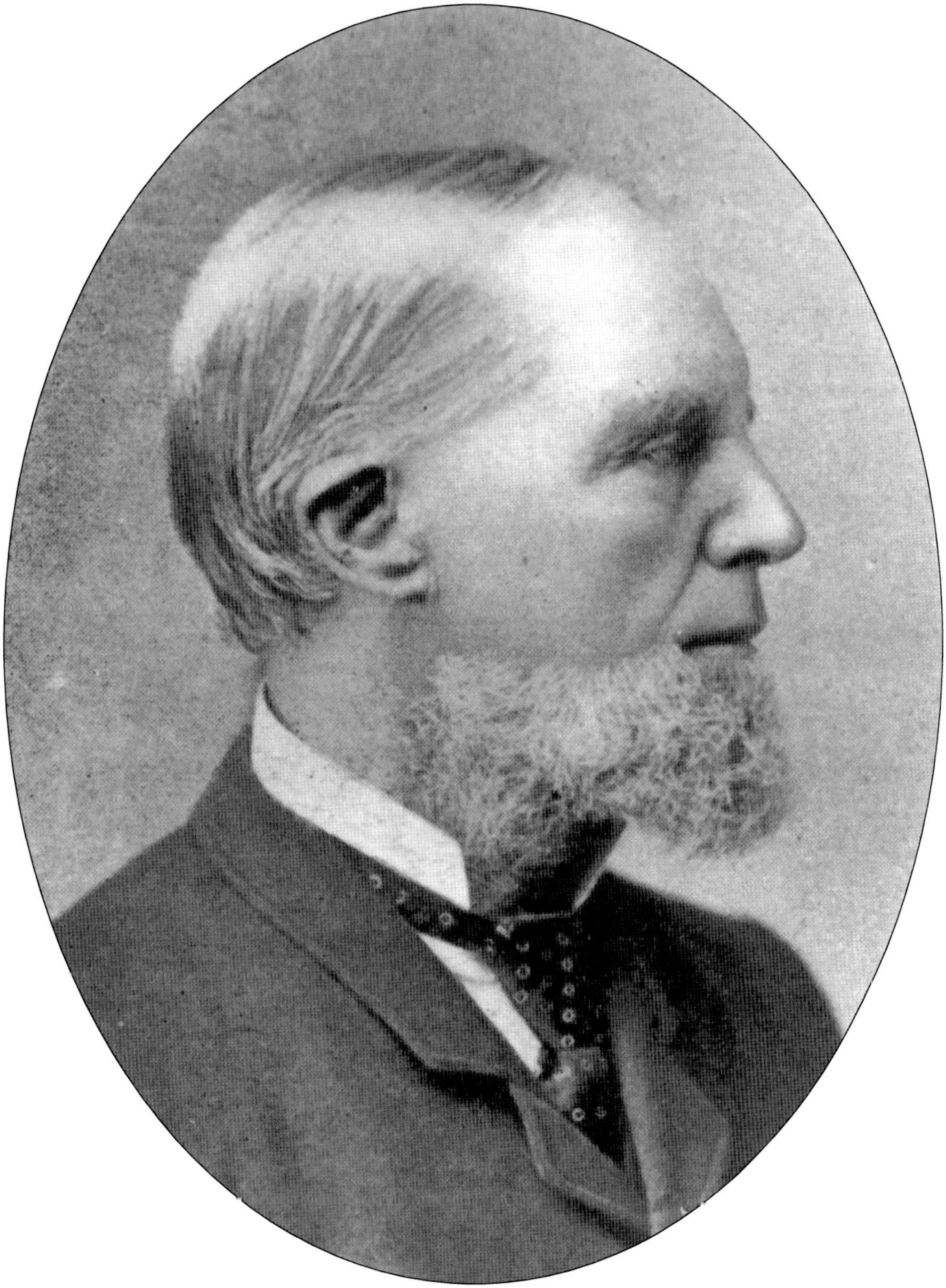

One of the city's prominent businessmen, Lewis Pughe was born in Wales in 1829. After his arrival to the United States as a young boy, he was educated in the local public schools. He later became the poor director in Scranton and served for many years as school director. (Courtesy of Forest Hill Archives.)

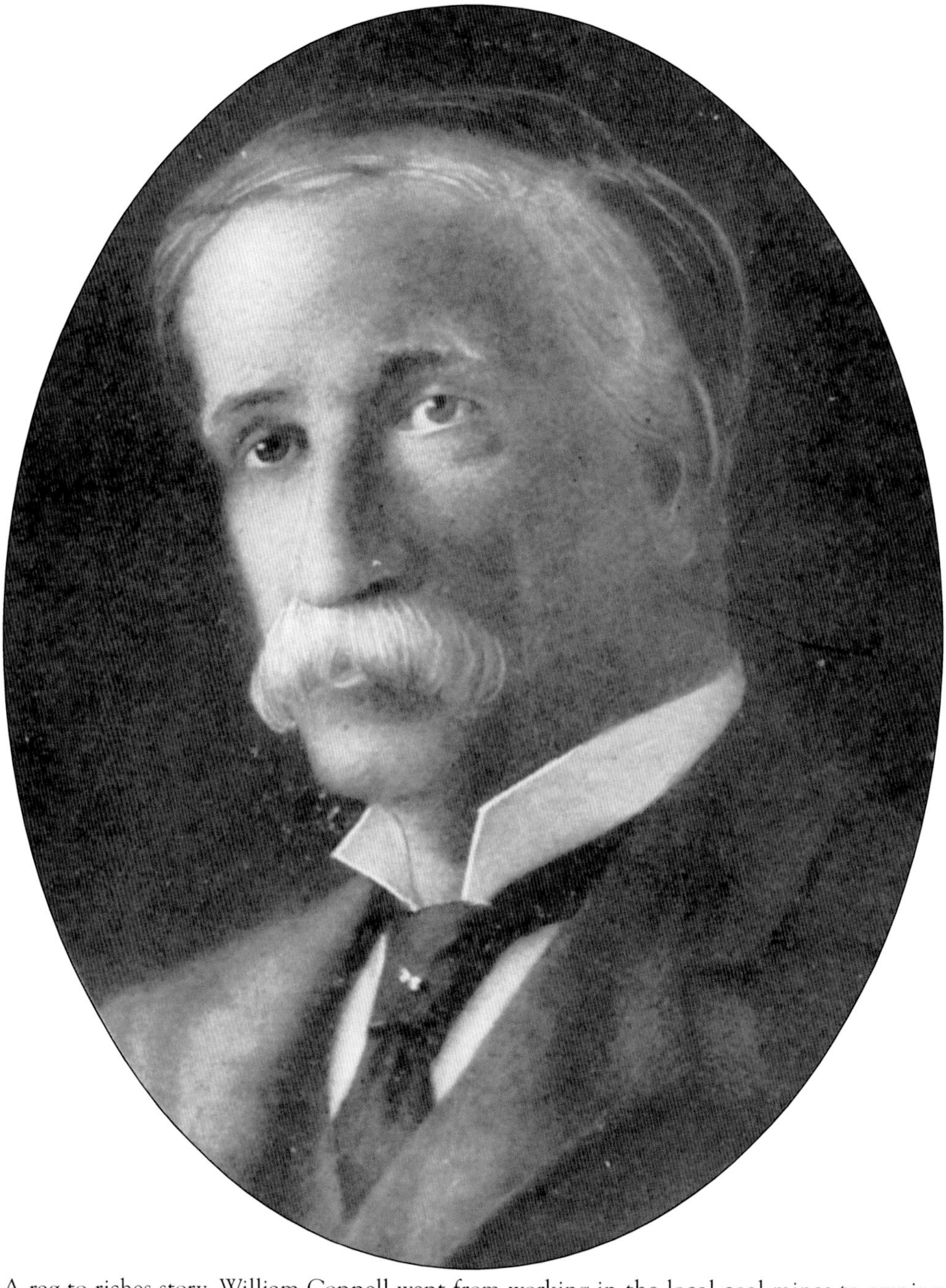

A rag-to-riches story, William Connell went from working in the local coal mines to owning several of them by the time he was 30. Three qualities that had been contributed to his success: energy, independence and his heritage to a long line of Scotch ancestors. In 1872, he founded the Third National Bank of Scranton and the firm of William Connell and Company. The Connell Building in Scranton still stands proudly today in honor of this man. (Courtesy of Forest Hill Archives.)

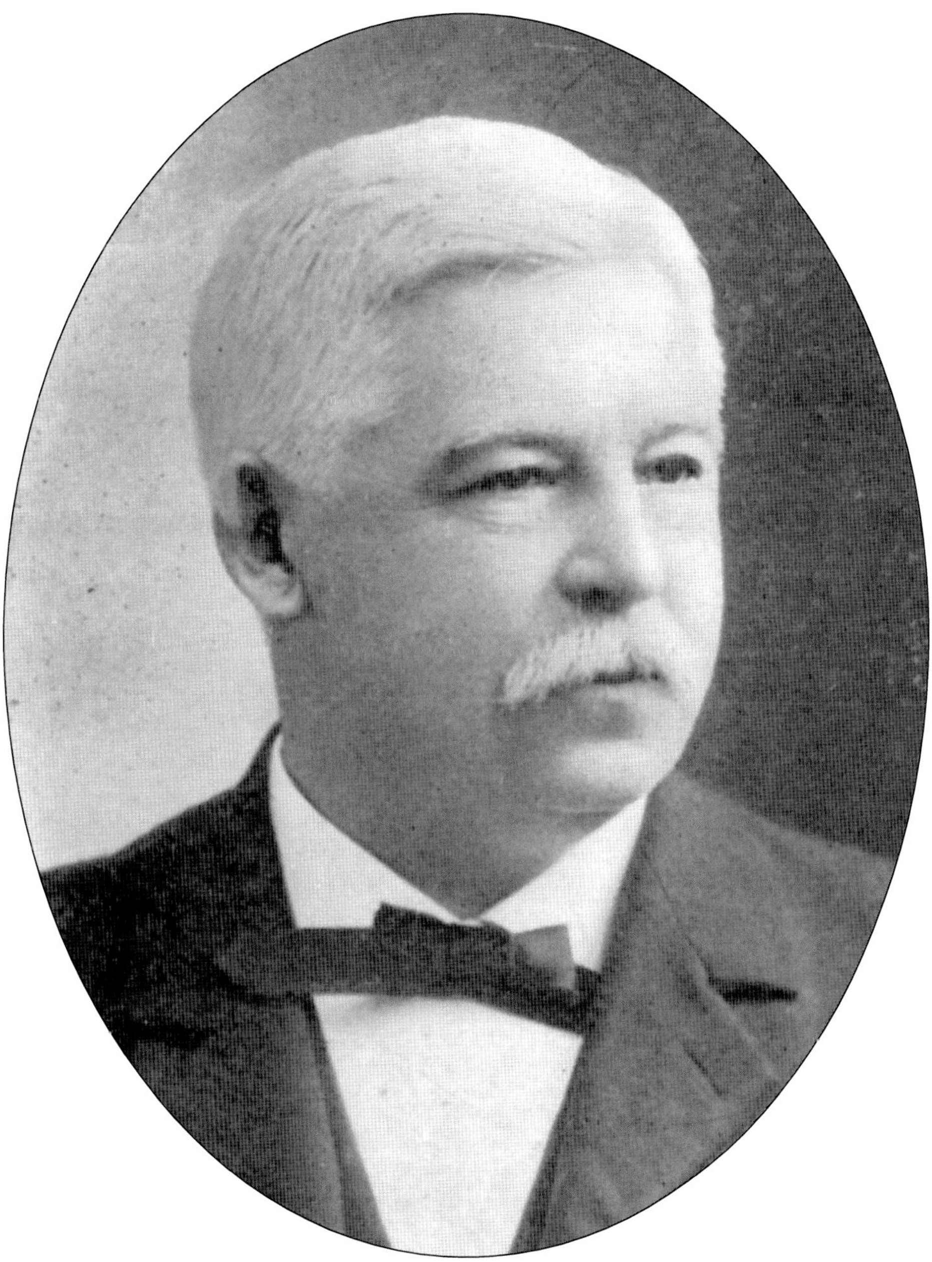

Thomas Jefferson "T.J." Foster moved to Scranton, Pennsylvania, in 1891 and founded the International Correspondence School (ICS). The school developed rapidly, adding language, business, and other study courses that were made available to all students throughout the world. Besides his fame for the ICS courses, Foster was primarily responsible for the enactment of safety mining laws, which made it necessary for foremen and officials to have knowledge of gas caves and mechanics before they could secure a position. Foster was also credited with originating the idea of the return address on envelopes in the upper left-hand corner. Foster coined the phrase, "We teach the world," and the legacy of his ICS still exists today. Penn Foster, named for its founder and the state it mainly operates in, is an accredited institution that still teaches the world through online courses for high school, career school, and college. (Author's collection.)

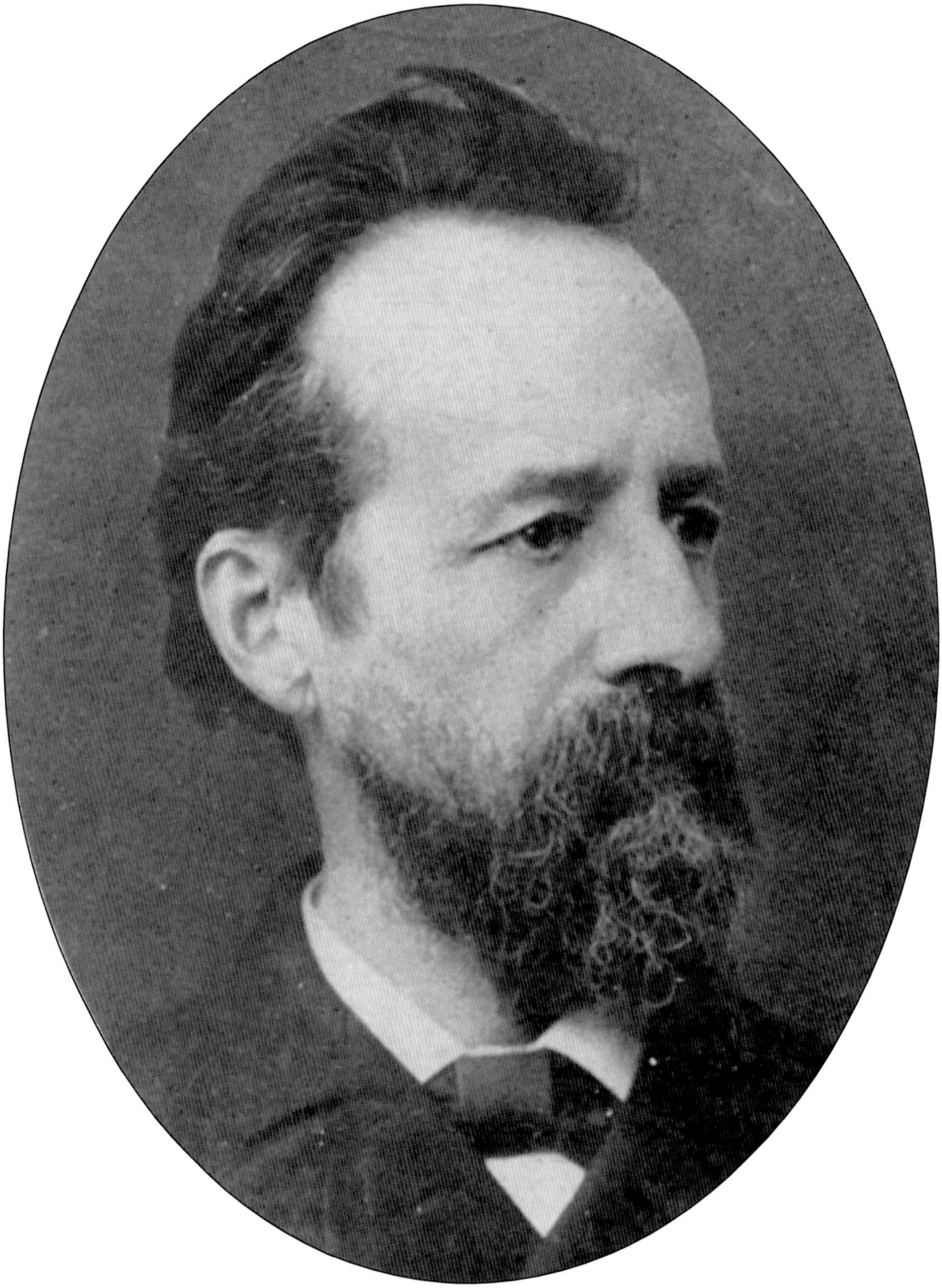

Dr. Jeremiah L. Fordham had been a resident of Green Ridge for 40 years and was considered one of its pioneers having played an important part in Scranton's growth. He was born in Southampton and received his medical training at Amherst College. He had acquired quite an enviable reputation as having one of the only skilled dental practices in the territory, which he shared with Dr. W.A. Taft at 104 North Washington Avenue. For many years, he was a prominent member of the Susquehanna Dental Association and had frequently read some scholarly papers at meetings of that body. (Author's collection.)

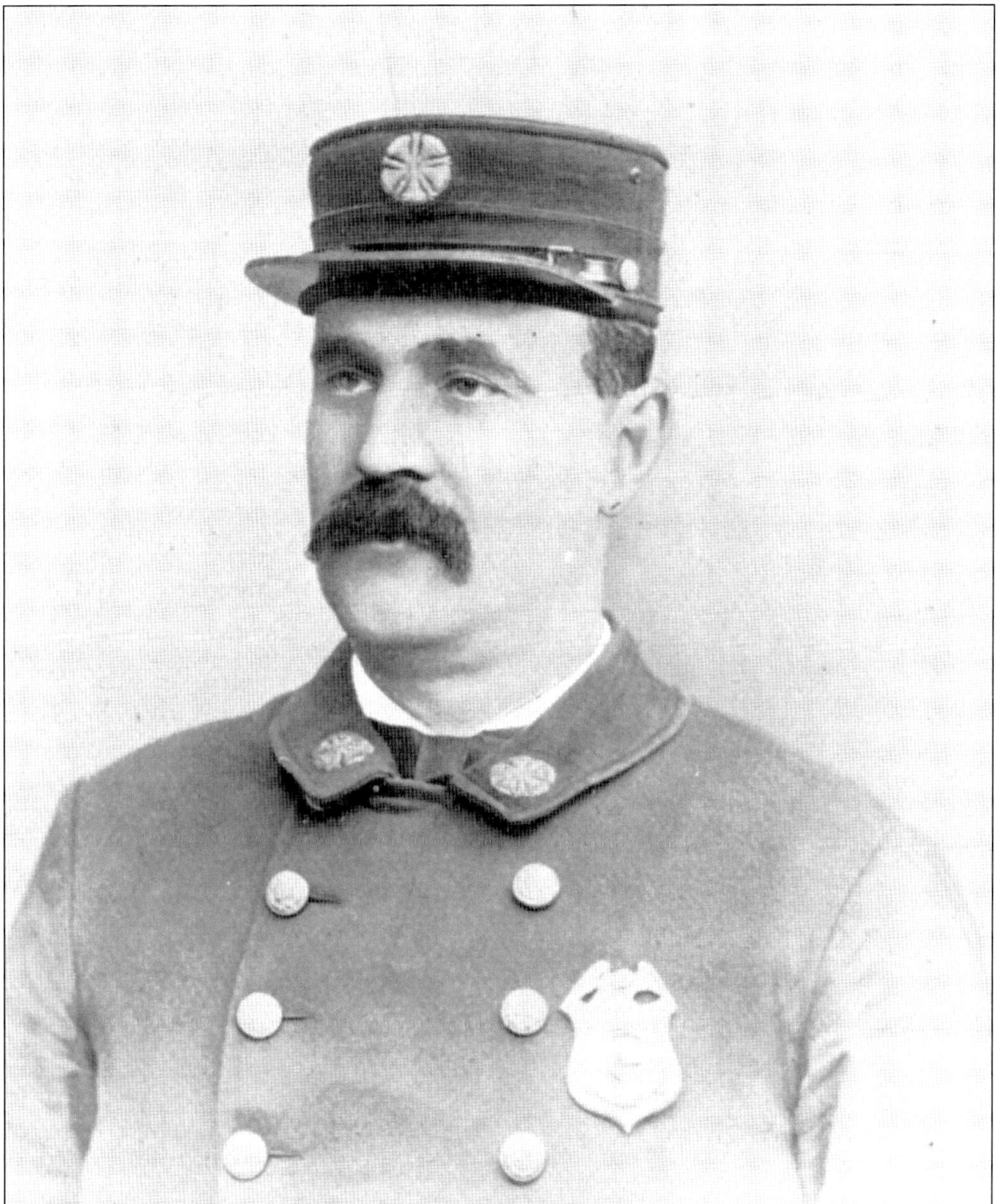

Henry F. Ferber was born in Pittsburgh, Pennsylvania on April Fool's Day in 1853. Henry was the son of A.C. Ferber, and like his police chief father, he spent many years protecting and serving the city. From 1868 until his retirement in 1916, Fire Chief Ferber was connected with the fire department. His last service was at the fire that destroyed Clarke Brother's Store in West Scranton. As always, Chief Ferber was the first man to arrive on the scene and assisted the other firemen in battling the blaze. It has been said that no man in the region had a better reputation as a skilled firefighter and leader of firemen than Chief Ferber. Pictured here is Ferber's shield badge. It has been described as having a silver center and gold edging, indicative of his position. (Courtesy of Forest Hill Archives.)

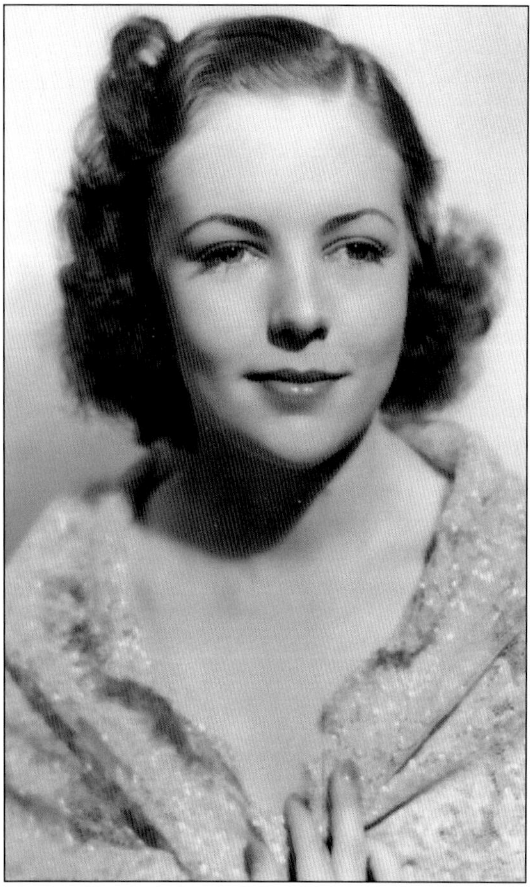

Jeanne Madden Martin, former film and stage star, was born in Scranton. She was bitten by the acting bug very early on and had been chosen for many leading roles in her high school plays at Central High. Martin was only 18 years old when she starred in her first film, *Stage Struck,* with Dick Powell and Joan Blondell, under the direction of Busby Berkeley. Martin played the role of Ruth Williams and sang "Fancy Meeting You" with Dick Powell. *Stage Struck* premiered at the Strand Theatre in Scranton on August 29, 1936, and the large crowd was so excited that they broke through police lines to greet the young hometown starlet. A year before, Martin performed as a singer on the NBC Radio Network and, in 1938, starred in the Broadway play *Knickerbocker Holiday* alongside Walter Houston. Martin made two more films, *Talent Scout* and *Sea Racketeers,* before taking time off to raise her family. In her later years, she took over as proprietor of the Holland Hotel. She is the mother of local television personality Keith Martin. Jeanne Madden Martin is pictured at left, and below is a ticket stub to the opening of *Stage Struck* at the Ritz. (Both, author's collection.)

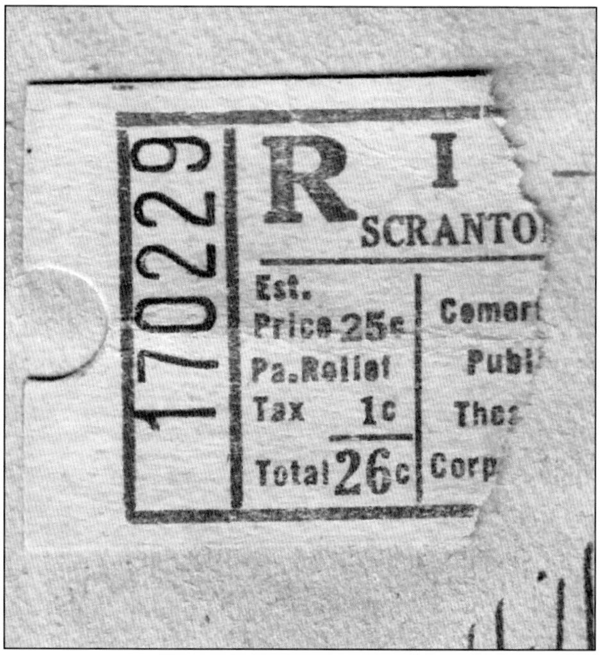

Jeannie Madden Martin's mother and father were local celebrities in their own rights. Harry Madden (right) was the owner and proprietor of the Holland and Nash Hotels as well as a musical and civic leader. Harry's public career began in 1903, when he became director of the Scranton Boys Club. He possessed a beautiful baritone voice and was very active in musical activities such as being a member of the Anthracite Male Quartet. He was also soloist with famous evangelists Dr. McKinney, Dr. George Wood Anderson, and Dr. Ernest Crabell. Harry ran both hotels until 1917 and then gave his attention exclusively to the Hotel Holland until his death in 1936. Grace Browning Madden (below) became owner and manager of the Hotel Holland after her husband's death. She was a graduate of the Scranton Conservatory of Music and had taken part in a variety of the city's musical activities, especially concerts and choral work as accompanist. (Author's collection.)

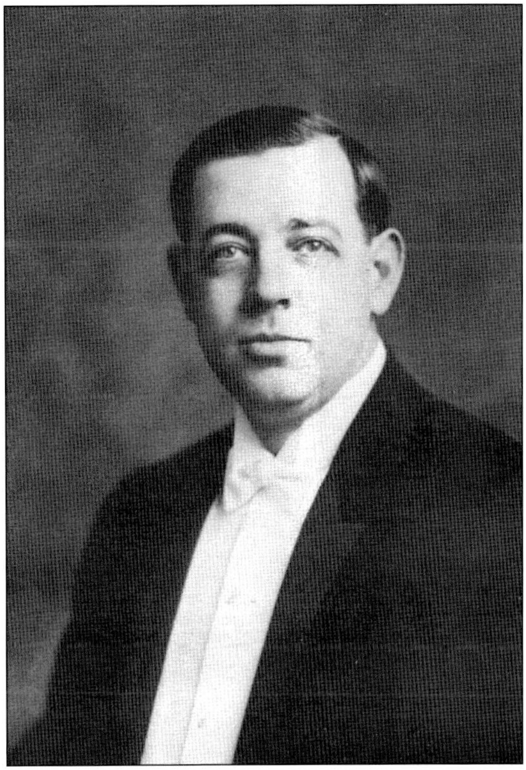

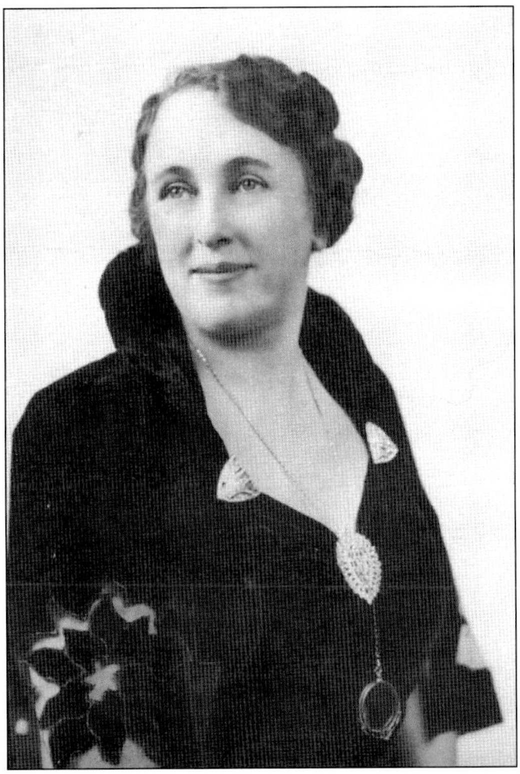

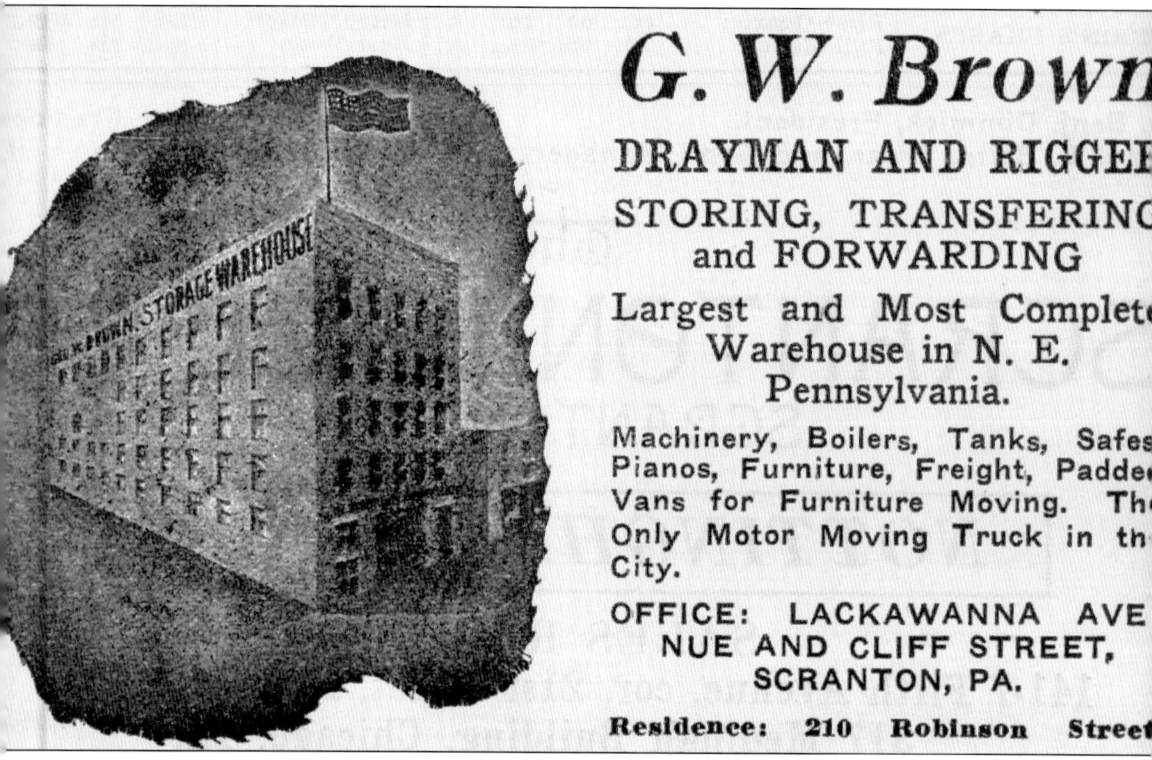

G.W. Brown started out with a single horse and wagon. Because of his untiring efforts and determination, he had established a trucking, hoisting, rigging, and storage business that was a credit to Scranton. Brown passed away from heart disease as the G.W. Brown Draying Company was flourishing on Cliff Street. Afterwards, his wife, Louise Tanner Brown, took over the handling of the business. At the start, the business was operating with four motor trucks and two teams, and eleven people were under her employment. Some seven years later, in 1930, a total of 14 motor trucks plied the streets of Scranton, and 22 people were in her employ. The business became even bigger under Louise's direction, but not without its share of difficulties. There was a lack of capital, and in order to establish credit with a trucking company to buy the first truck, Louise had to state her case rather convincingly to the manager of the company. Then there was the perplexing problem of labor; some of the white, male truck drivers refused to work for an African American woman. Harmony was achieved by the establishment of union scale wages and the division of employees equally between black and white. This practice eliminated race antagonism. (Courtesy of the Forest Hill Archives.)

Ezra F. Wickham, partner of Wickham Brothers Mayonnaise and Potato Chip Manufacturers was a native of Honesdale, Pennsylvania, but lived most of his life on Adams Avenue in Dunmore, Pennsylvania. Wickham's Products was founded in 1900 by Ezra and his brother Alfred. They were known for their mayonnaise, sandwich spreads, relishes, sauces, and mustard. (Author's collection.)

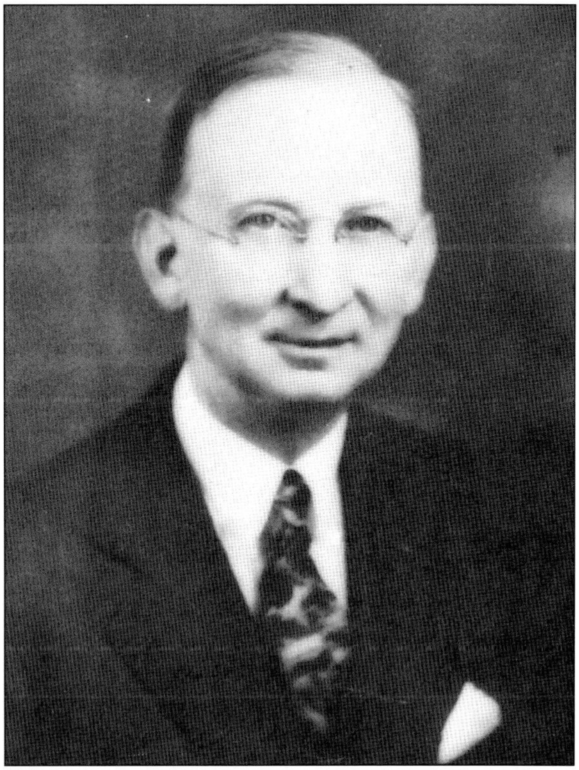

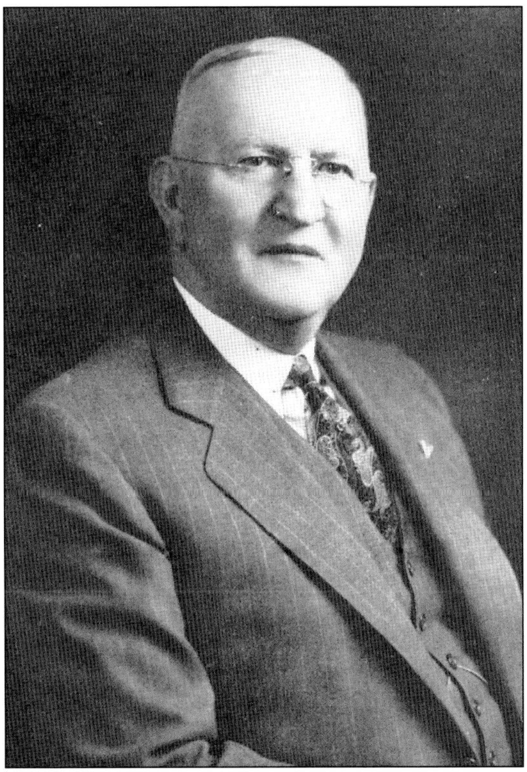

The brother of Ezra, Alfred F. Wickham was also born in Wayne County near Honesdale, Pennsylvania. Their ancestors came from Wickham, England, in 1735. The brothers' business was conducted as a partnership until 1932, when it became incorporated. Alfred was very active in civic organizations. He was a member of the Elm Park Methodist Church Kiwanis Chamber of Commerce, Independent Order of Odd Fellows (IOOF), and the Knights of Malta. Alfred resided at 1726 Jefferson Avenue in Scranton. The Wickham Brothers' business was located at the corner of Green Ridge Street and Albright Avenue. (Author's collection.)

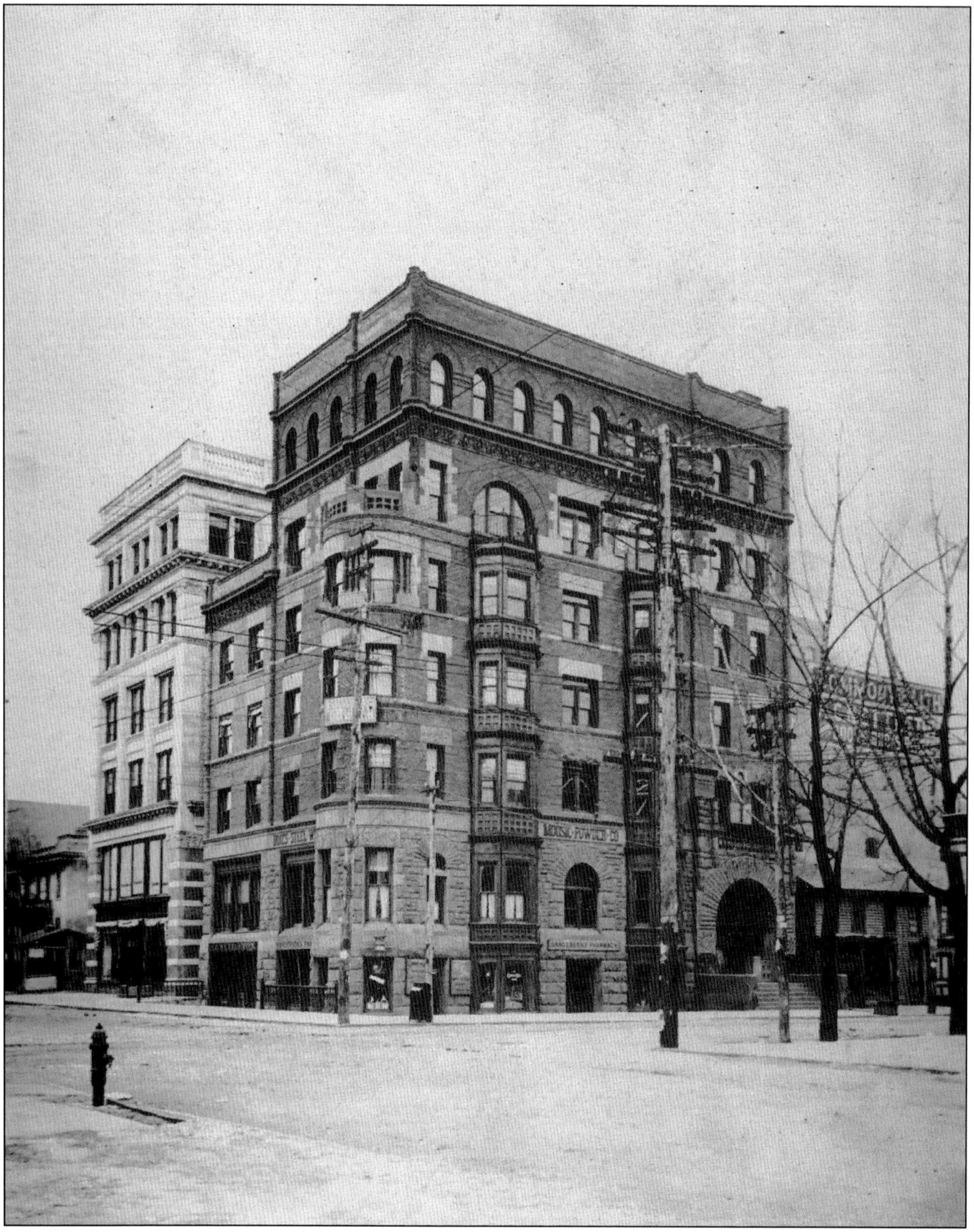

James Hall Rittenhouse was a civil and mining engineer who, for over 30 years, resided in the Green Ridge section of Scranton. James came from a very prominent family; he was a descendant of David Rittenhouse, the famous 18th-century astronomer. James married Ida Cole, the daughter of Rev. Leonard Cole, in April 1878. They came to live in Scranton 10 years later. Their marriage produced four children: Lucia, Ralph, Karl, and Leonard. The Rittenhouse family does not have a stone to mark their graves, but it is known for certain that they are buried in Forest Hill. Pictured is the Commonwealth Building in downtown Scranton. Today, it is known as the Brooks Building; the offices of J.H. Rittenhouse were located there in the late 19th century. (Author's collection.)

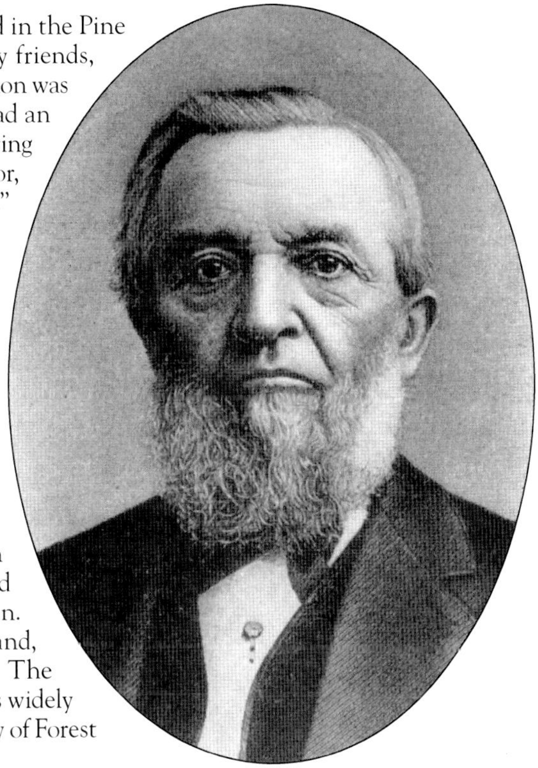

Benjamin Throop, the good doctor, is buried in the Pine Hill section of the cemetery, surrounded by friends, family, and acquaintances. His chosen profession was that of physician and surgeon, but he also had an honorable record of his service in the Army during the Civil War and the brilliancy as an author, having penned "A Half Century in Scranton." (Courtesy of Forest Hill Archives.)

Henry G. Diller was the leader of a band in Germany when he was only 18 years old and a player in the Dodsworth Band of New York, a famous musical organization known around the country. By the time he reached Scranton, Henry was a well-polished musician. He became the leader of Scranton's first band, Diller's Silver Coronets String Orchestra. The band gained much fame and success and was widely known throughout the East Coast. (Courtesy of Forest Hill Archives.)

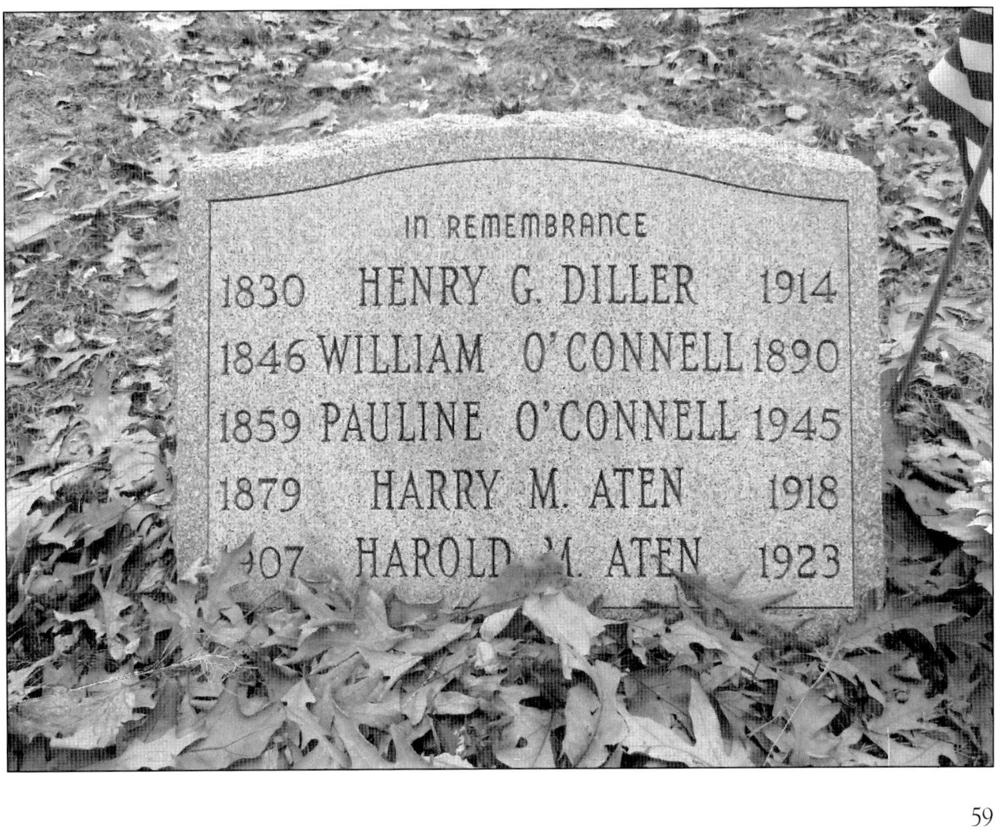

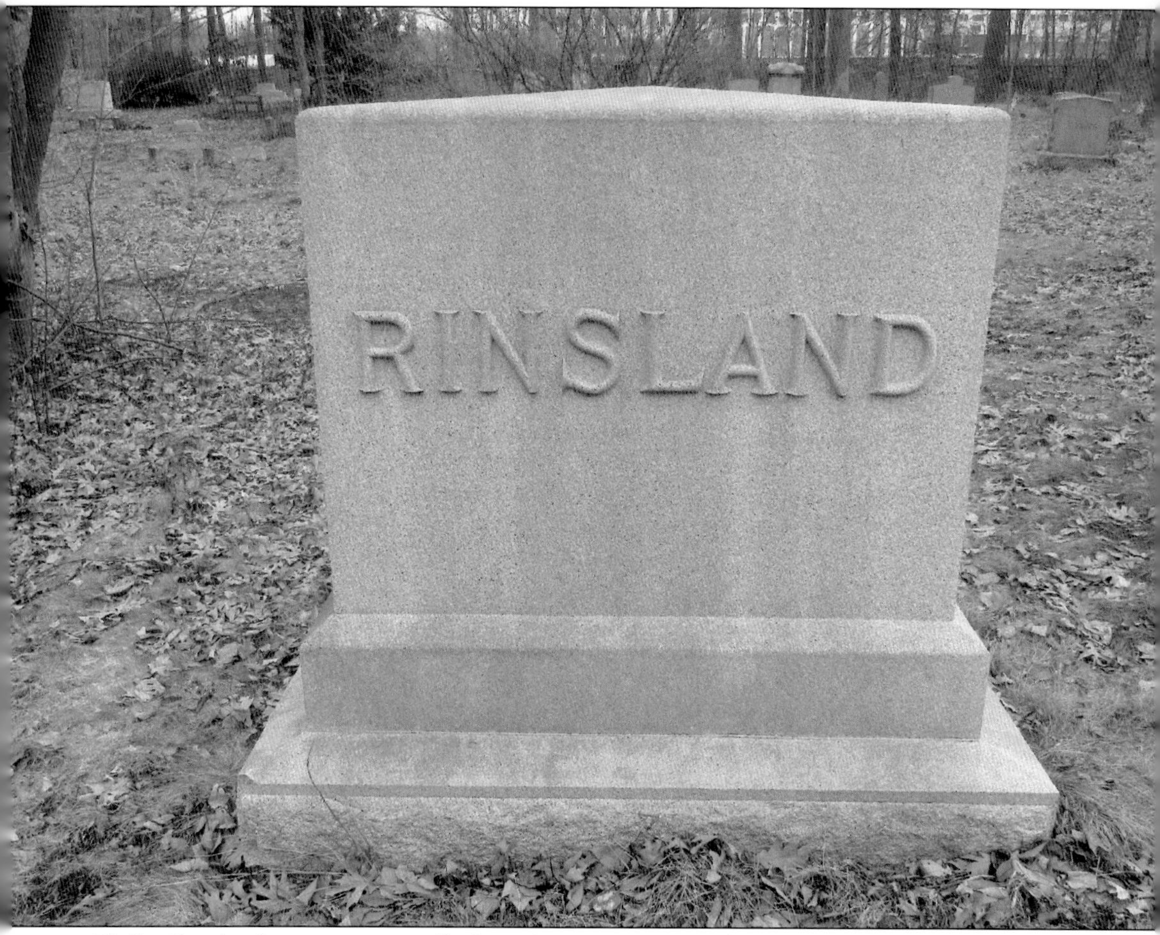

Phillip Rinsland was not originally from Scranton. He was born in Callicoon, New York, the son of a locomotive engineer. After his father was killed in a train accident, the family moved to Carbondale, Pennsylvania, when Phillip was only five years old. As a young man, he worked as an apprentice in a barbershop. Some years later, he opened his own shop called the Turkish Bath Barber Shop on Linden Street in downtown Scranton. Phillip threw his hat in local politics in 1899 and was elected to the position of city assessor. He had been described as having a keen eye for poor conditions in the city and went on to help many of its under privileged residents. (Author's collection.)

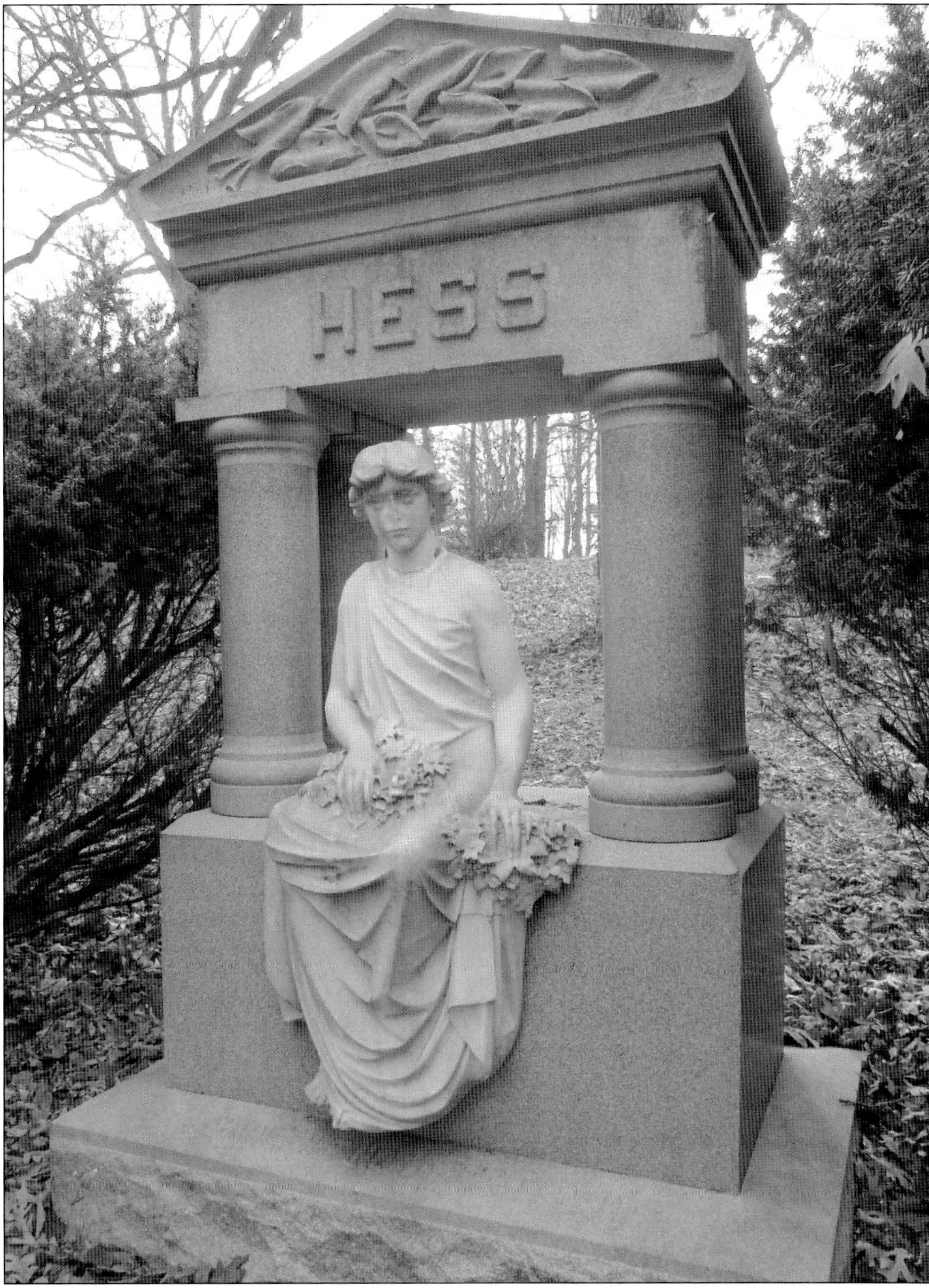

The monument was designed in the likeness of 18-year-old Edith Hess and is one of the most visited stones in Forest Hill. Hess perished on July 4, 1912, in the worst rear-end collision in railroading history, known as the Gibson Train Wreck. The accident occurred three miles of Corning, New York, and claimed the lives of 39 people, 4 of which were Scrantonians. Hess was laid to rest at Forest Hill on July 8, 1912. (Author's collection.)

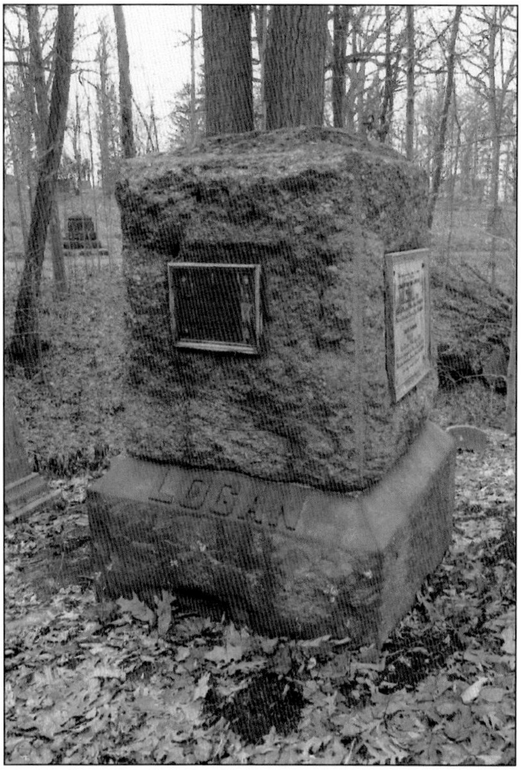

The Logans were a very prominent family in the area during the 19th century. Patriarch Samuel Crothers Logan served as reverend for the First Presbyterian Church in Scranton for more than 25 years. His eldest son, Harry V. Logan, was a physician who had a very successful practice until the day he died at the early age of 58. The youngest Logan, Arthur, was a lawyer but for only for a brief time due to a respiratory ailment that robbed him of fulfilling his life's dream. (Author's collection.)

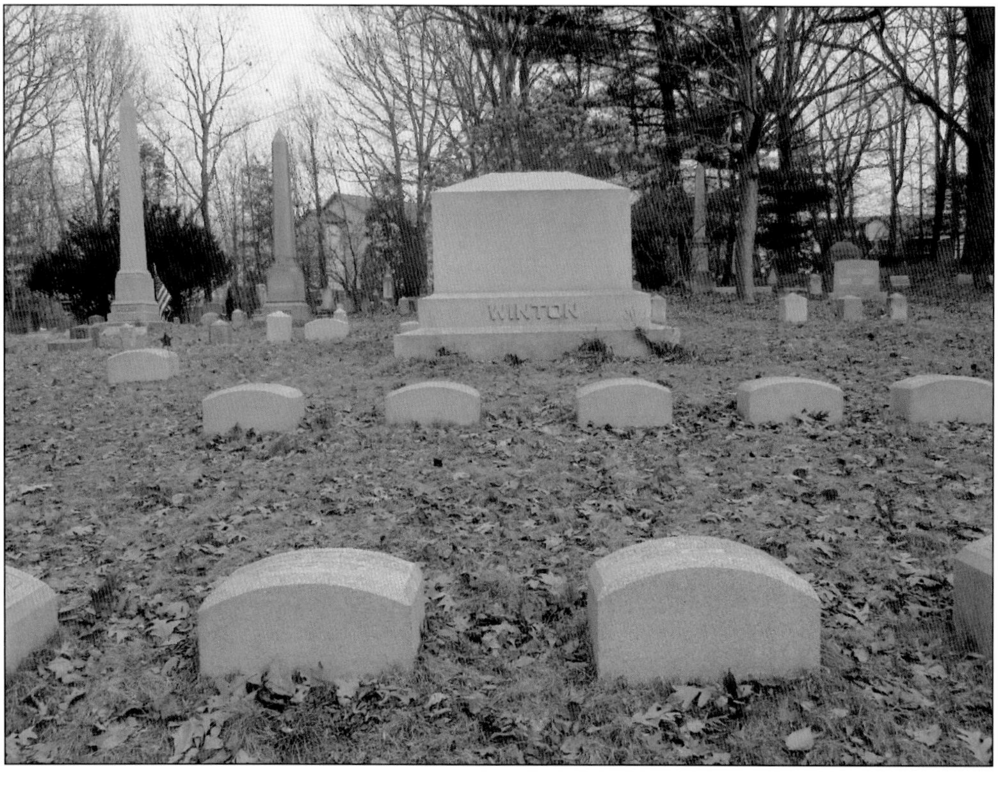

Some would consider the Wintons the first family of Providence. Their story began with William Wilander "W.W" Winton, who was born in 1815 and came to settle in the area with his family in 1833. By 1850, W.W. was very secure in his holdings, which included owning a good amount of land. Over the following two decades, W.W. opened many businesses, including a popular general store and one of the first banks in Providence. (Author's collection.)

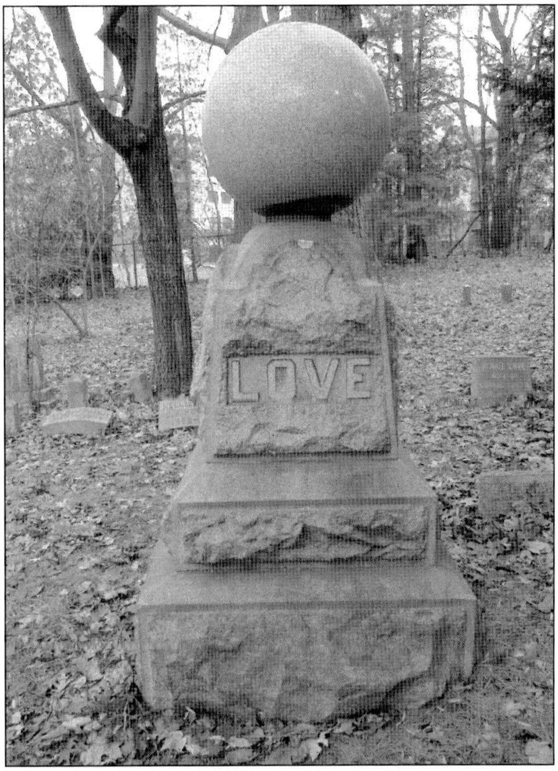

William Love was a resident of North Scranton for nearly 60 years and was considered one of its pioneer citizens. He and his wife, Marcia, had two daughters, both of whom died before them. Horsemen throughout Northern Pennsylvania knew William Love as an expert blacksmith. His shop in Providence was the mecca for the turfmen of that section. (Author's collection.)

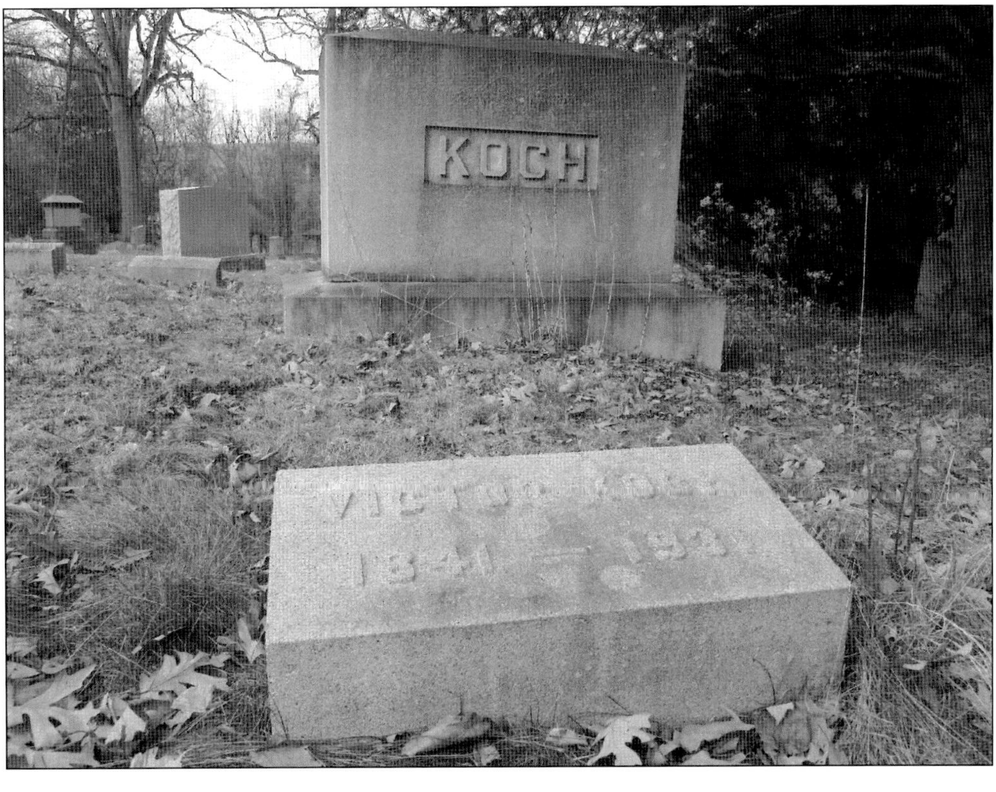

Victor Koch was born in Germany on November 21, 1841, and educated in their public schools. Upon his arrival in America, he met and married Caroline Trust. Victor became proprietor of the Scranton House in 1870. He built a 27-room mansion in 1894 at the corner of Madison Avenue and Mulberry Street. Today, it is the site of the Chipak Funeral Home. (Author's collection.)

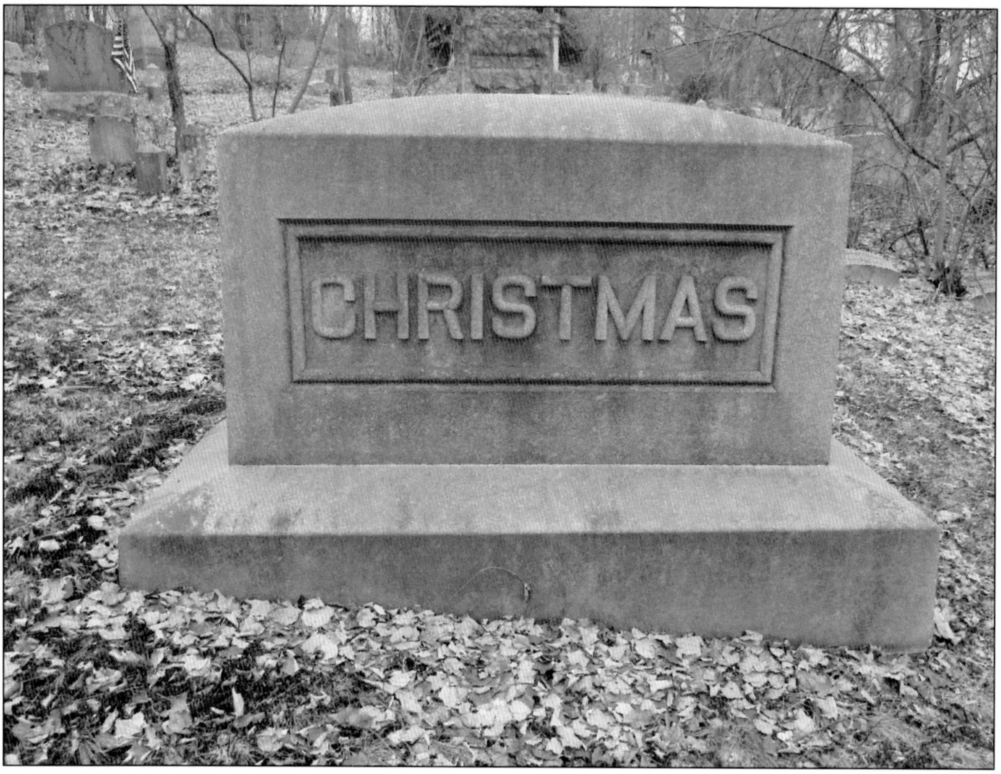

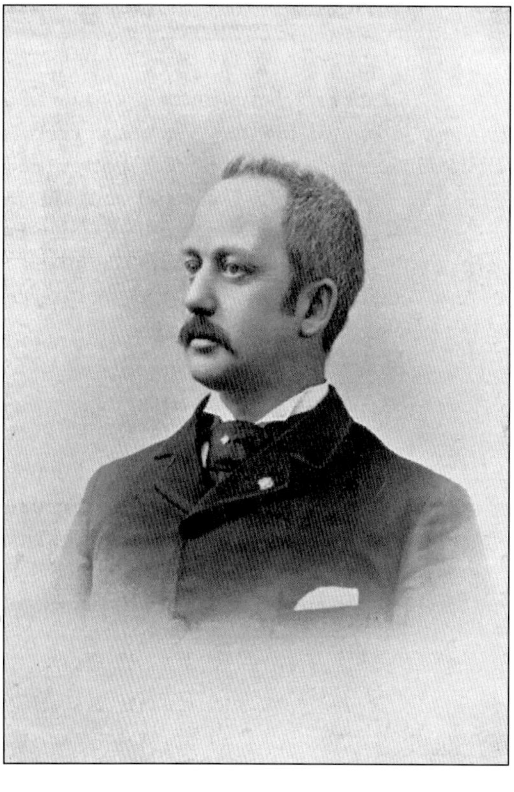

In 1848, Henry Christmas left his birth home in Bryn Mawr, South Wales, and settled in Pottsville, Pennsylvania. Soon after, he relocated to Scranton to open a shoemaking establishment near the local ore mine. He employed 10 men, but after the mine became abandoned he sought a more profitable field as a machinist in Clarks Breaker in nearby Providence. The first Welsh sermon in Providence was preached in the home of Henry Christmas. (Author's collection.)

James G. Bailey owned and operated a general store at 401 Penn Avenue. He was a self-made man and would come to have one of the largest grocery trades in Scranton. Bailey later ran and was elected Scranton's mayor from 1896 to 1899. (Courtesy of the Albright Memorial Library.)

In the spring of 1868, D.W. Connolly embarked on the study of law in Scranton. At the end of his studies, he passed an arduous examination before Judges Lewis Jones, Alfred Hand, and W.G. Ward. He was admitted to practice in the mayor's court for the city of Scranton in May 1870. Throughout his career, Connolly maintained an unblemished reputation and was universally respected by all classes. (Courtesy of Forest Hill Archives.)

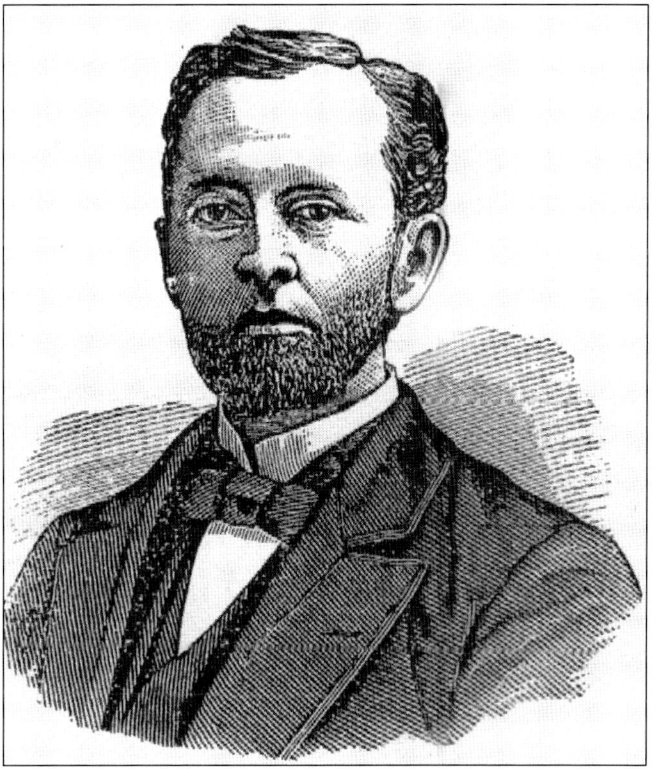

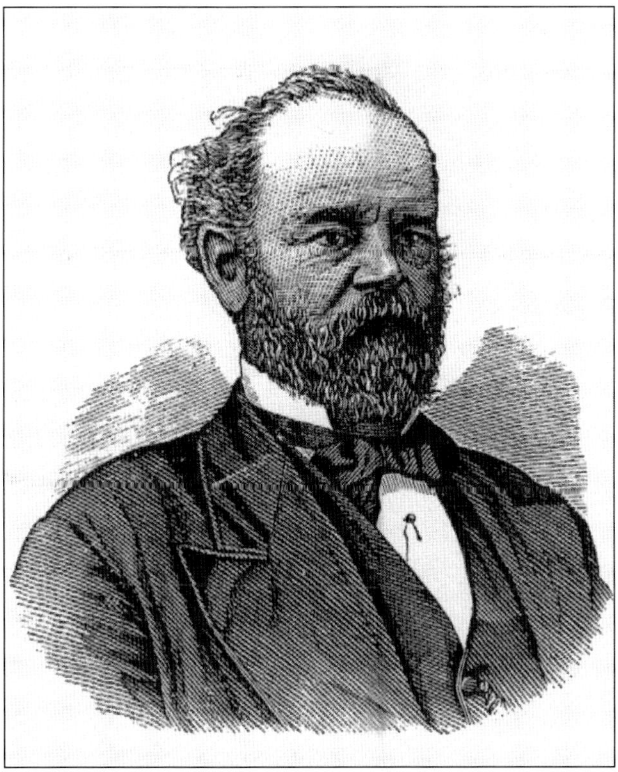

Dr. John Wilson Gibbs Jr. was one of the older physicians in Scranton during the time of his practice. He was born October 10, 1823, near Newark, New Jersey; settled in Hyde Park in 1857; and began a lucrative career in medicine and surgery. He was elected as coroner to the old county of Luzerne during the Civil War. (Courtesy of Forest Hill Archives.)

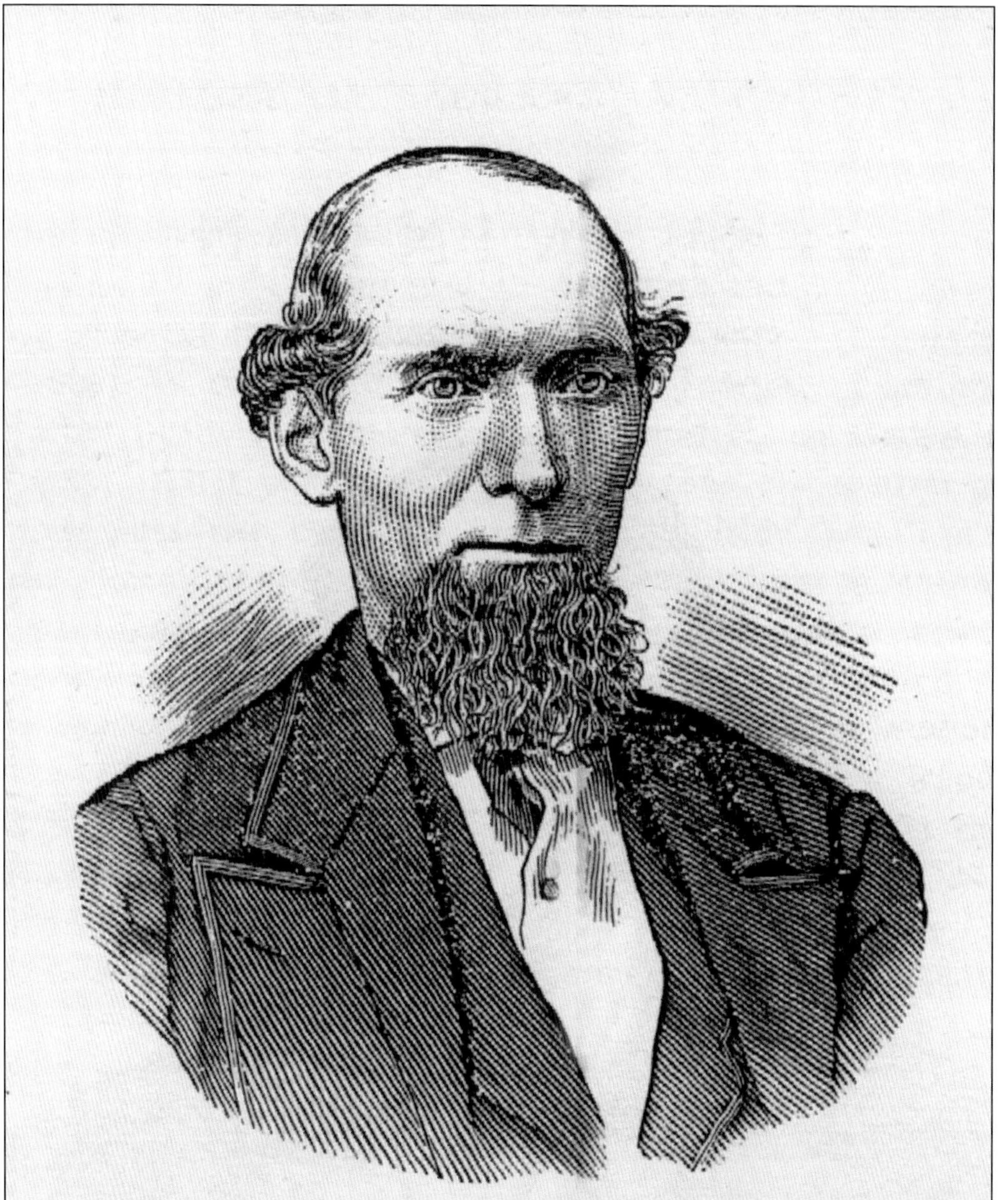

William S. Jones was born in Booneville, Oneida County, New York, in 1832 to poor parents who emigrated to the United States from North Wales two years prior to his birth. William was the first of his family to be born in America. He began working in the mines loading coal at the age of 13. He worked in the mines until adulthood, when he enlisted to fight in the Civil War. In 1864, after the war ended, William returned to his Hyde Park home and resumed working in the mines until his health began to fail from the poor working conditions. For several years, he was employed by the Banner American Company as managing editor of *Banner America*, a Welsh weekly newspaper. (Courtesy of Forest Hill Archives.)

Dr. Ludwig Wehlau graduated from the Würzburg Medical College in Bavaria, in 1874. He relocated to America in 1876 and settled in Scranton, where he opened his medical practice. He was ranked high among the medical professionals in the area. (Courtesy of Forest Hill Archives.)

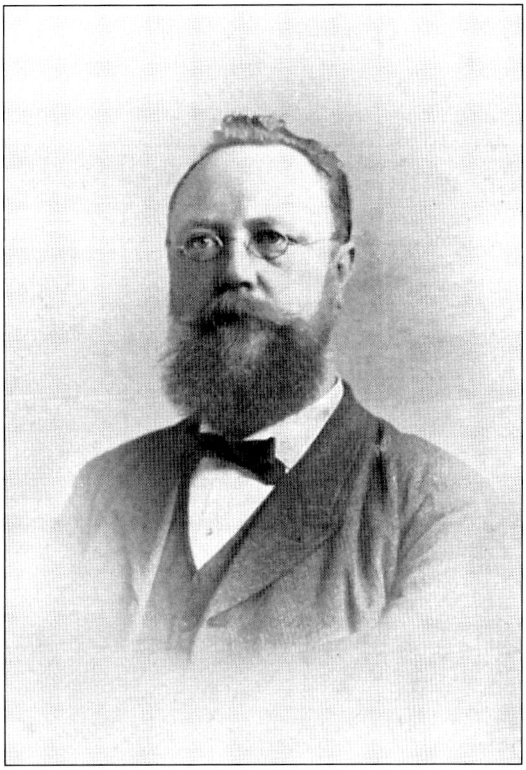

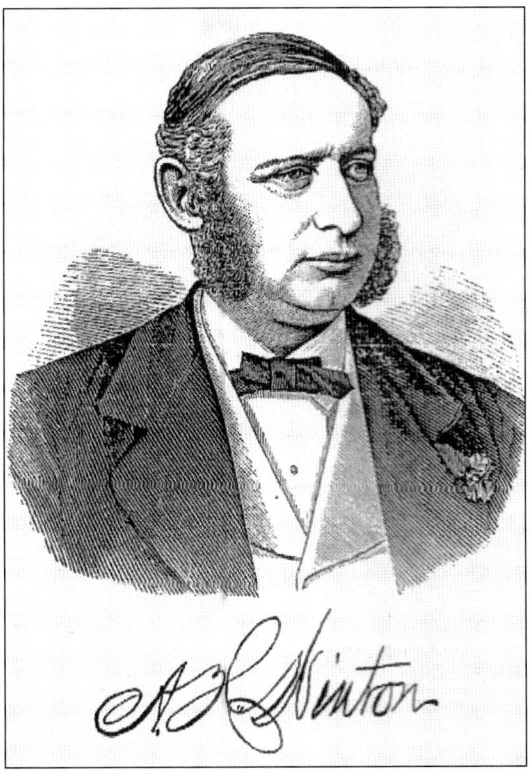

A.H. Winton was another renowned lawyer of his time in the city of Scranton. Born in Scranton in 1838, Winton was well educated throughout his early life, and after he entered the bar, he began a partnership with M. Harding, the late president judge of Luzerne County. Winton's reputation as a lawyer grew when he stood in defense for former Scranton mayor F.A. Beamish in what is known as the Free Press libel suit. Winton secured Beamish's acquittal. He was known as an eloquent speaker and was extremely involved in the Temperance Movement and establishing Lackawanna County in 1878. (Courtesy of Forest Hill Archives.)

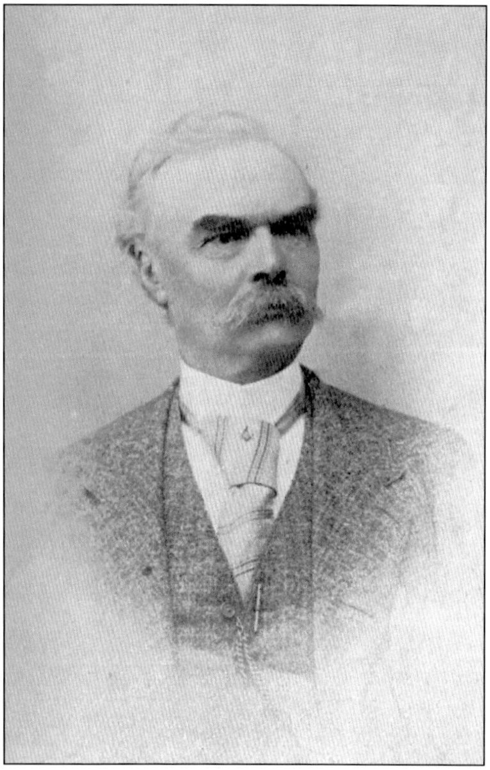

Samuel Griffith Kerr was of the firm Kerr & Siebecker, Carpet and Curtain Dealers. He was born in Ireland, and in 1873 he moved to Scranton and opened a carpet store on August 14 of that year. In 1877, he enlisted as a private in Company C of the 13th Regiment NGP (National Guard Pennsylvania). His store was the first devoted entirely to carpets in Scranton. (Courtesy of Albright Memorial Library.)

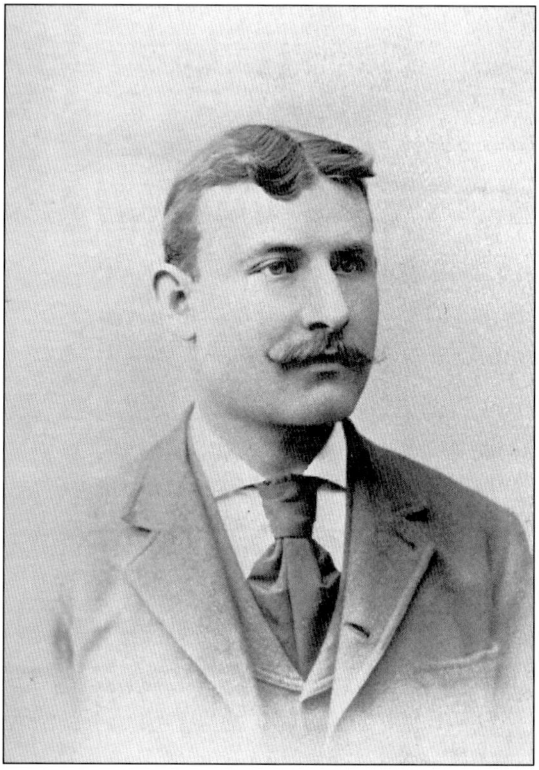

Charles W. Blume was the junior member of the firm of William Blume & Son, Manufacturers of and Dealers in Carriages, Buggies, Phaetons, Traps, and Business Wagons. Blume was a representative of his generation whose indomitable thrift, energy, and intelligence combined with good judgement helped the family enterprises to flourish. (Courtesy of Albright Memorial Library.)

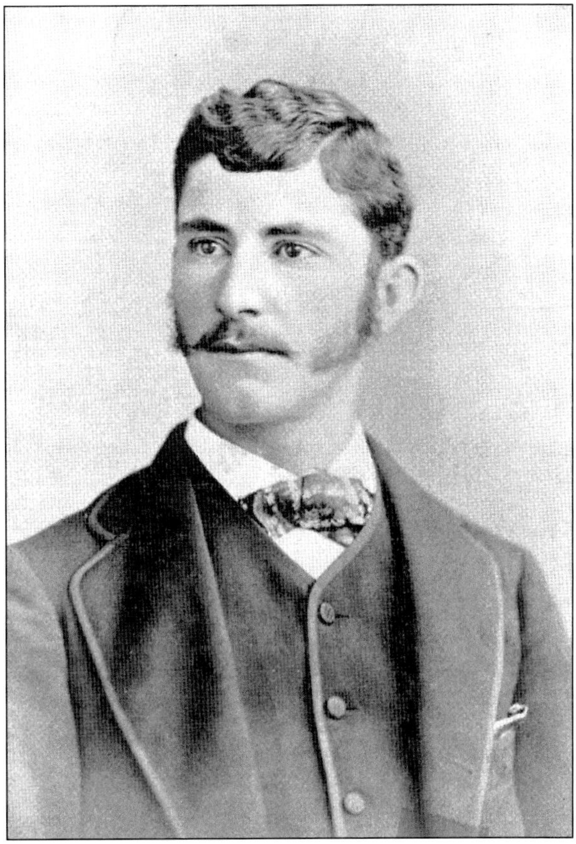

Thomas B. McClintock rented a property on Monroe Avenue, between Vine and Olive Streets, where he opened his first greenhouse. In 1889, he purchased a larger tract of land on Jefferson Avenue and Electric Street, where he built Commodious Conservatory. During his time in Scranton, he established one of the most successful florists' business in Scranton. Below is an advertisement for McClintock's Florists. (Courtesy of Forest Hill Archives.)

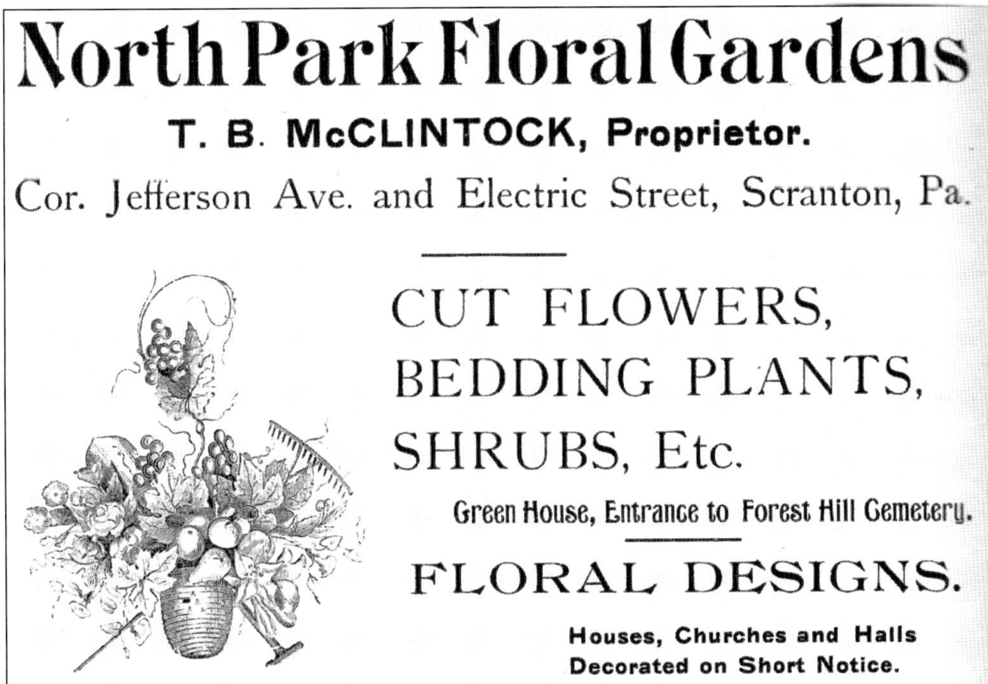

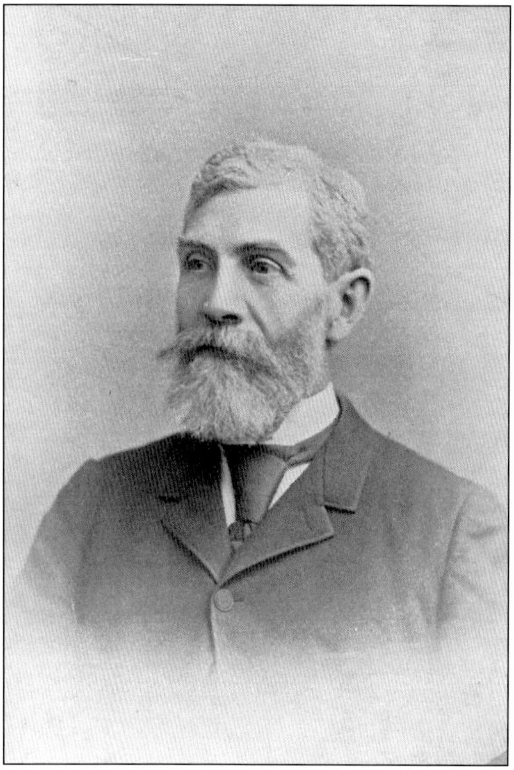

A familiar face to the 19th-century businessmen of Scranton, Smith B. Mott was a native of the city. Mott acquired a reputation unequaled in this section of the state for expert accounting and trustworthiness. His knowledge in local banking was impeccable. He was employed as a cashier for the Second National Bank. (Courtesy of Forest Hill Archives.)

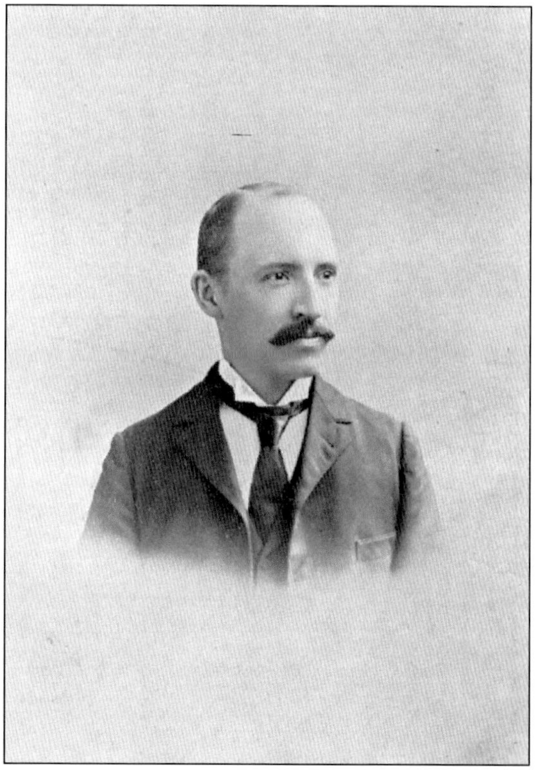

Born in Pottsville, Pennsylvania, Louis Conrad entered a gentlemen's furnishing store, as a clerk, after his schooling. He opened up his own place of business on 305 Lackawanna Avenue. In later years, he became better known as Louis Conrad, "the Hatter." (Courtesy of Albright Memorial Library.)

Jasper C. Taylor was the county superintendent of schools. Born in 1857 in Scott Township, Lackawanna County, he was a teacher for 16 years. In May 1893, he was elected as the county superintendent of schools. (Courtesy of Albright Memorial Library.)

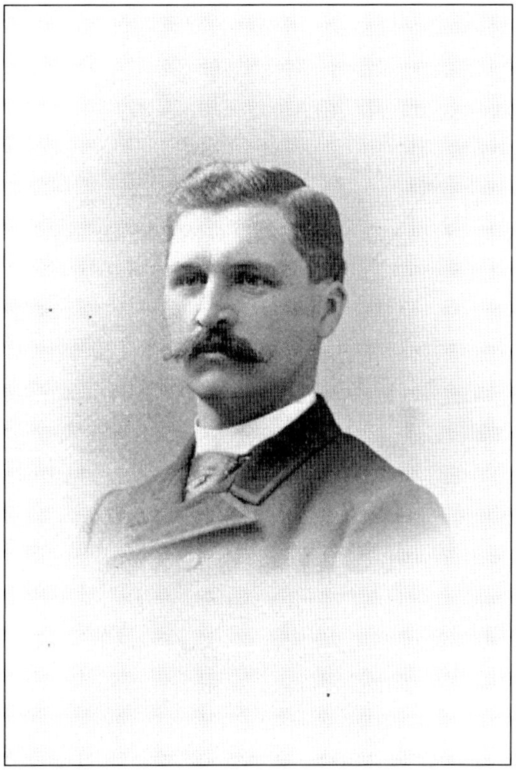

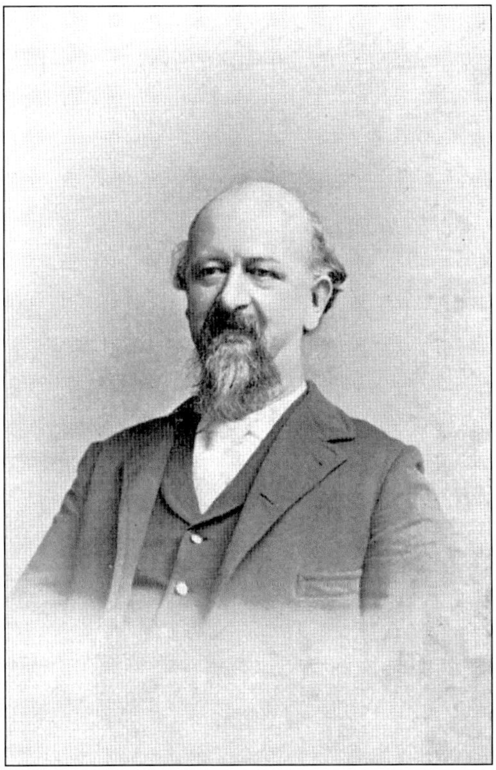

Fred Wagner entered the printing trade in 1852. He took charge of the *Scranton Wochenblatt* in 1865, making it the leading German newspaper in the state. (Courtesy of the Albright Memorial Library.)

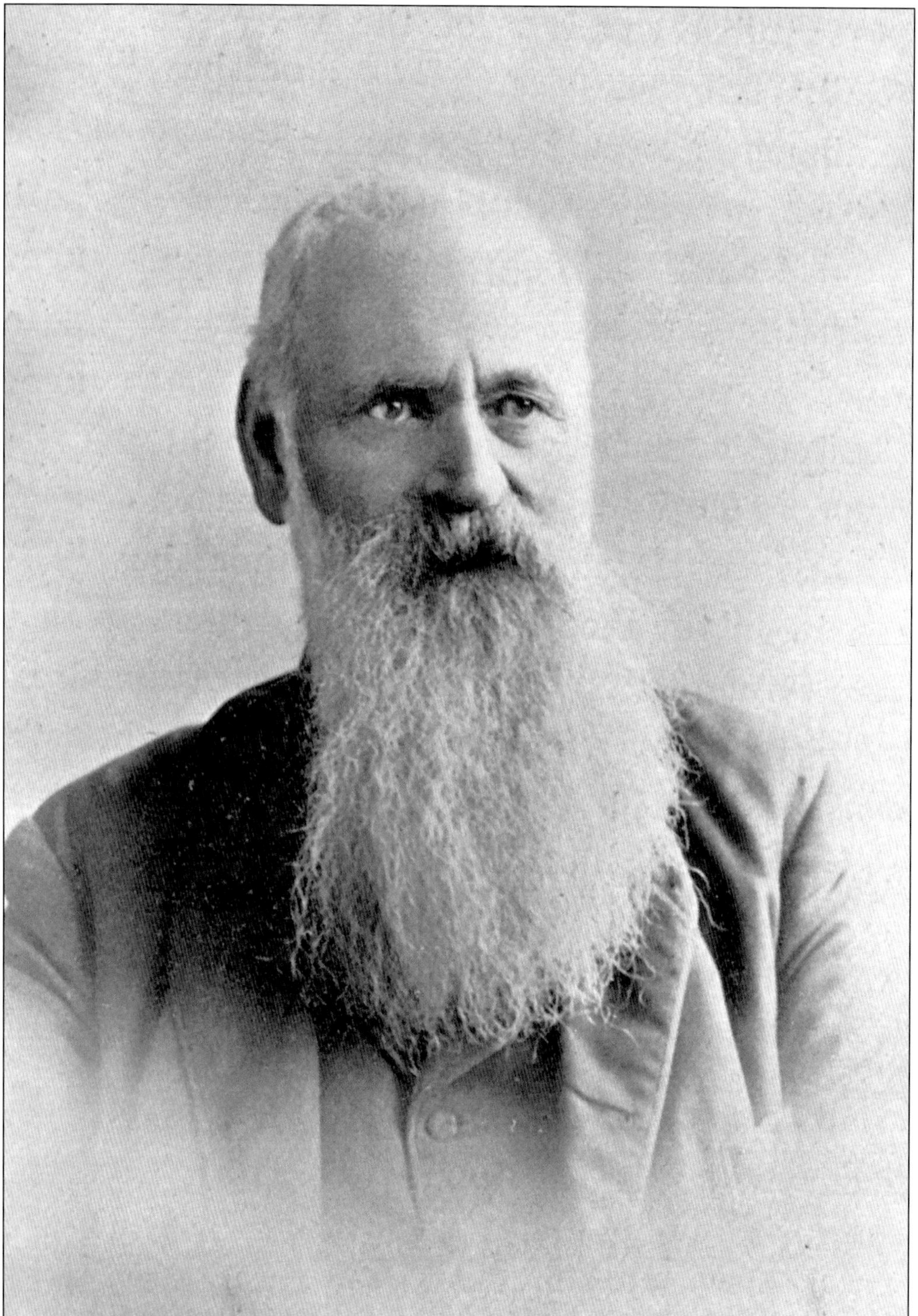

Dr. Peter Winter was a prominent physician of Dunmore. As a young man, he taught school for three years, but he was determined to become a physician, so he entered the University of New York and graduated in 1863. (Courtesy of the Albright Memorial Library.)

Four

CEMETERY EPHEMERA AND MEMORABILIA

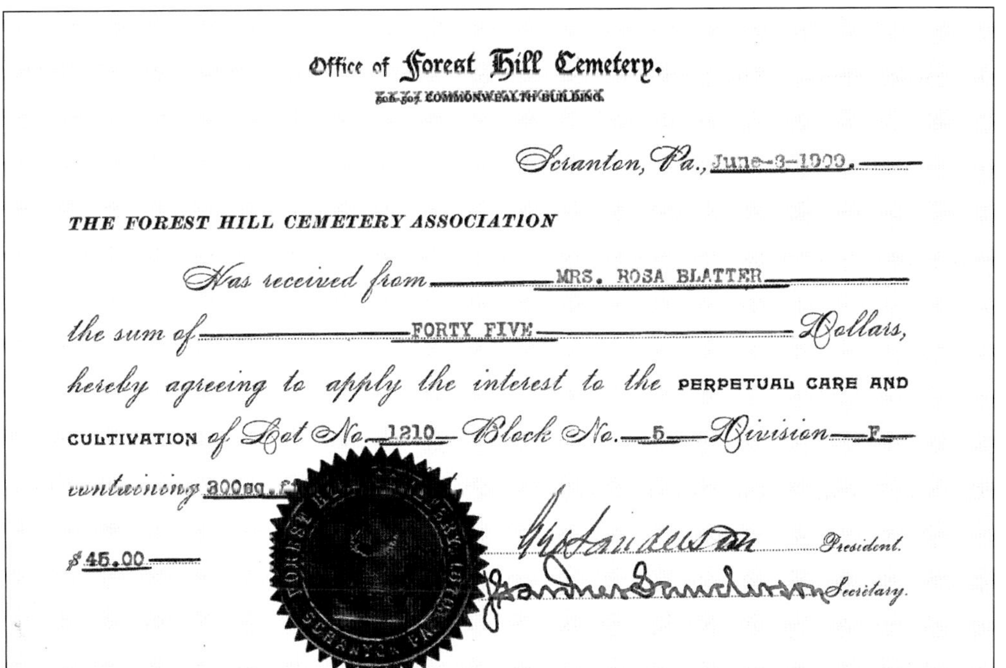

Office of Forest Hill Cemetery.

505-507 COMMONWEALTH BUILDING

Scranton, Pa., June-3-1909.

THE FOREST HILL CEMETERY ASSOCIATION

Has received from MRS. ROSA BLATTER

the sum of FORTY FIVE Dollars,

hereby agreeing to apply the interest to the PERPETUAL CARE AND CULTIVATION of Lot No. 1210 Block No. 5 Division F

containing 300sq.f

$45.00

President.

Secretary.

This perpetual care certificate dated 1909 is for Rose Blatter in the sum of $45. In general, perpetual care funds are used for the maintenance and repair of burial lots. Many cemeteries offer this service, but in some states, it is required by law. (Courtesy of Forest Hill Archives.)

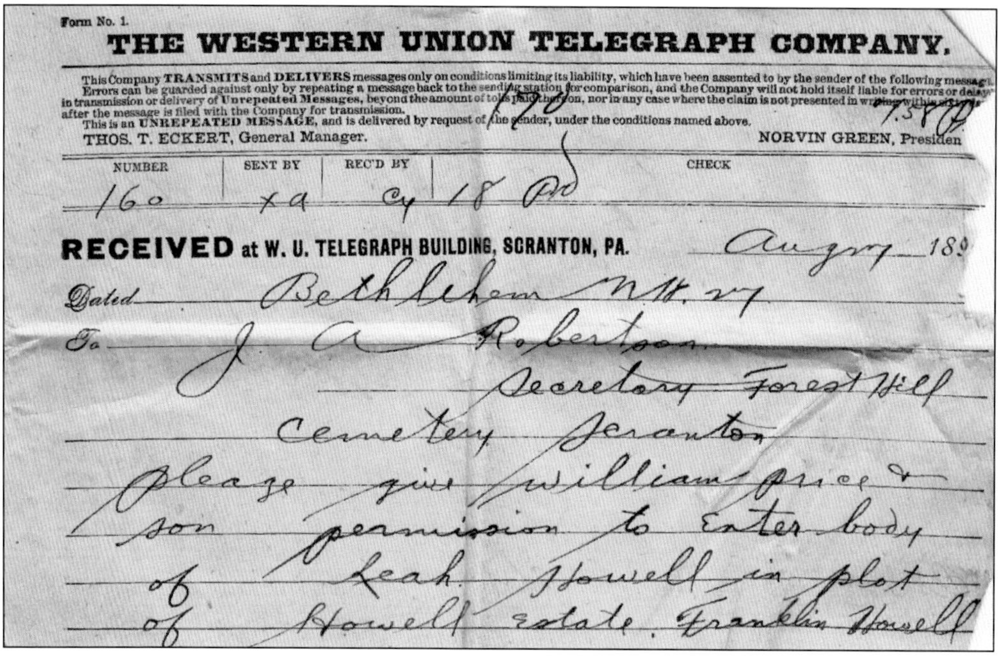

Form No. 1.

THE WESTERN UNION TELEGRAPH COMPANY.

This Company TRANSMITS and DELIVERS messages only on conditions limiting its liability, which have been assented to by the sender of the following message. Errors can be guarded against only by repeating a message back to the sending station for comparison, and the Company will not hold itself liable for errors or delays in transmission or delivery of Unrepeated Messages, beyond the amount of tolls paid thereon, nor in any case where the claim is not presented in writing within sixty days after the message is filed with the Company for transmission.
This is an UNREPEATED MESSAGE, and is delivered by request of the sender, under the conditions named above.

THOS. T. ECKERT, General Manager. NORVIN GREEN, President

NUMBER	SENT BY	REC'D BY		CHECK
160	xa	Cy	18 Pd	

RECEIVED at W. U. TELEGRAPH BUILDING, SCRANTON, PA. Aug 27 189

Dated Bethlehem N.H. 27

To J. A. Robertson
Secretary Forest Hill
Cemetery Scranton

please give William Price & son permission to enter body of Leah Howell in plot of Howell estate. Franklin Howell

J.A. Robertson served as Forest Hill's secretary for a time. Pictured here is a note that granted permission to William Price via Western Union to inter the body of Leah Howell in the plot of the Howell estate. (Courtesy of Forest Hill Archives.)

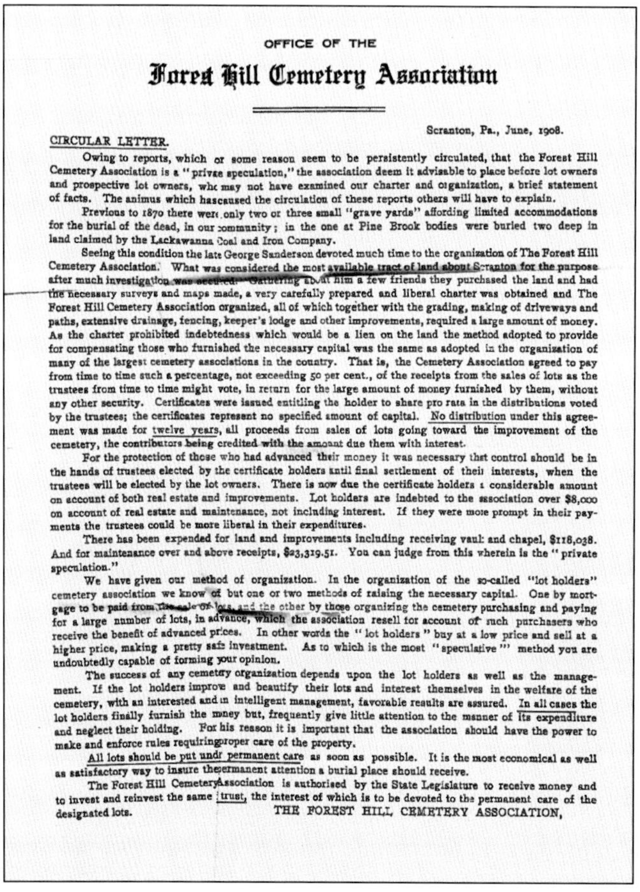

OFFICE OF THE

Forest Hill Cemetery Association

Scranton, Pa., June, 1908.

CIRCULAR LETTER.

Owing to reports, which or some reason seem to be persistently circulated, that the Forest Hill Cemetery Association is a "privae speculation," the association deem it advisable to place before lot owners and prospective lot owners, whc may not have examined our charter and organization, a brief statement of facts. The animus which hascaused the circulation of these reports others will have to explain.

Previous to 1870 there were only two or three small "grave yards" affording limited accommodations for the burial of the dead, in our community; in the one at Pine Brook bodies were buried two deep in land claimed by the Lackawanna Coal and Iron Company.

Seeing this condition the late George Sanderson devoted much time to the organization of The Forest Hill Cemetery Association. What was considered the most available tract of land about Scranton for the purpose after much investigation was secured. Gathering about him a few friends they purchased the land and had the necessary surveys and maps made, a very carefully prepared and liberal charter was obtained and The Forest Hill Cemetery Association organized, all of which together with the grading, making of driveways and paths, extensive drainage, fencing, keeper's lodge and other improvements, required a large amount of money. As the charter prohibited indebtedness which would be a lien on the land the method adopted to provide for compensating those who furnished the necessary capital was the same as adopted in the organization of many of the largest cemetery associations in the country. That is, the Cemetery Association agreed to pay from time to time such a percentage, not exceeding 50 per cent., of the receipts from the sales of lots as the trustees from time to time might vote, in return for the large amount of money furnished by them, without any other security. Certificates were issued entitling the holder to share pro rata in the distributions voted by the trustees; the certificates represent no specified amount of capital. No distribution under this agreement was made for twelve years, all proceeds from sales of lots going toward the improvement of the cemetery, the contributors being credited with the amount due them with interest.

For the protection of those who had advanced their money it was necessary that control should be in the hands of trustees elected by the certificate holders until final settlement of their interests, when the trustees will be elected by the lot owners. There is now due the certificate holders a considerable amount on account of both real estate and improvements. Lot holders are indebted to the association over $8,000 on account of real estate and maintenance, not including interest. If they were more prompt in their payments the trustees could be more liberal in their expenditures.

There has been expended for land and improvements including receiving vault and chapel, $118,038. And for maintenance over and above receipts, $23,319.51. You can judge from this wherein is the "private speculation."

We have given our method of organization. In the organization of the so-called "lot holders" cemetery association we know of but one or two methods of raising the necessary capital. One by mortgage to be paid from the sale of lots, and the other by those organizing the cemetery purchasing and paying for a large number of lots, in advance, which the association resell for account of such purchasers who receive the benefit of advanced prices. In other words the "lot holders" buy at a low price and sell at a higher price, making a pretty safe investment. As to which is the most "speculative" method you are undoubtedly capable of forming your opinion.

The success of any cemetery organization depends upon the lot holders as well as the management. If the lot holders improve and beautify their lots and interest themselves in the welfare of the cemetery, with an interested and in intelligent management, favorable results are assured. In all cases the lot holders finally furnish the money but, frequently give little attention to the manner of its expenditure and neglect their holding. For his reason it is important that the association should have the power to make and enforce rules requiringproper care of the property.

All lots should be put undr permanent care as soon as possible. It is the most economical as well as satisfactory way to insure thepermanent attention a burial place should receive.

The Forest Hill CemeteryAssociation is authorised by the State Legislature to receive money and to invest and reinvest the same in trust, the interest of which is to be devoted to the permanent care of the designated lots.

THE FOREST HILL CEMETERY ASSOCIATION,

Pictured is a circular letter dated June 1908 from the office of Forest Hill Cemetery. In this letter, the writer explains why the Forest Hill Cemetery Association is not a "private speculation." (Courtesy of the Forest Hill Archives.)

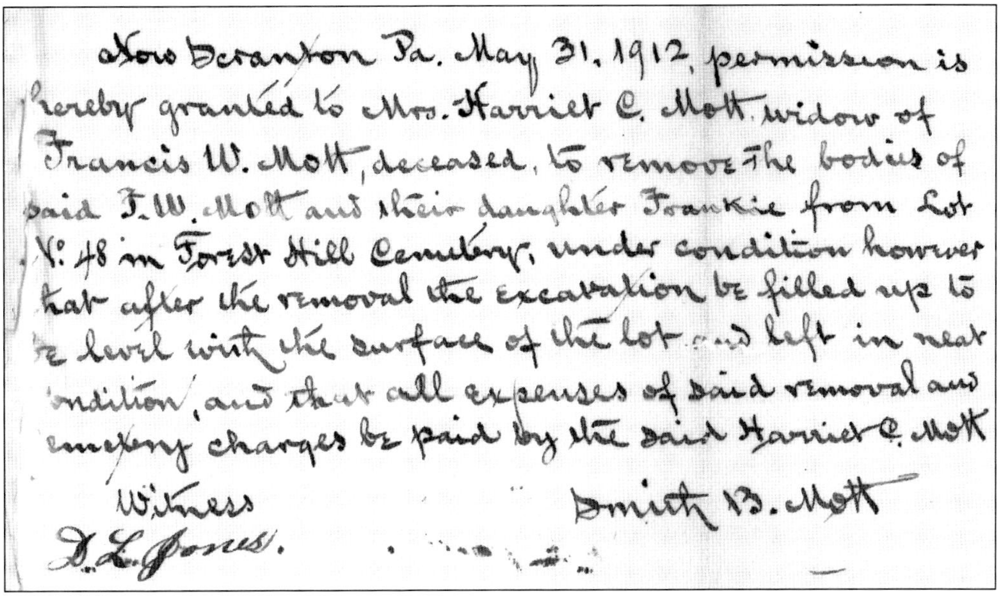

Now Scranton Pa. May 31, 1912, permission is hereby granted to Mrs. Harriet C. Mott, widow of Francis W. Mott, deceased, to remove the bodies of said F.W. Mott and their daughter Frankie from Lot No. 48 in Forest Hill Cemetery, under condition however that after the removal the excavation be filled up to a level with the surface of the lot and left in neat condition, and that all expenses of said removal and emptying charges be paid by the said Harriet C. Mott

Witness
D.L. Jones.

Smith B. Mott

The c. 1912 certificate is for the removal of F.W. Mott and his daughter from Lot No. 48 in Forest Hill to another cemetery. It was witnessed by D.L. Jones and signed by Smith B. Mott, who is a resident of the cemetery. (Courtesy of Forest Hill Cemetery Archives.)

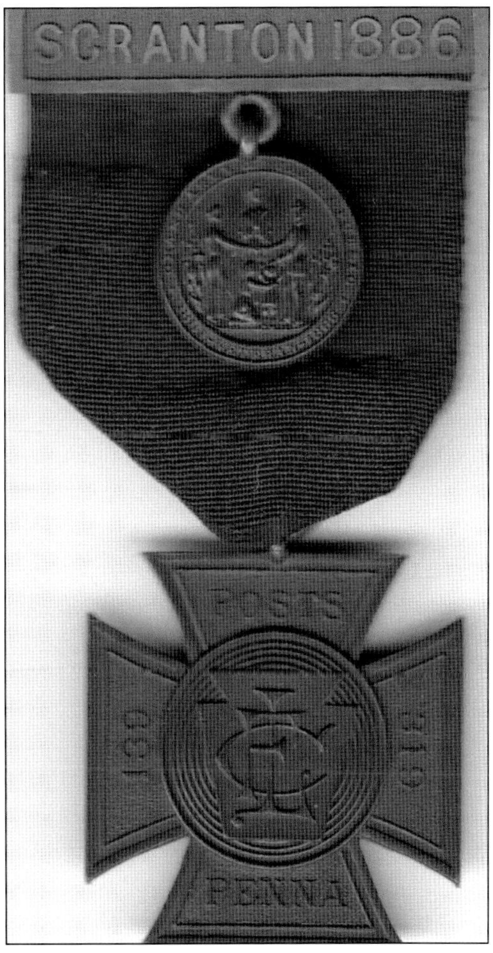

This Women's Relief Corps medal was owned by Lavina Albro, wife of Civil War veteran, William F. Albro. In 1893, the Women's Relief Corp was recognized as the ladies' auxiliary to the Grand Army of the Republic. (Courtesy of Forest Hill Archives.)

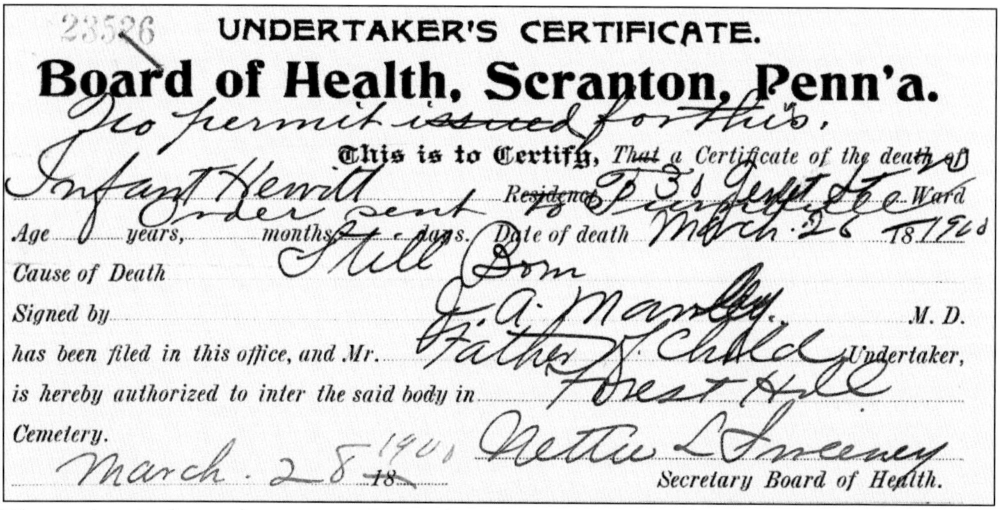

23526 **UNDERTAKER'S CERTIFICATE.**

Board of Health, Scranton, Penn'a.

No permit issued for this.

This is to Certify, *That a Certificate of the death of* Infant Hewitt *Residence* 731 Jeff Ave *Ward*

Age 0 *years,* *months* *days.* *Date of death* March 26 *18*1901

Cause of Death Still Born

Signed by J. A. Manley *M. D.*

has been filed in this office, and Mr. Father of child *Undertaker,*

is hereby authorized to inter the said body in Forest Hill

Cemetery.

March 28 *18*1901 Nettie L. Sweeney

Secretary Board of Health.

This undertaker's certificate states that no burial permit was issued. However, the father is listed as the undertaker. It was custom in those times for the father of a stillborn or a child only a few years old to be named as the undertaker. (Courtesy of Forest Hill Archives.)

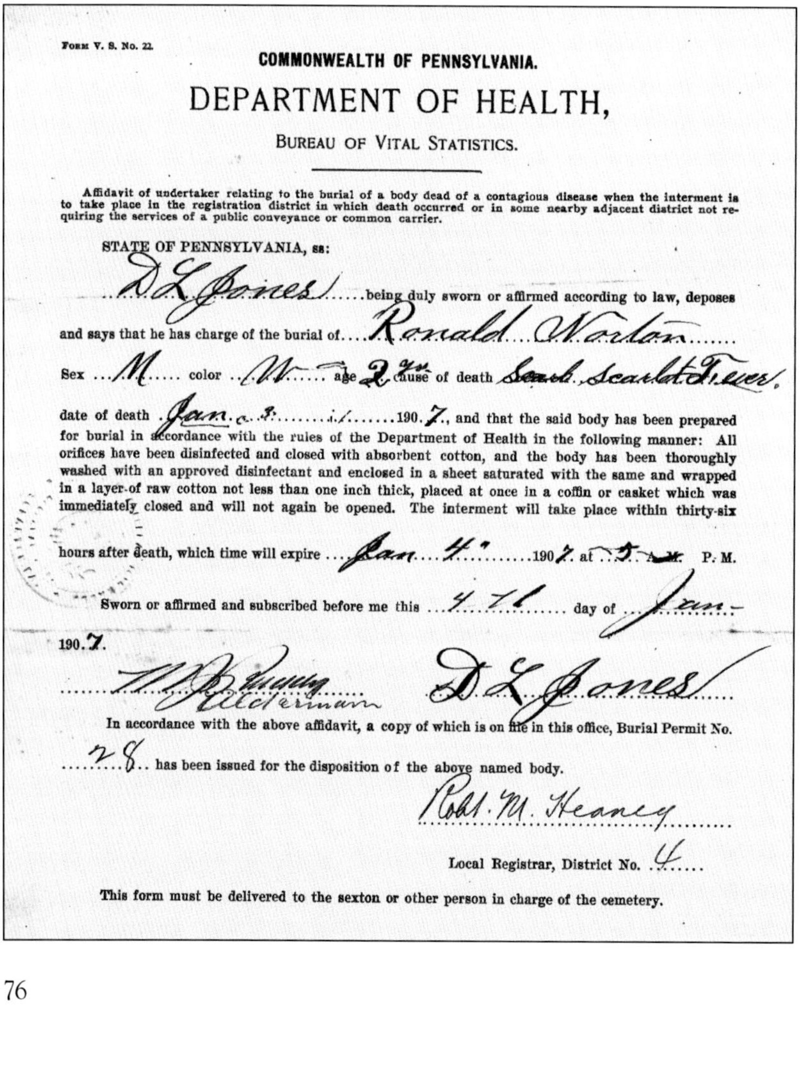

FORM V. S. No. 22.

COMMONWEALTH OF PENNSYLVANIA.

DEPARTMENT OF HEALTH,

BUREAU OF VITAL STATISTICS.

Affidavit of undertaker relating to the burial of a body dead of a contagious disease when the interment is to take place in the registration district in which death occurred or in some nearby adjacent district not requiring the services of a public conveyance or common carrier.

STATE OF PENNSYLVANIA, ss:

D L Jones being duly sworn or affirmed according to law, deposes and says that he has charge of the burial of Ronald Norton

Sex M color W age 2 yrs cause of death Scarlet Fever

date of death Jan 3 190 7, and that the said body has been prepared for burial in accordance with the rules of the Department of Health in the following manner: All orifices have been disinfected and closed with absorbent cotton, and the body has been thoroughly washed with an approved disinfectant and enclosed in a sheet saturated with the same and wrapped in a layer of raw cotton not less than one inch thick, placed at once in a coffin or casket which was immediately closed and will not again be opened. The interment will take place within thirty-six hours after death, which time will expire Jan 4th 1907 at 5 P. M.

Sworn or affirmed and subscribed before me this 4th day of Jan 1907.

Alderman D L Jones

In accordance with the above affidavit, a copy of which is on file in this office, Burial Permit No. 28 has been issued for the disposition of the above named body.

Robt. M. Heaney

Local Registrar, District No. 4

This form must be delivered to the sexton or other person in charge of the cemetery.

Pictured is a Department of Health certificate from around 1907. D.L. Jones was the undertaker; he was the son of D.D. Jones, who had funeral homes in Hyde Park and downtown Scranton. (Courtesy of Forest Hill Archives.)

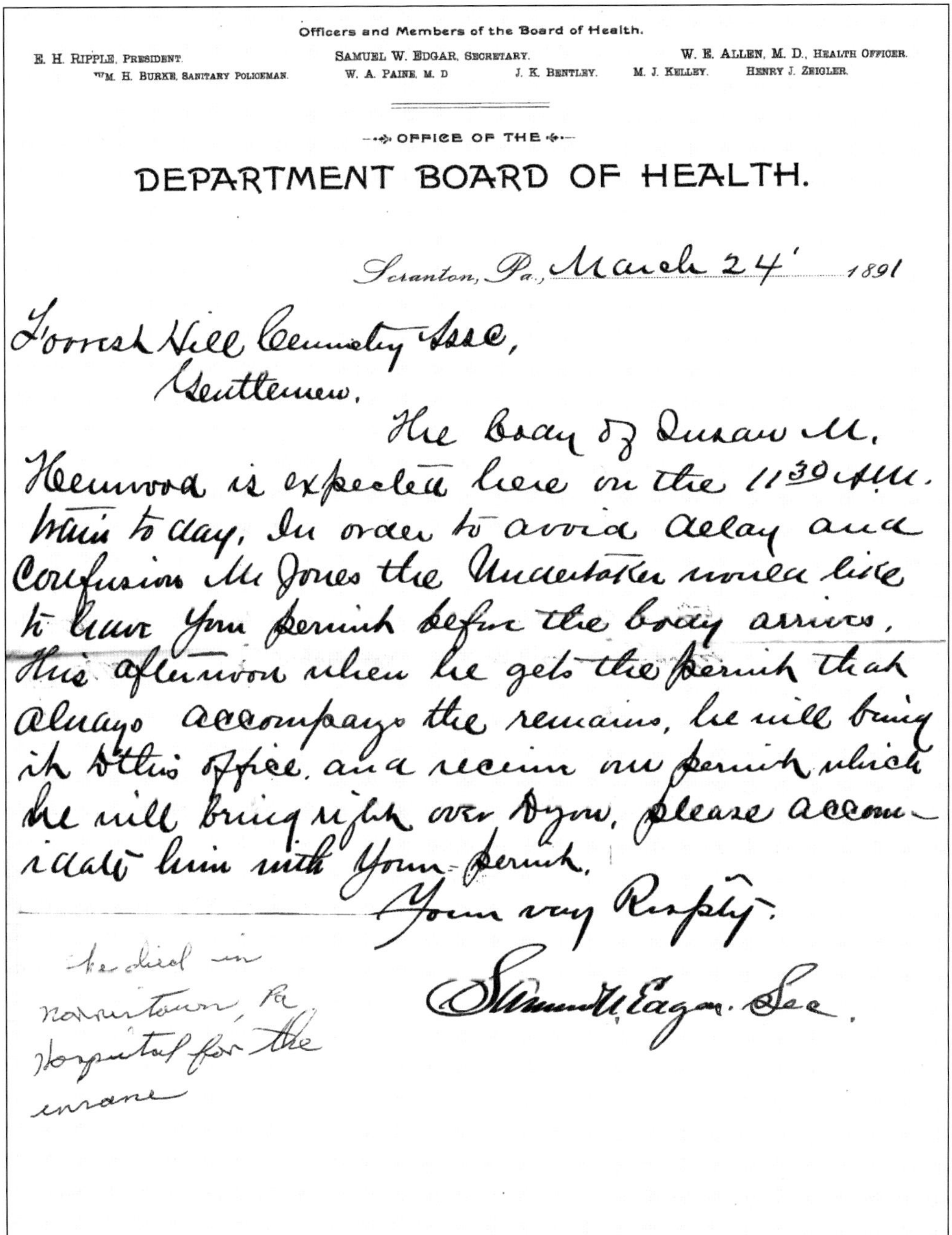
Officers and Members of the Board of Health.

E. H. RIPPLE, PRESIDENT. SAMUEL W. EDGAR, SECRETARY. W. E. ALLEN, M. D., HEALTH OFFICER.
WM. H. BURKE, SANITARY POLICEMAN. W. A. PAINE, M. D. J. K. BENTLEY. M. J. KELLEY. HENRY J. ZEIGLER.

— OFFICE OF THE —

DEPARTMENT BOARD OF HEALTH.

Scranton, Pa., March 24' 1891

Forest Hill Cemetery Assc,
Gentlemen,
The Body of Susan M.
Henwood is expected here on the 11.30 A.M.
train to day. In order to avoid delay and
confusion Mr Jones the Undertaker would like
to have your permit before the body arrives.
This afternoon when he gets the permit that
always accompanys the remains, he will bring
it to this office and receive our permit which
he will bring right over to you. Please accom-
modate him with your permit.
Your very Respty.

Saml W. Edgar. Sec.

she died in
Norristown, Pa.
Hospital for the
insane

This board of health certificate states that Isabelle Henwood died in the Norristown, Pennsylvania, Hospital for the insane. She was interred at Forest Hill Cemetery, as is Samuel W. Edgar, undertaker. (Courtesy of Forest Hill Archives.)

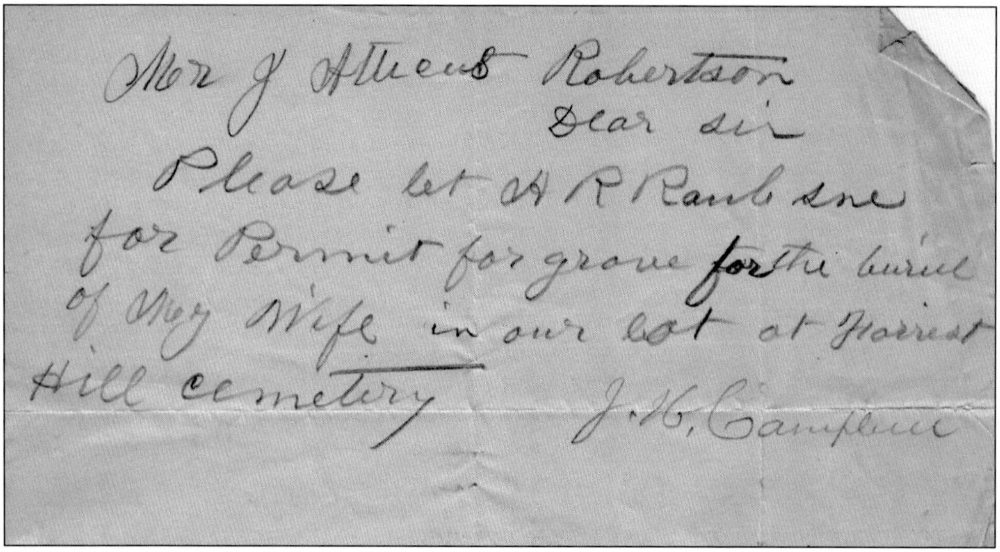

Mr J Atticus Robertson
Dear sir
Please let H R Raub see
for Permit for grave for the burial
of my Wife in our lot at Forrest
Hill cemetery J. H. Campbell

This letter states J.H. Campbell gave written permission to H.R. Raub for the burial of his wife at Forest Hill Cemetery. Below is the letterhead of J.H. Campbell, president of the Wyoming Manufacturing Company, located in Scranton. (Both, courtesy of Forest Hill Archives.)

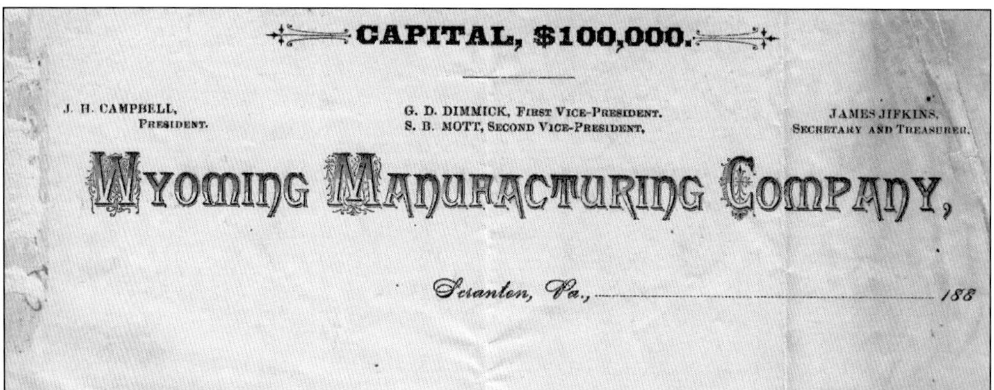

CAPITAL, $100,000.

J. H. CAMPBELL, PRESIDENT.
G. D. DIMMICK, FIRST VICE-PRESIDENT.
S. B. MOTT, SECOND VICE-PRESIDENT.
JAMES JIFKINS, SECRETARY AND TREASURER.

WYOMING MANUFACTURING COMPANY,

Scranton, Pa., ... 188

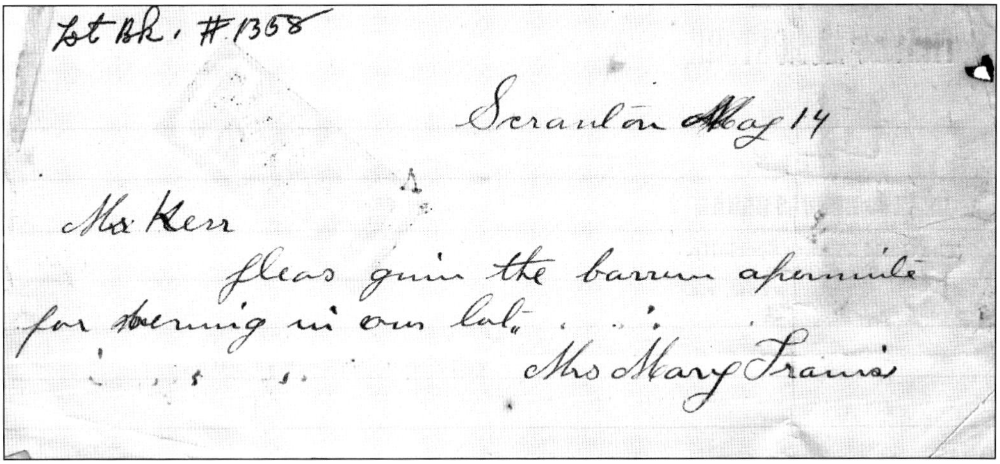

1st Bk. #1358

Scranton May 14

Mr Kerr

pleas give the barrer a permite
for berring in our lot.

Mrs Mary Travis

Mary Travis gave permission to the bearer to bury her loved ones. Below is the letterhead of Traviss' Music Store located at 428 Spruce Street in Scranton. Today, the Scranton Mattress Company resides at the address. These documents are from 1885. (Both, courtesy of Forest Hill Archives.)

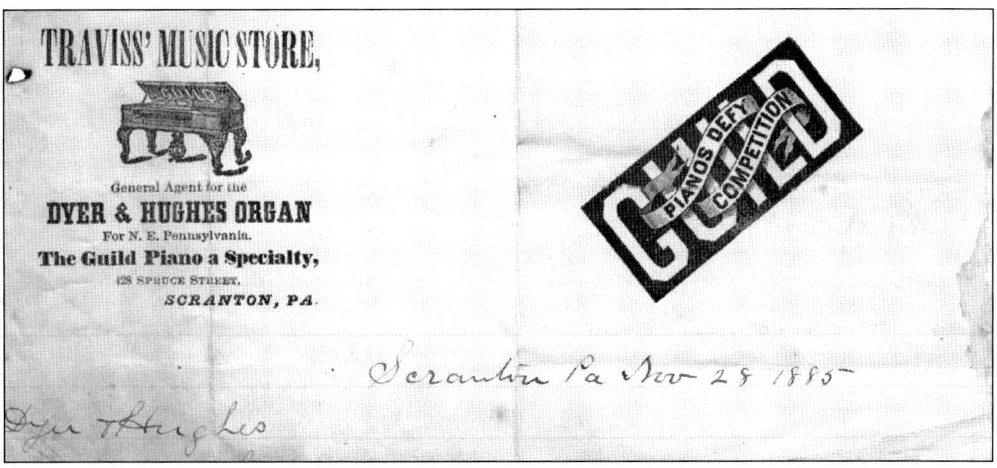

TRAVISS' MUSIC STORE,

General Agent for the

DYER & HUGHES ORGAN

For N. E. Pennsylvania.

The Guild Piano a Specialty,

428 Spruce Street,

SCRANTON, PA.

GUILD PIANOS DEFY COMPETITION

Scranton Pa Nov 28 1885

Dyer & Hughes

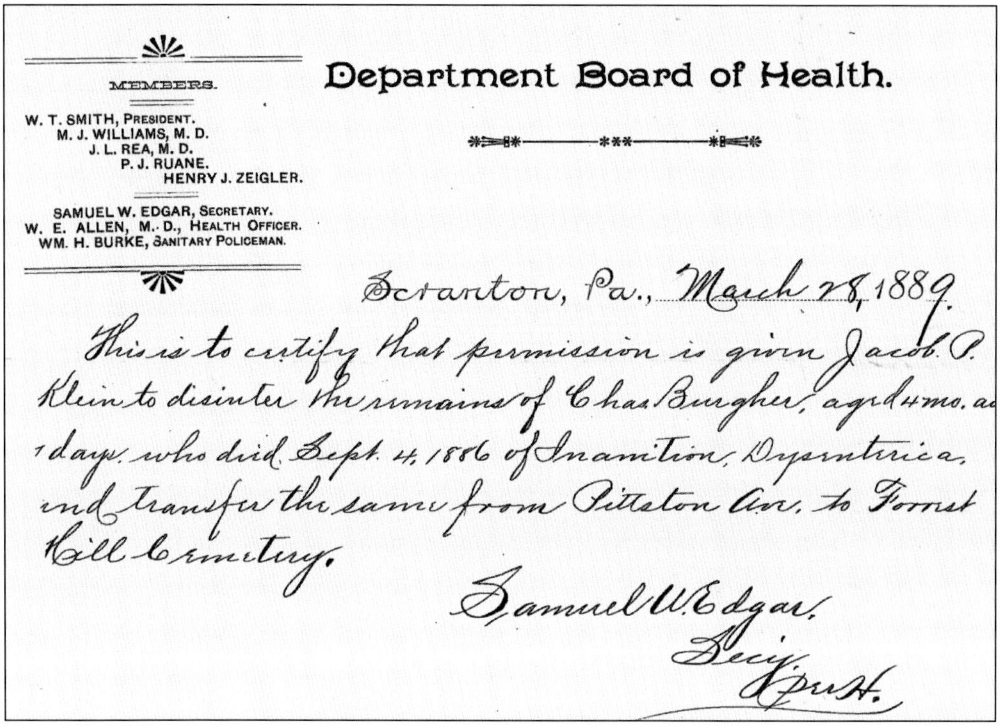

MEMBERS.

W. T. SMITH, PRESIDENT.
M. J. WILLIAMS, M. D.
J. L. REA, M. D.
P. J. RUANE.
HENRY J. ZEIGLER.

SAMUEL W. EDGAR, SECRETARY.
W. E. ALLEN, M. D., HEALTH OFFICER.
WM. H. BURKE, SANITARY POLICEMAN.

Department Board of Health.

Scranton, Pa., March 28, 1889.

This is to certify that permission is given Jacob P. Klein to disinter the remains of Chas Burgher, aged 4 mo. and 1 days, who died Sept. 4, 1886 of Inanition, Dysentria, and transfer the same from Pittston Ave. to Forrest Hill Cemetery.

Samuel W. Edgar,
Secy.
Dpt. H.

This notice of reburial is from the Pittston Avenue Cemetery, which is located in South Scranton. J.L. Rea, MD, Samuel W. Edgar, and W.E. Allen, MD, are all residents of Forest Hill. (Courtesy of Forest Hill Archives.)

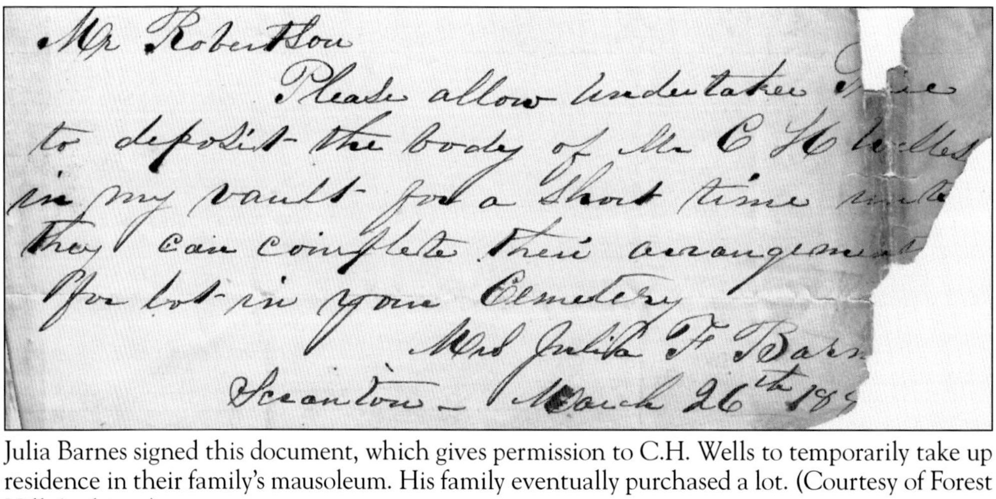

Mr Robertson

Please allow undertaker to deposit the body of Mr C H Wells in my vault for a short time until they can complete their arrangements for lot in your Cemetery

Mrs Julia F Barn

Scranton – March 26th 18

Julia Barnes signed this document, which gives permission to C.H. Wells to temporarily take up residence in their family's mausoleum. His family eventually purchased a lot. (Courtesy of Forest Hill Archives.)

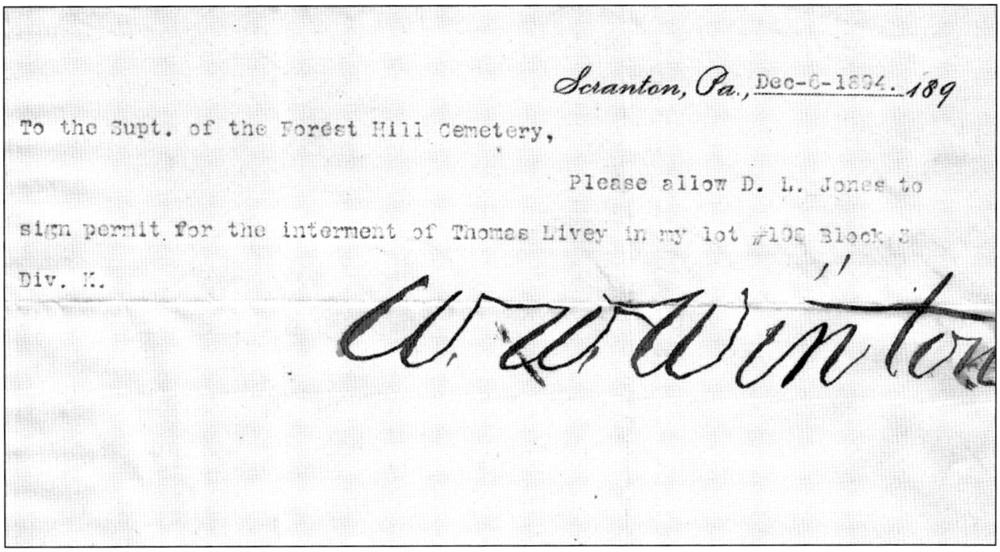

Scranton, Pa., Dec-6-1894. 189

To the Supt. of the Forest Hill Cemetery,

Please allow D. L. Jones to sign permit for the interment of Thomas Livey in my lot #100 Block B Div. K.

W. W. Winton

In 1894, W.W. Winton of the prominent Providence family writes to give permission to D.L. Jones to inter his son-in-law Thomas Livey. He was asking for Livey to be interred in Lot 100, Block B, Division K. (Courtesy of Forest Hill Archives.)

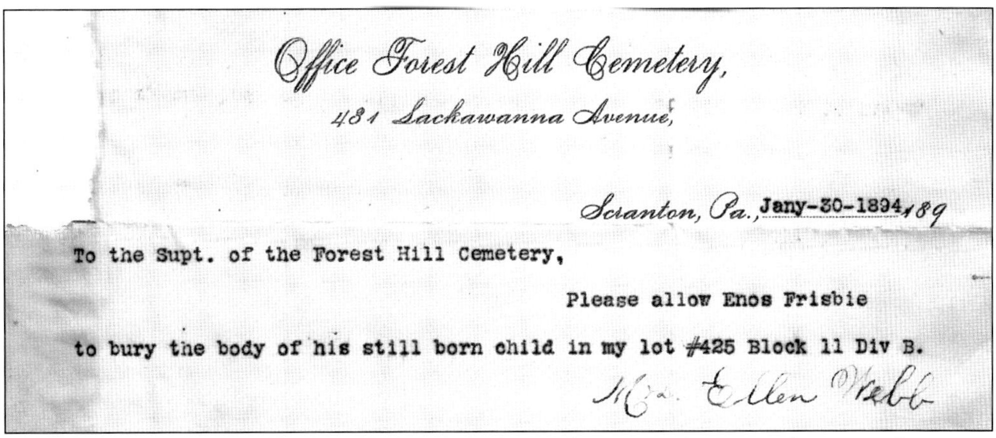

Office Forest Hill Cemetery,

481 Lackawanna Avenue,

Scranton, Pa., Jany-30-1894 189

To the Supt. of the Forest Hill Cemetery,

Please allow Enos Frisbie to bury the body of his still born child in my lot #425 Block 11 Div B.

Mrs. Ellen Webb

In 1894, the offices of Forest Hill Cemetery were located at 481 Lackawanna Avenue in Scranton. This letter granted permission to Enos Frisbie to bury his stillborn child. (Courtesy of Forest Hill Archives.)

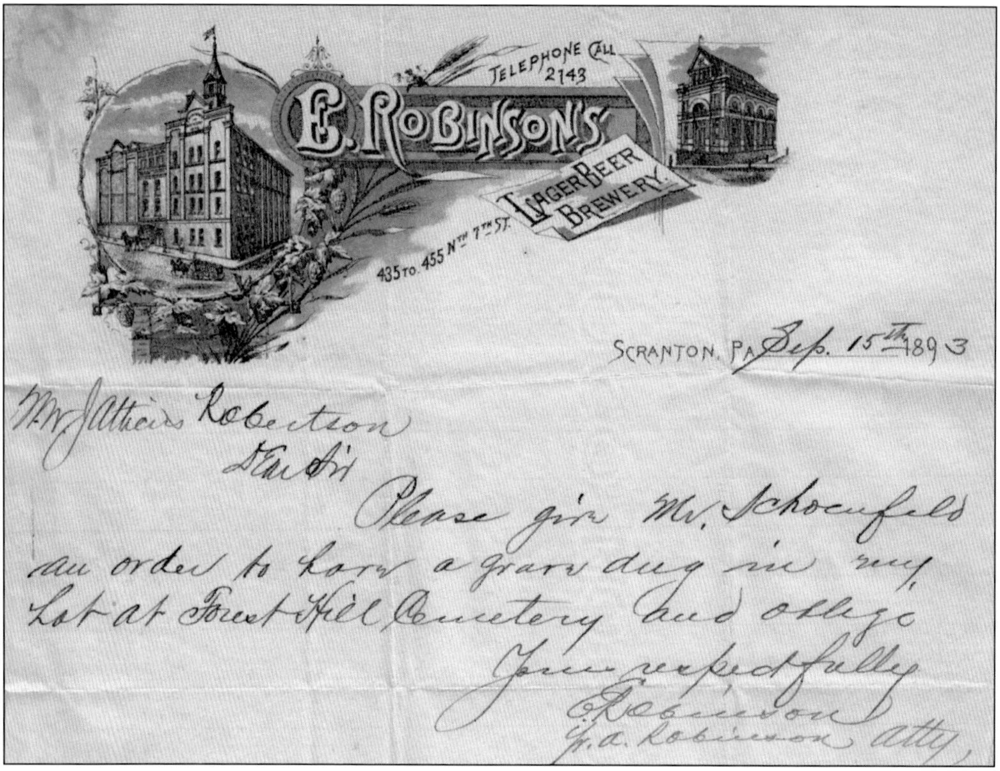

TELEPHONE CALL 2143

E. ROBINSON'S

LAGER BEER BREWERY

435 TO 455 NTH 7TH ST.

SCRANTON, PA. Sep. 15th 1893

Mr J Atticus Robertson
Dear Sir

Please give Mr. Schoenfeld an order to have a grave dug in my Lot at Forest Hill Cemetery and oblige

Yours respectfully
E. Robinson
J. A. Robinson atty

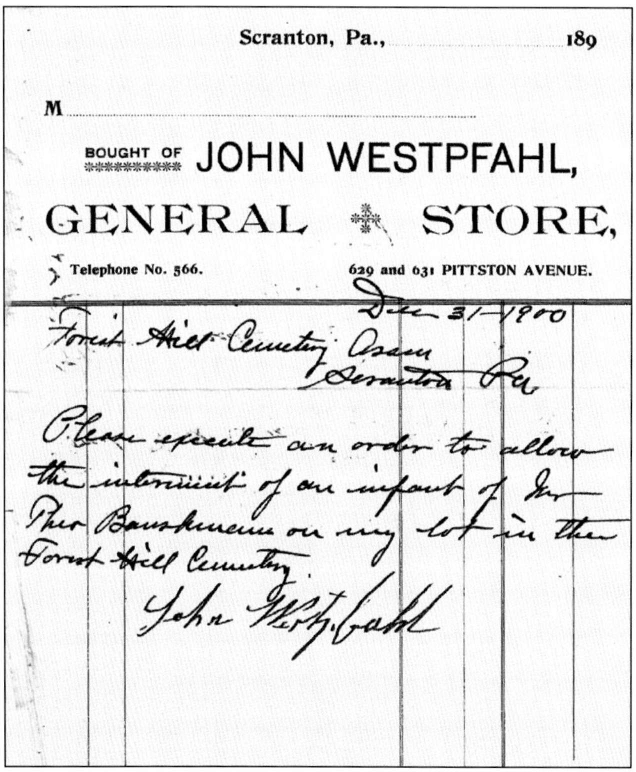

Scranton, Pa., ... 189

M ....

BOUGHT OF JOHN WESTPFAHL,

GENERAL STORE,

Telephone No. 566. 629 and 631 PITTSTON AVENUE.

Dec 31 - 1900

Forest Hill Cemetery Assn
Scranton Pa

Please execute an order to allow the internment of an infant of Mr Peter Bauschmann on my lot in the Forest Hill Cemetery.

John Westpfahl

Elizabeth Robinson, sister-in-law to Mina Robinson best known for operating her husband's south-side brewery after he passed, wrote this letter to one of the founders of the cemetery, J. Atticus Robertson. She was writing because of concerns about her burial lot. (Courtesy of Forest Hill Archives.)

John Westpfahl sent this note to the cemeteries association, asking for the internment of an infant. In 1883, Westpfahl opened a general store on the 700 block of Pittston Avenue in South Scranton. Westpfahl's store was considered one of the best concerns on this side of the Roaring Brook. John Westpfahl died on November 11, 1903, and was buried in Forest Hill. (Courtesy of Forest Hill Archives.)

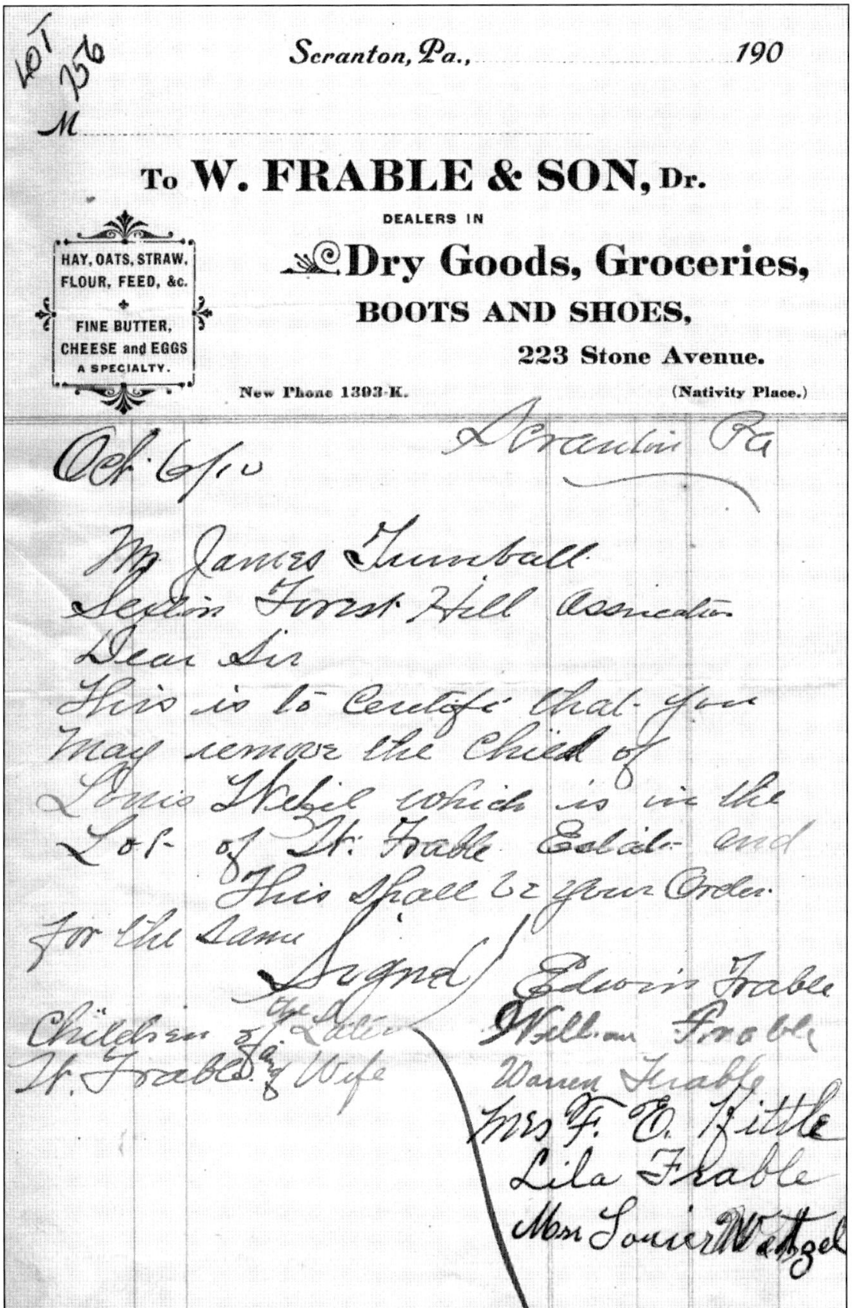

Lot 756

Scranton, Pa., ... 190

M ....

To **W. FRABLE & SON,** Dr.

DEALERS IN

Dry Goods, Groceries,

BOOTS AND SHOES,

223 Stone Avenue.

HAY, OATS, STRAW, FLOUR, FEED, &c.

FINE BUTTER, CHEESE and EGGS A SPECIALTY.

New Phone 1393-K.

(Nativity Place.)

Oct 6/10 Scranton Pa

Mr James Turnball
Sexton Forest Hill Association
Dear Sir
This is to Certify that you
May remove the Child of
Louis Wetzel which is in the
Lot of W. Frable Estate and
This shall be your Order
for the same
Signed) Edwin Frable
William Frable
Warren Frable
Mrs F. E. Kittle
Lila Frable
Mrs Louis Wetzel
Children of the Late
W. Frable & Wife

In this letter, William Frable grants permission to James Turnball for the removal of a body. "A substantial citizen of Dunmore" was how local historian Thomas Murphy described James Turnball in his book *The History of Lackawanna County*. On September 10, 1874, Turnball was the first person to accept the position of general manager at Forest Hill Cemetery. He remained in their employ for 45 years. Both he and his wife, Agnes, were the first residents to live in the cemetery's gate house. It was there on July 23, 1919, that Turnball took his last breath at the age of 86. (Courtesy of Forest Hill Archives.)

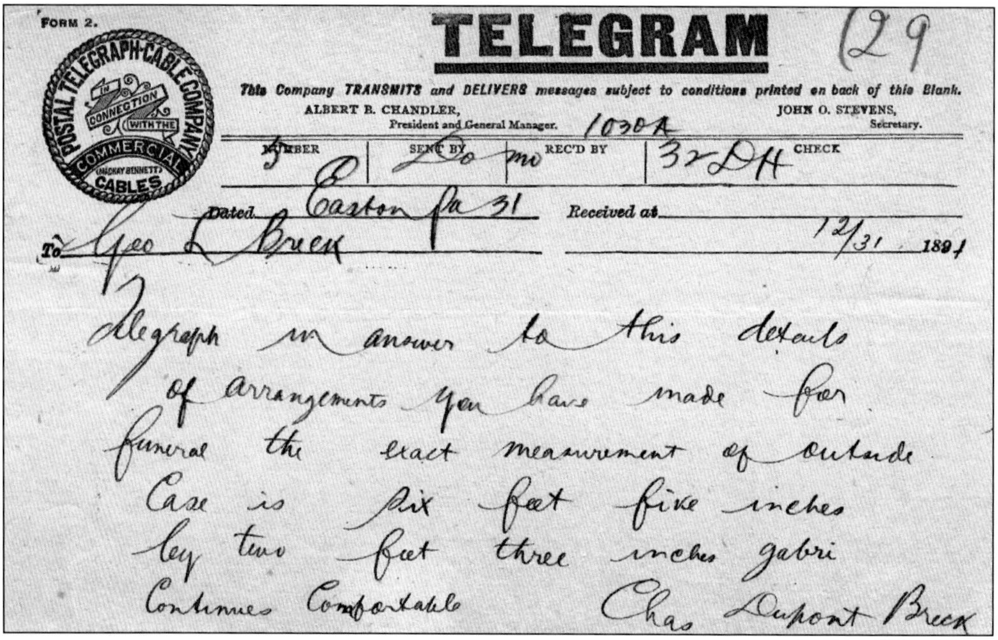
FORM 2.

TELEGRAM

(29

POSTAL TELEGRAPH-CABLE COMPANY. IN CONNECTION WITH THE COMMERCIAL (MACKAY-BENNETT) CABLES.

This Company TRANSMITS and DELIVERS messages subject to conditions printed on back of this Blank.

ALBERT B. CHANDLER, President and General Manager. 1030A JOHN O. STEVENS, Secretary.

NUMBER 5 SENT BY Do mo REC'D BY 32 DH CHECK

Dated Easton Pa 31 Received at

To Geo L Breck 12/31 1891

Telegraph in answer to this details of arrangements you have made for funeral the exact measurement of outside case is six feet five inches by two feet three inches gabri continues comfortable Chas Dupont Breck

This telegram, dated 1891, was sent to George Breck with the details for the funeral arrangements of Amelia E. Swift. She was only 11 years old. Her grandfather William Breck was one of the original founders, and Charles Dupont Breck was the young girl's uncle. (Courtesy of Forest Hill Archive.)

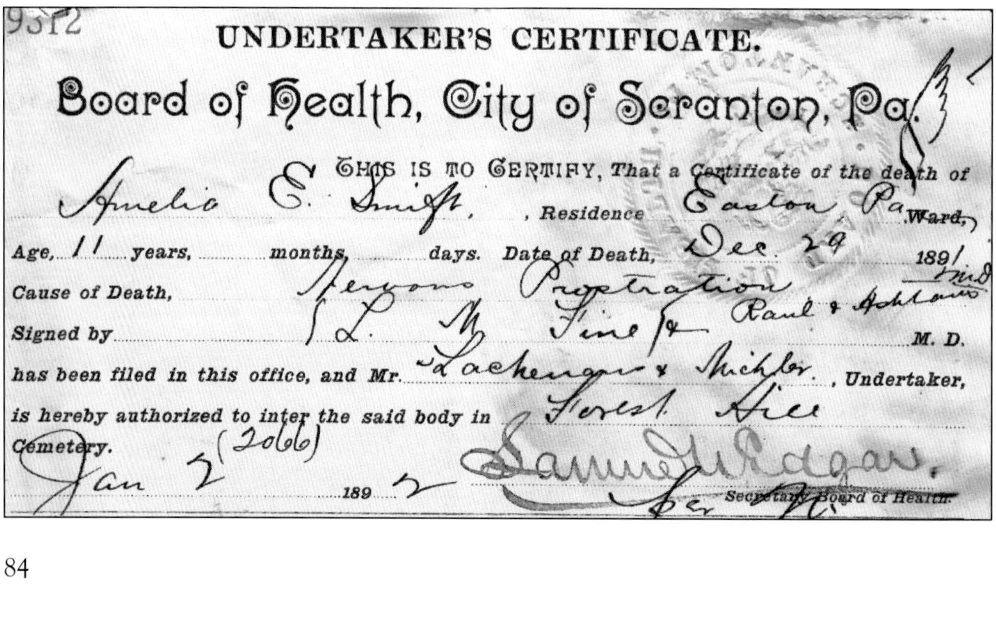
9512

UNDERTAKER'S CERTIFICATE.

Board of Health, City of Scranton, Pa.

THIS IS TO CERTIFY, That a Certificate of the death of Amelia E. Swift, Residence Easton Pa Ward,

Age, 11 years, months, days. Date of Death, Dec 29 1891

Cause of Death, Nervous Prostration

Signed by J. L. M. Fine Jr M. D.

has been filed in this office, and Mr. Lackenger & Michler, Undertaker,

is hereby authorized to inter the said body in Forest Hill Cemetery.

Jan 2 (2066) 1892 Samuel W. Edgar, Secretary Board of Health.

Five

Always Remembered

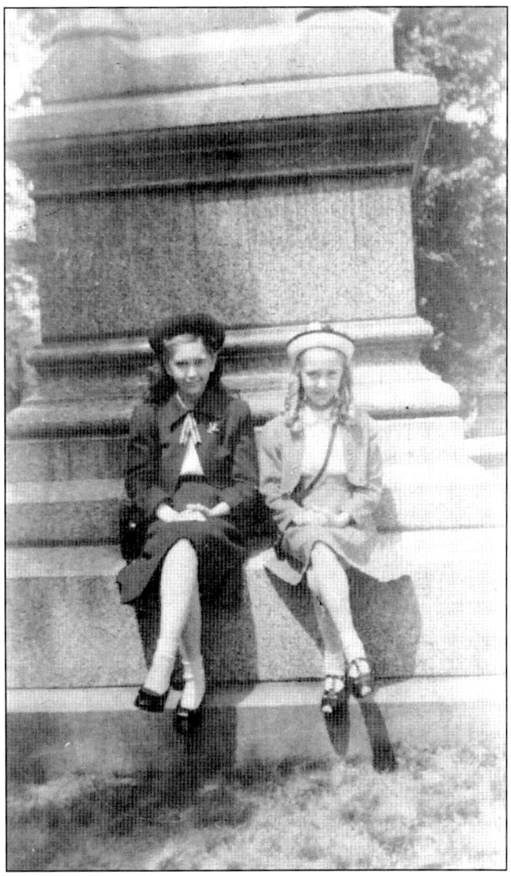

Nancy (right) and Shirley Cawley (left) would visit the cemetery every Sunday. This photograph was taken on Easter Sunday 1947. Back in the day, people would often visit and picnic on Sunday afternoons in cemeteries. (Courtesy of Nancy Phillips.)

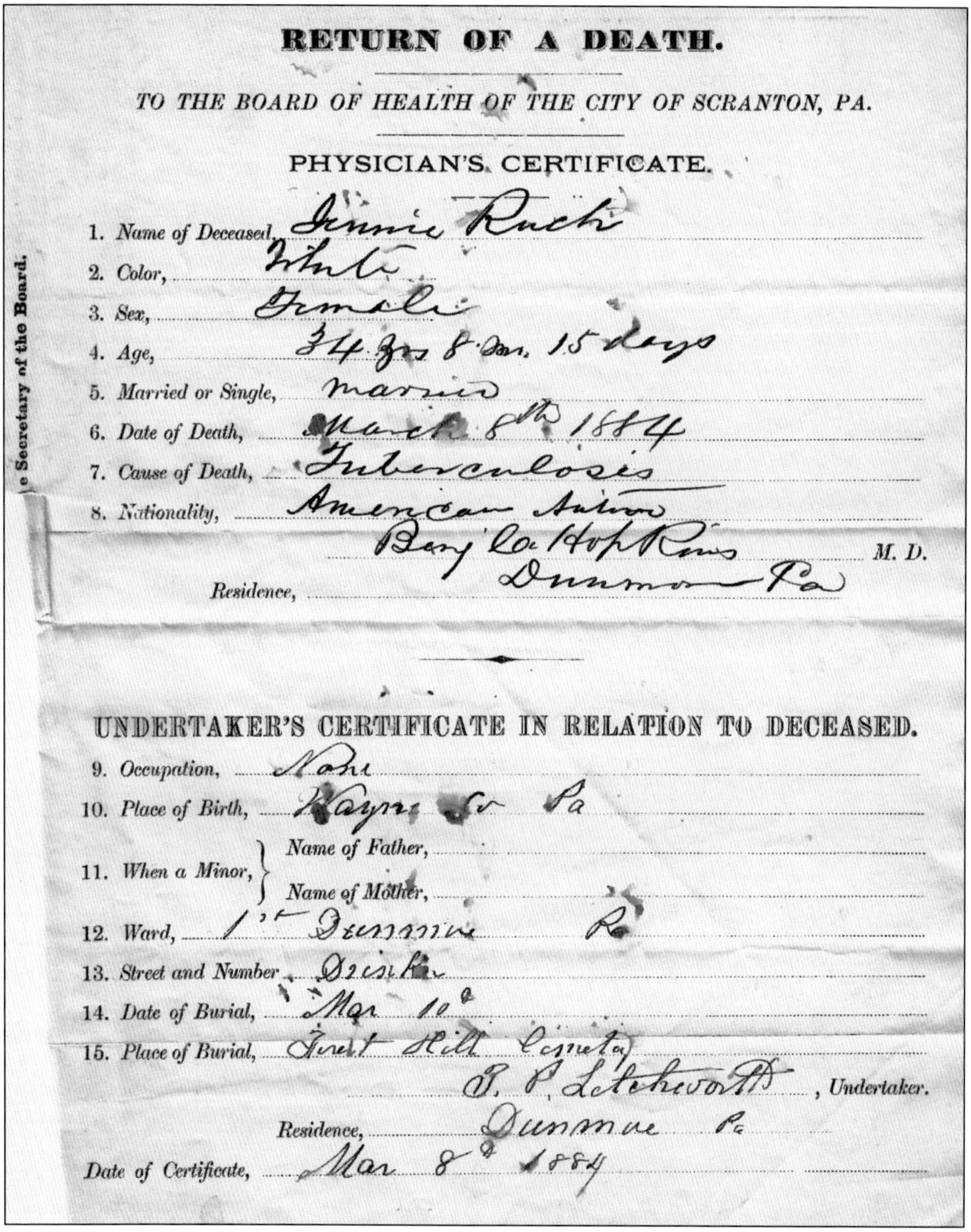

RETURN OF A DEATH.

TO THE BOARD OF HEALTH OF THE CITY OF SCRANTON, PA.

PHYSICIAN'S CERTIFICATE.

1. *Name of Deceased,* Jennie Ruch
2. *Color,* White
3. *Sex,* Female
4. *Age,* 34 yrs 8 mo. 15 days
5. *Married or Single,* married
6. *Date of Death,* March 8th 1884
7. *Cause of Death,* Tuberculosis
8. *Nationality,* American Nation

Benj'a Hopkins M. D.

Residence, Dunmore Pa

e Secretary of the Board.

UNDERTAKER'S CERTIFICATE IN RELATION TO DECEASED.

9. *Occupation,* None
10. *Place of Birth,* Wayne Co Pa
11. *When a Minor,* *Name of Father,* / *Name of Mother,*
12. *Ward,* 1st Dunmore Pa
13. *Street and Number* Drinker
14. *Date of Burial,* Mar 10th
15. *Place of Burial,* Forest Hill Cemetery

P. P. Letchworth, *Undertaker.*

Residence, Dunmore Pa

Date of Certificate, Mar 8th 1884

This is the death certificate of Jennie Ruch, who died of tuberculosis on March 8, 1884. She was a resident of Dunmore and was only 34 years old when she passed away. (Courtesy of Forest Hill Archives.)

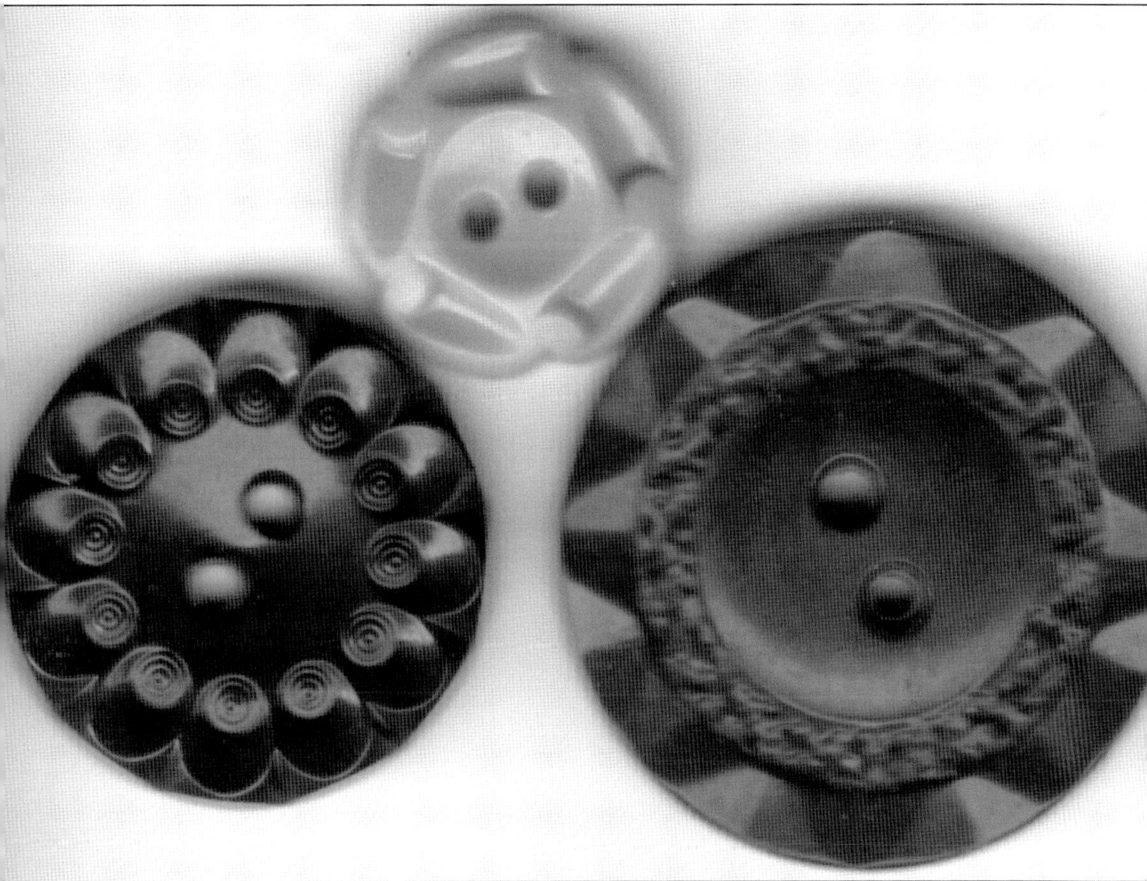

Nancy Phillips's father worked at William Connell's button mill in South Scranton. Shown in the photograph are some of the original buttons. The buttons were distributed around the world. (Courtesy of Nancy Phillips.)

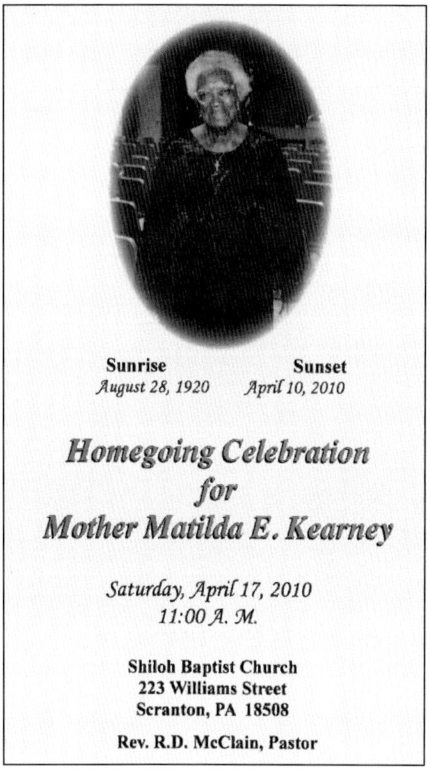

Sunrise
August 28, 1920

Sunset
April 10, 2010

Homegoing Celebration
for
Mother Matilda E. Kearney

Saturday, April 17, 2010
11:00 A. M.

Shiloh Baptist Church
223 Williams Street
Scranton, PA 18508

Rev. R.D. McClain, Pastor

Matilda E. "Tillie" Kearney (left) moved to Scranton with her parents when she was eight years old and received her formal education in the city's school system. In 1937, she married Walter "Pat" Kearney (pictured below). The couple were blessed with five children. Matilda spent many years working as a housekeeper and childcare provider. When she turned 50 years old, she embarked on a new career, working for the State of Pennsylvania in the Food Stamp Department and Low-Income Heating Program. She remained in the position until her retirement at the age of 77. A lifetime of service to the Pine Street Baptist Church and Shiloh Baptist Church, along with her selfless service to others, earned her the title of the beloved "Mother of Shiloh Baptist Church." (Both, courtesy of Nora Kearney.)

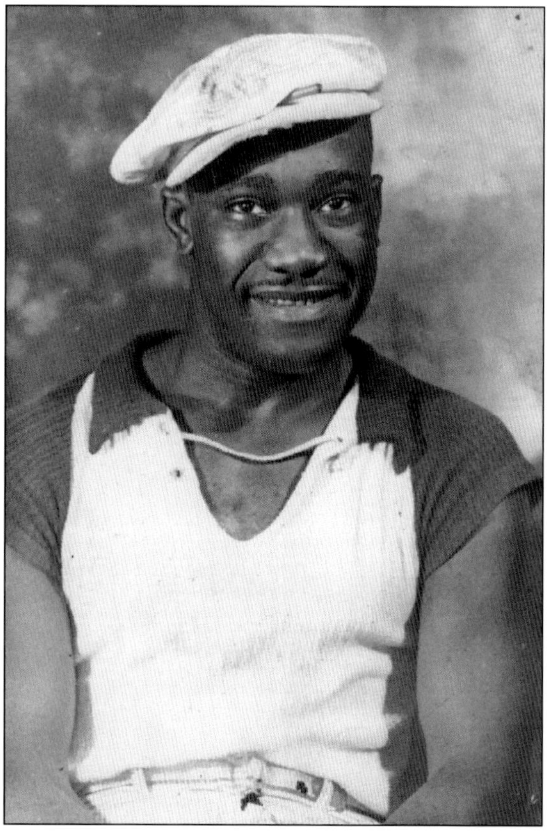

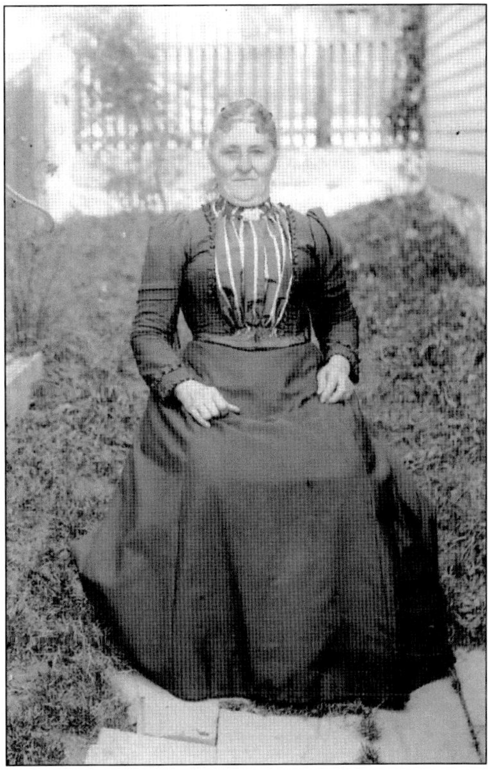

Minnie Uttrodt (right) was born in Scranton in 1847 and passed away in January 1926. Madeline Reidenbach and her brother Harry are pictured below. Harry, who worked as a manager in the offices of the Penn Transfer Company, died of asphyxiation in 1912. His story is a sad one. Harry asked his grandmother Minnie if he could work at night at Penn Transfer, because more messages came in at that time. Unfortunately, he had fallen asleep on the job and knocked over the gas heater. His lifeless body was found the next morning at his desk. Their granddaughter Bonnie O'Brien purchased a tombstone for both in 2015. (Both, courtesy of Bonnie O'Brien.)

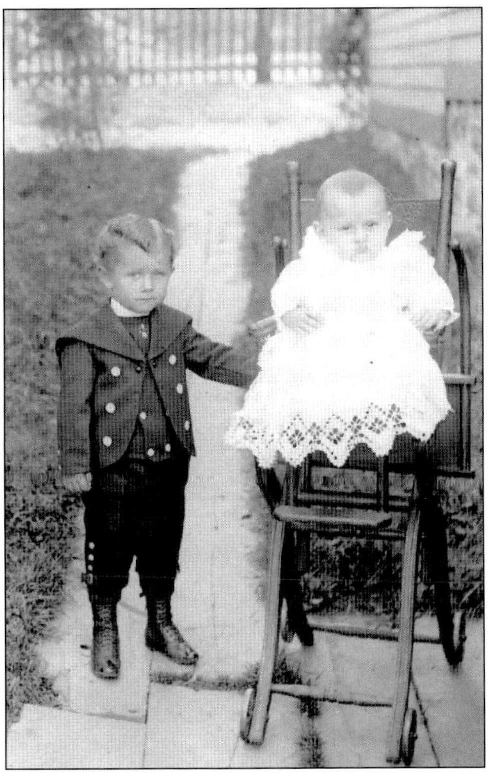

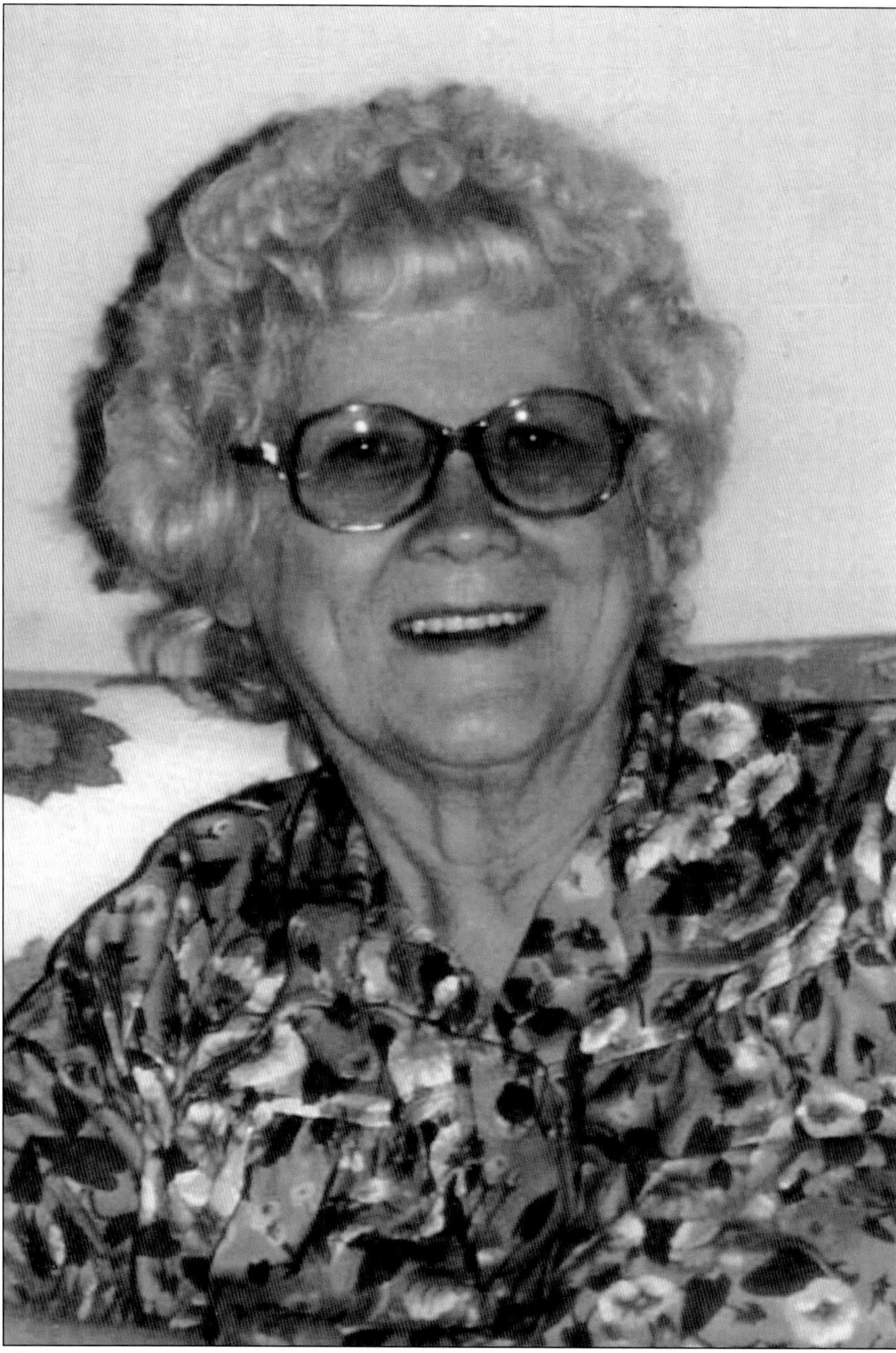

Ella Mae Detrick was the mother of Diane and Beverly. She was born March 14, 1902, and died on October 10, 1988. (Courtesy of Dorothy Loney.)

Diane (Detrick) Rogo, a resident of Scranton was born in 1940. Twenty-eight years later, on February 18, 1968, she was tragically killed in an automobile accident with her three-year-old daughter. Pictured from left to right are (kneeling) unidentified and Diane's brother George; (standing) Diane and unidentified. (Courtesy of Dorothy Loney.)

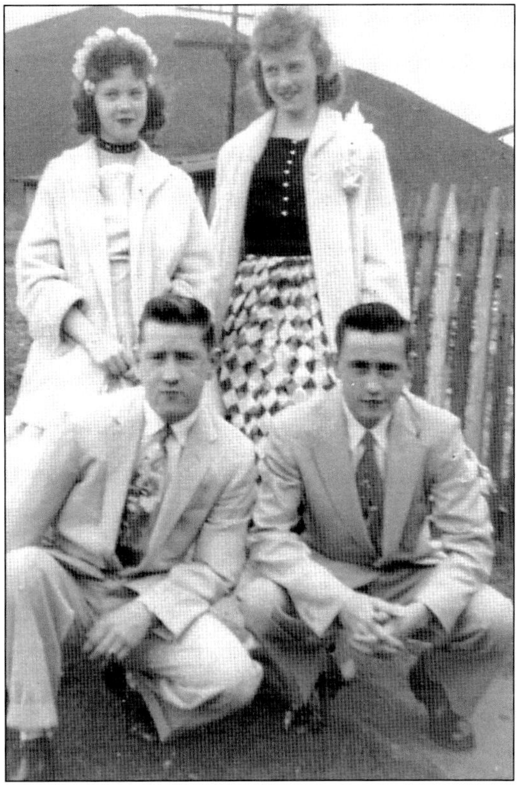

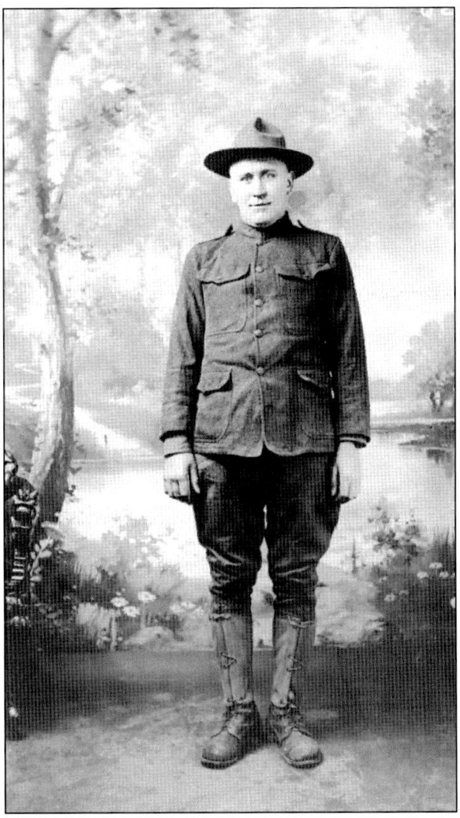

The doughboy pictured is Eugene Walter Pfurr, who served in World War I and worked in maintenance for a local coal company. He passed away in 1956 at the age of 64. (Courtesy of Debbie and Wendy Pfurr.)

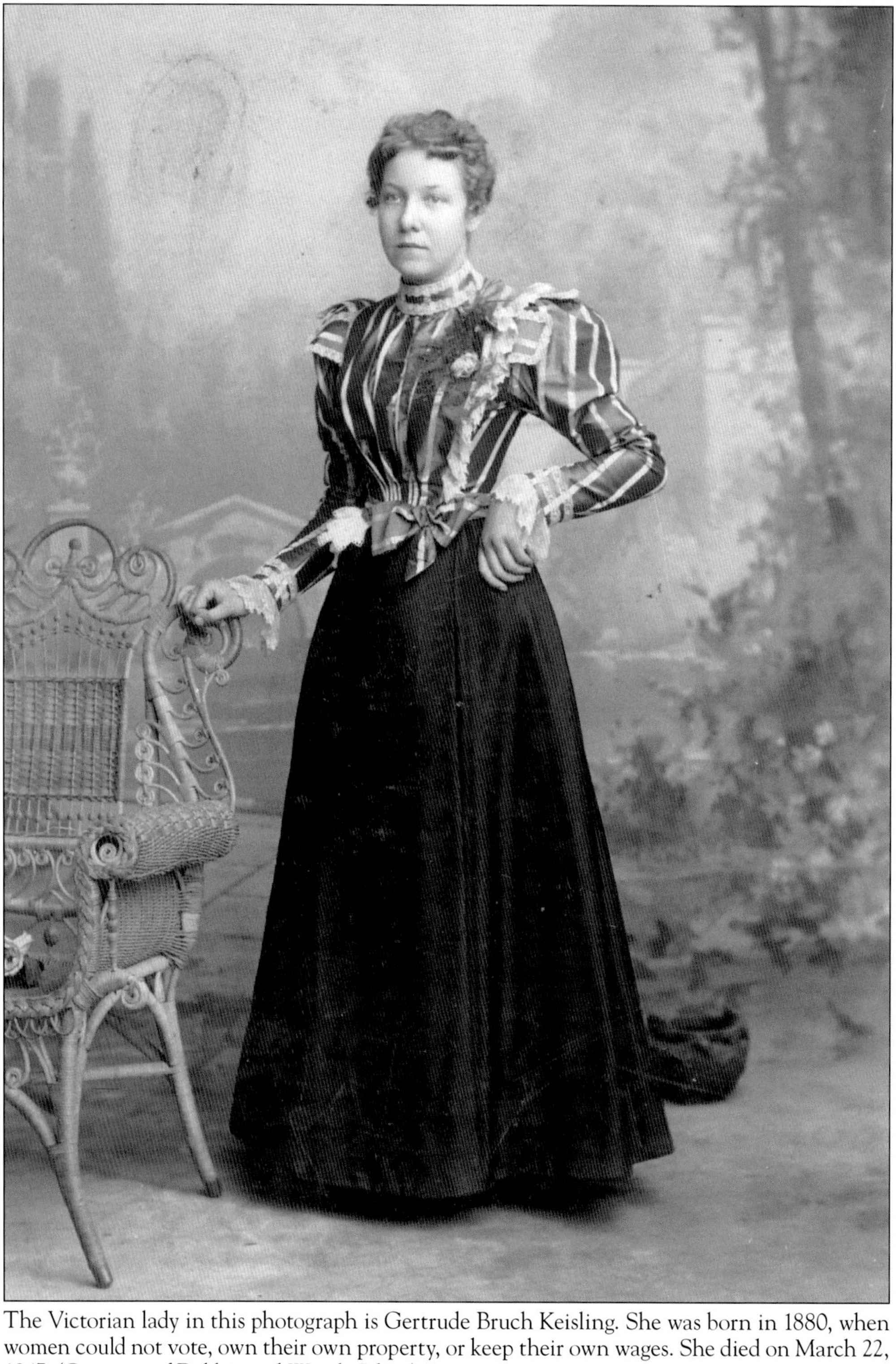

The Victorian lady in this photograph is Gertrude Bruch Keisling. She was born in 1880, when women could not vote, own their own property, or keep their own wages. She died on March 22, 1947. (Courtesy of Debbie and Wendy Pfurr.)

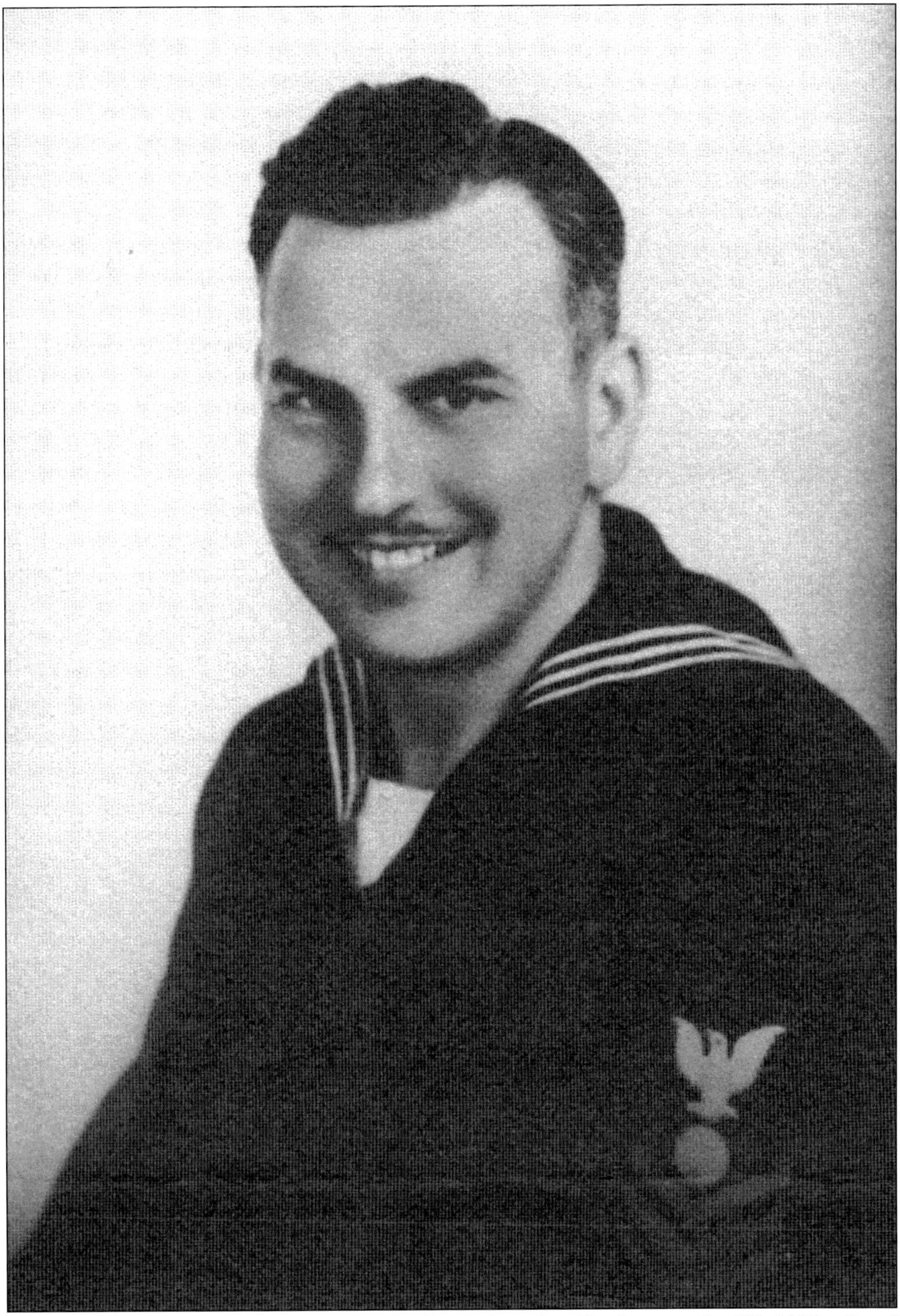

Charles A. Schroeder was the grandson of Adam Schroeder. Charles served in World War II and was killed on May 18, 1945, in the South Pacific. (Courtesy of Chuck Schroeder.)

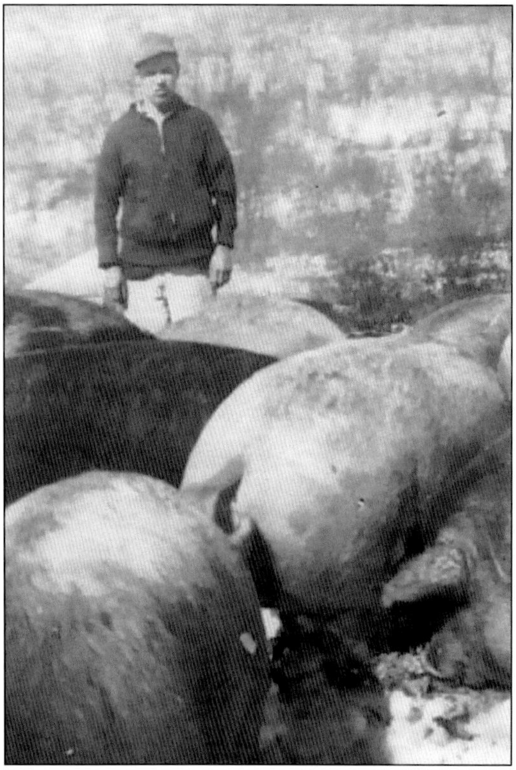

Peter Wells was born in Scranton on December 30, 1921. He was the son of Warren and Ellen Wells. Peter served his country in World War II. The Army veteran, seen in both photographs, passed away on August 1, 1978. (Both, courtesy of Linda Wells.)

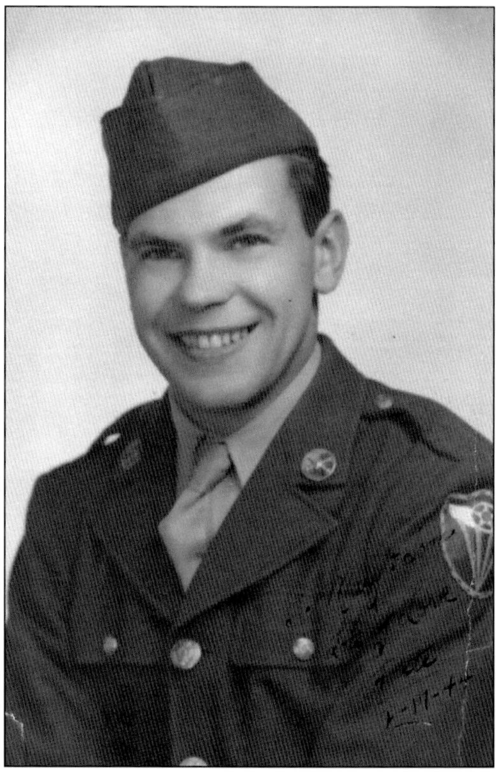

Albert K. Russel was Peter Wells's great-grandfather. At Forest Hill Cemetery, he resides in the GAR section, for the reason Albert served with a Pennsylvania Cavalry Unit in the Civil War from August 1861 to August 1862. Pictured are Albert (left) and an unidentified man. (Courtesy of Linda Wells.)

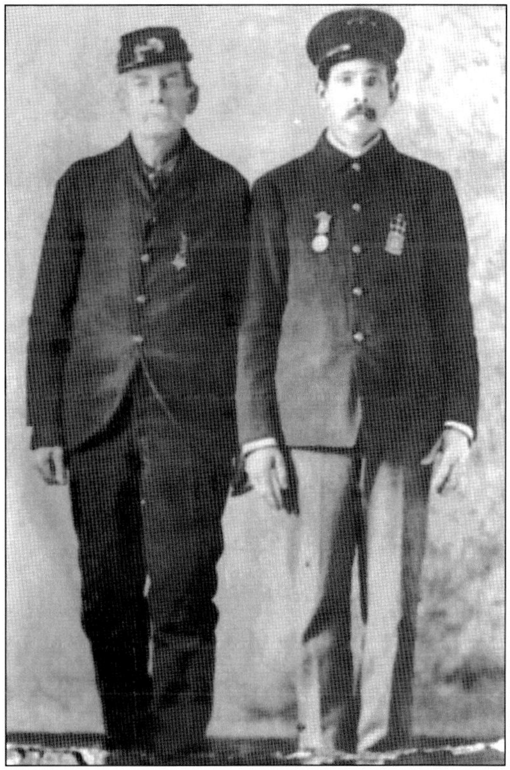

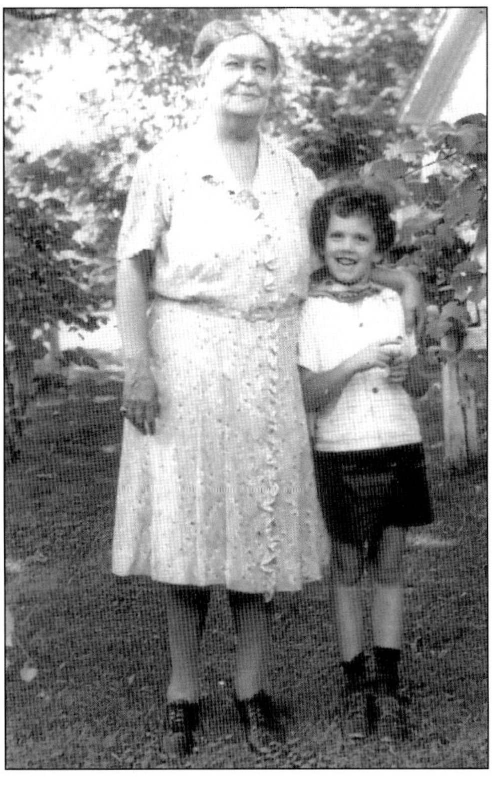

Victoria Connell Noecker Ruse, lovingly known to her family as "Aunt Vickie," was born in 1878. She was the sister of Robert Charles Connell. Here, she stands with little Linda Connell, around the 1940s. (Courtesy of Charles Connell.)

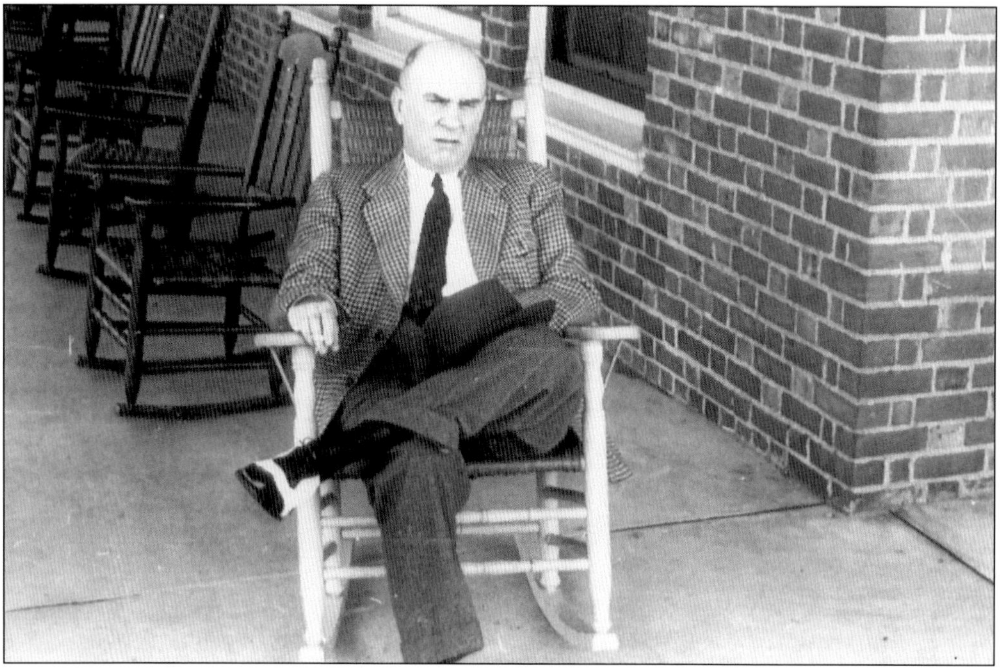

Robert Charles Connell Sr. (above) was a prominent attorney in the city. He was married to Teresa Nalen Connell (below). The couple had two sons: Robert J. Connell, president of the International Correspondence Schools International LTD, and Charles H. Connell. (Both, courtesy of Charles Connell.)

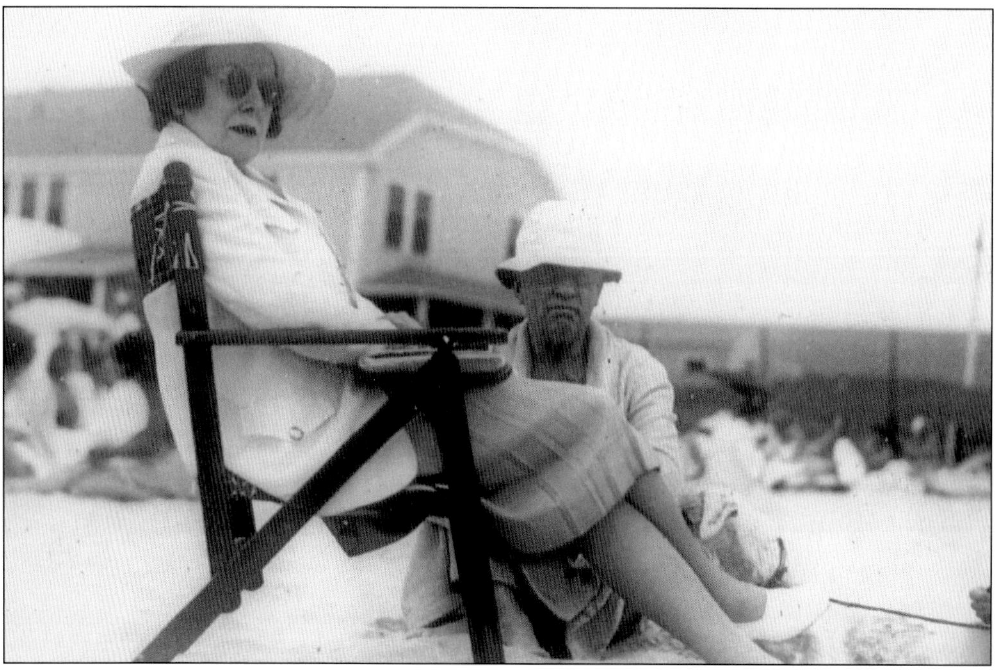

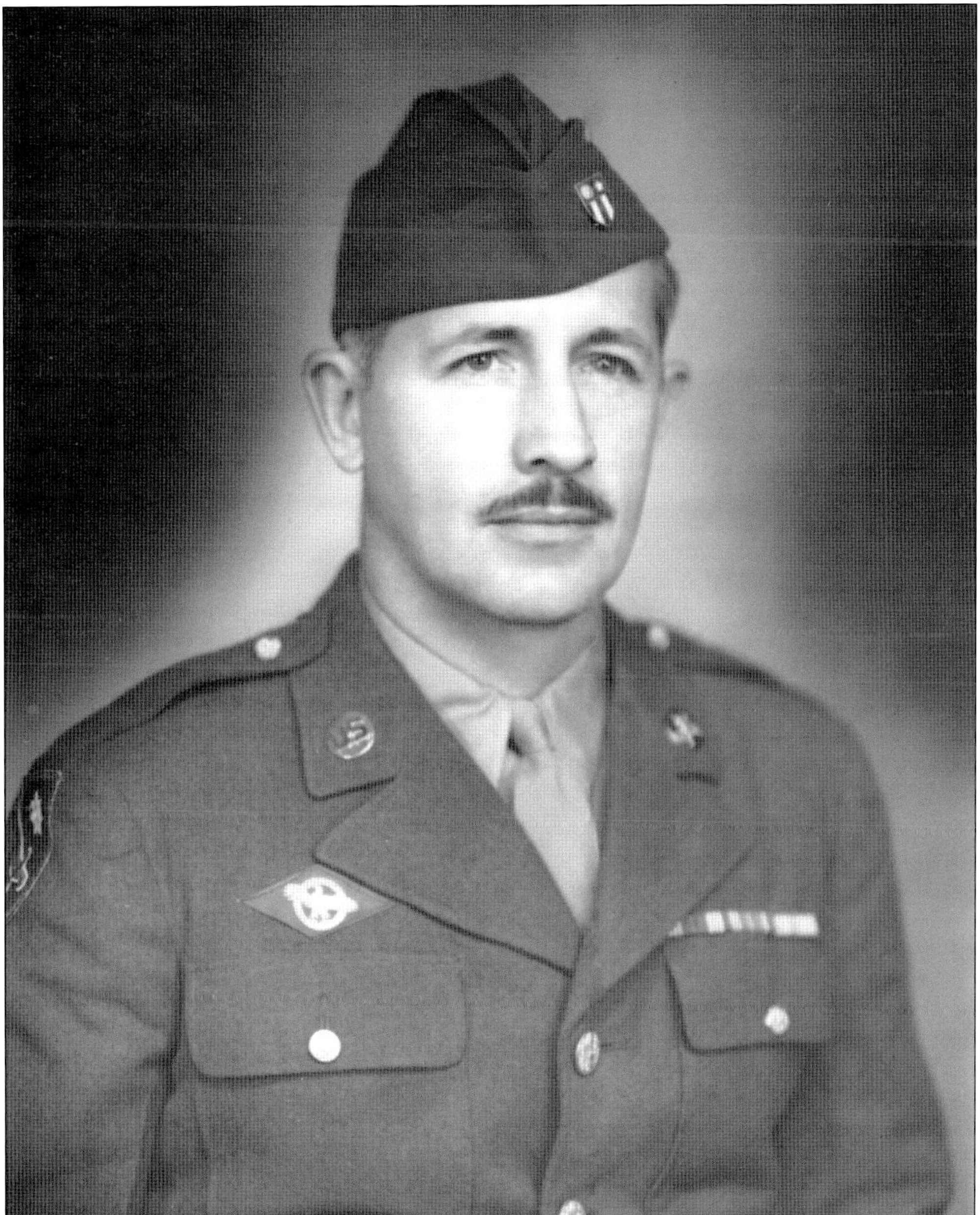

Andrew H. Kehrli was born on September 26, 1903, in Factoryville. His father, Andrew Sr., had emigrated from Switzerland and operated a hotel in the area. Andrew died on November 11, 1930. He was a veteran of World War II. (Courtesy of Ellen Sayers.)

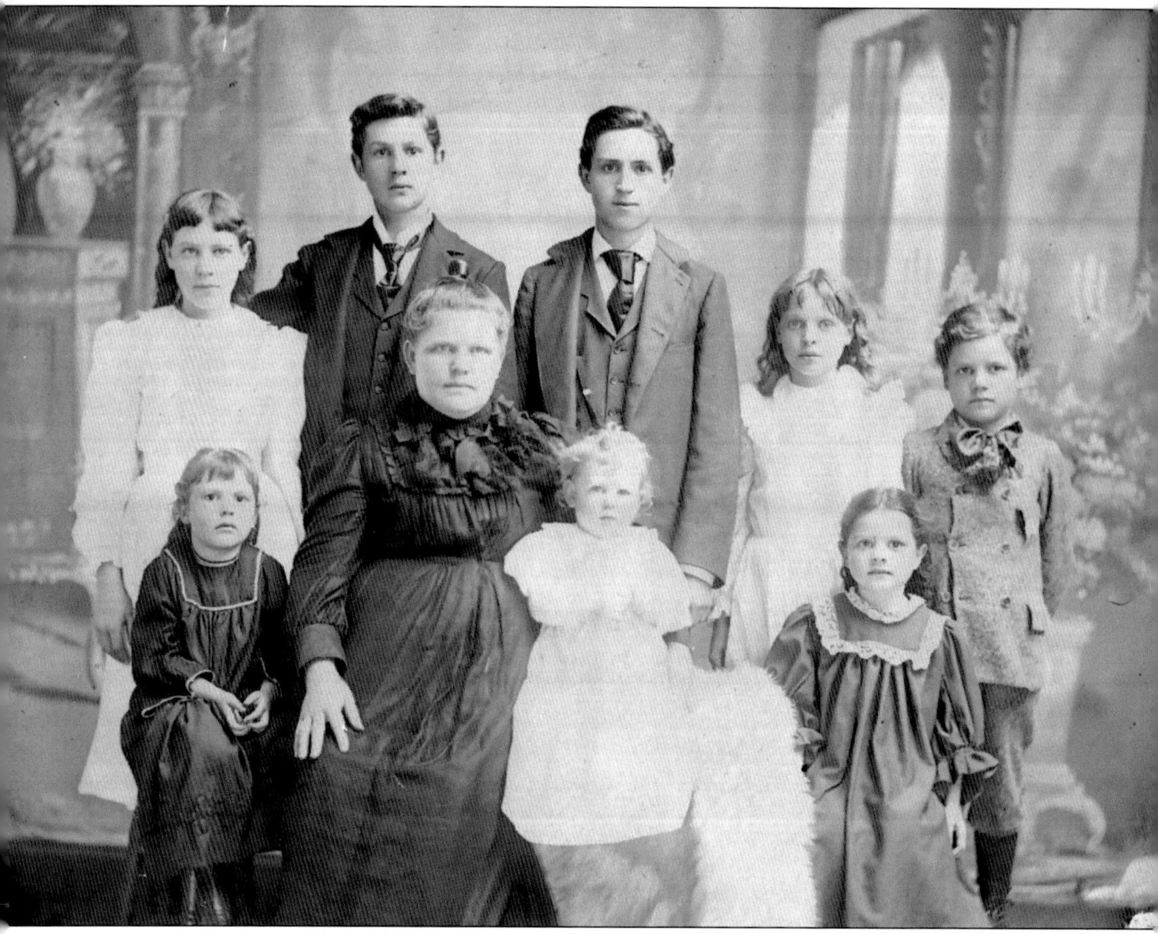

Pictured is Margaret Blatter (the woman seated in the first row; others are unidentified) with her beautiful family. The portrait was taken by their relative and photographer Henry Frey during the 19th century. (Courtesy of Ellen Sayers.)

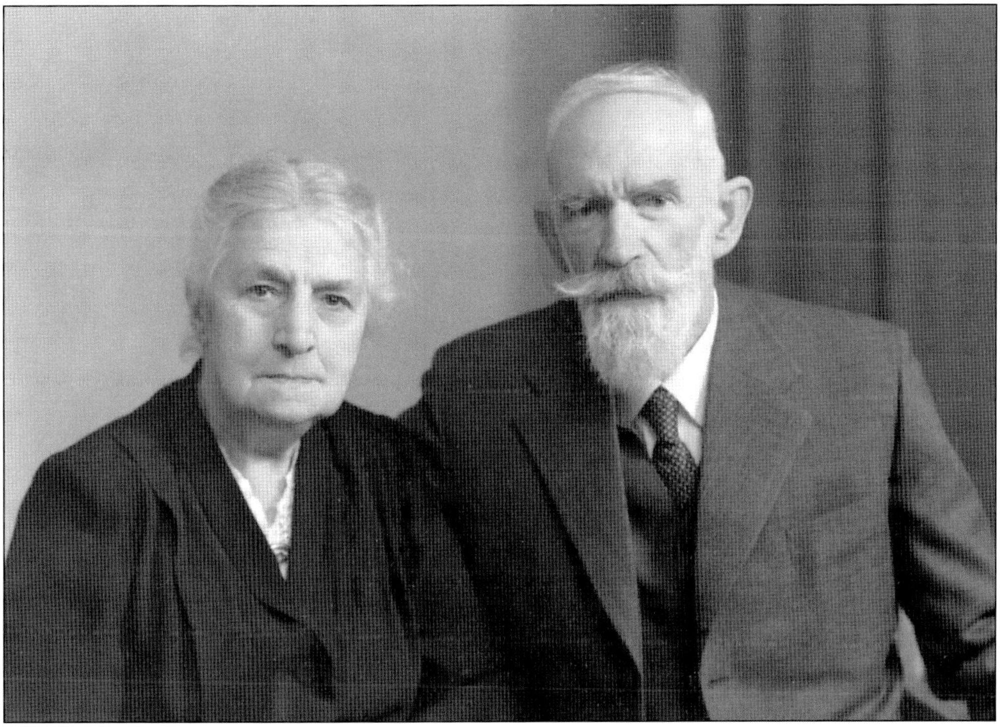

Henry Frey pictured above with his wife, Louise Blatter Frey. Henry was a well-known photographer in the city during the 19th century. Many photos found from that era have Frey's name embossed on them. His photography shop was located in Hyde Park. Pictured below is the Frey's residence at 519 Pine Street in Scranton. (Both, courtesy of Ellen Sayers.)

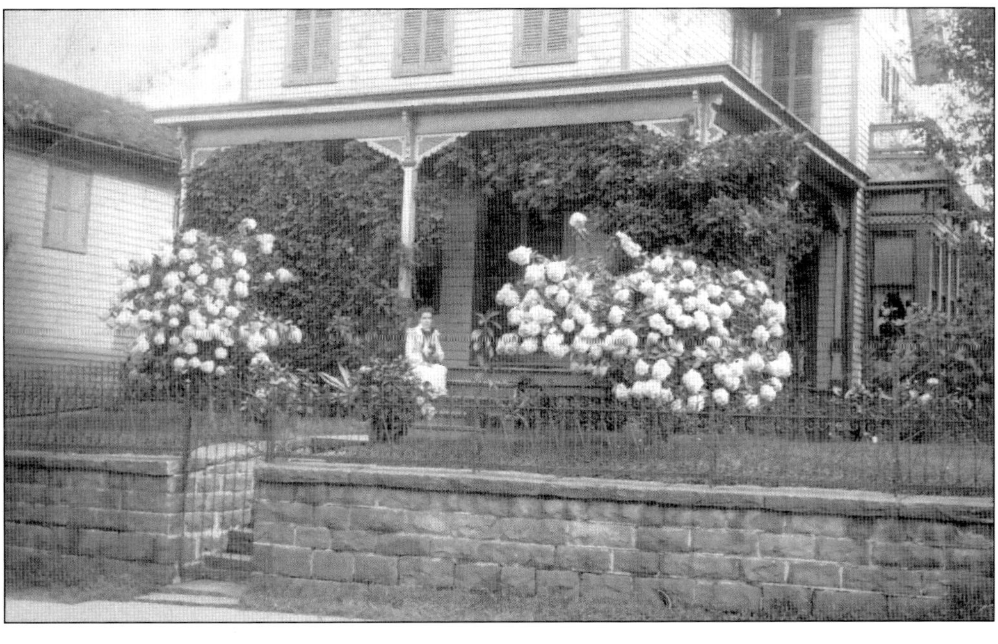

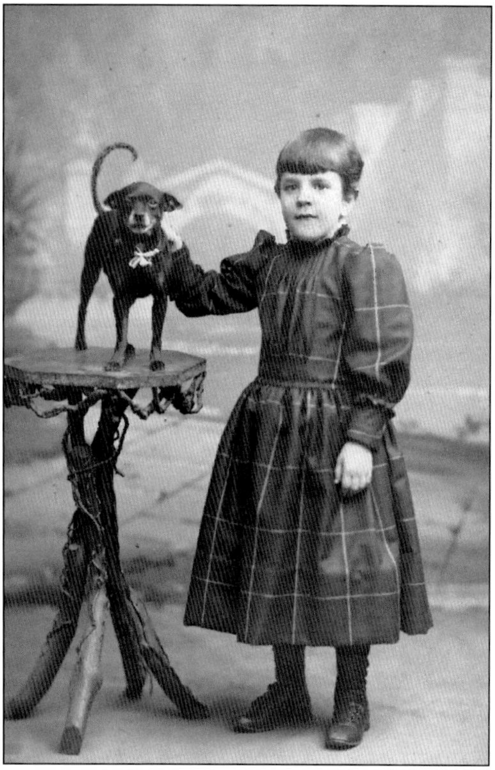

Henry and Louise Frey had one daughter, the beautiful Emma Rose, who they doted over. Emma was adopted by Henry, who was also her uncle. Both images were captured by Henry. The photograph below is a double exposure of Emma Rose. Henry was a man ahead of his times in the art of photography. (Both, courtesy of Ellen Sayers.)

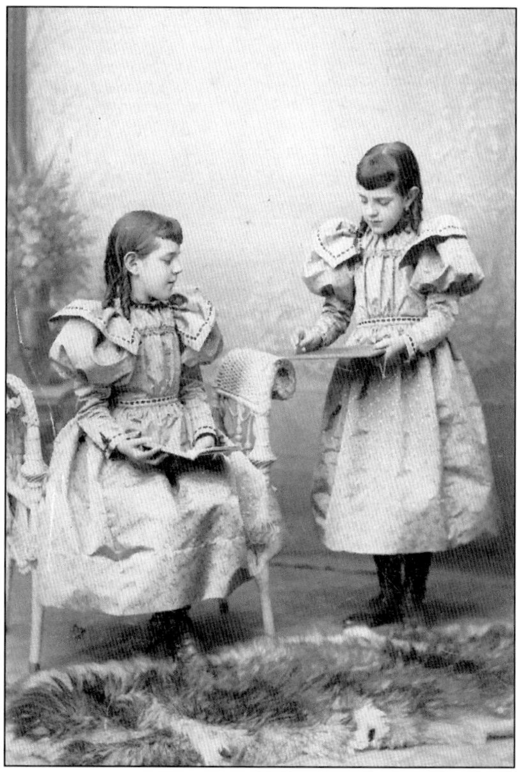

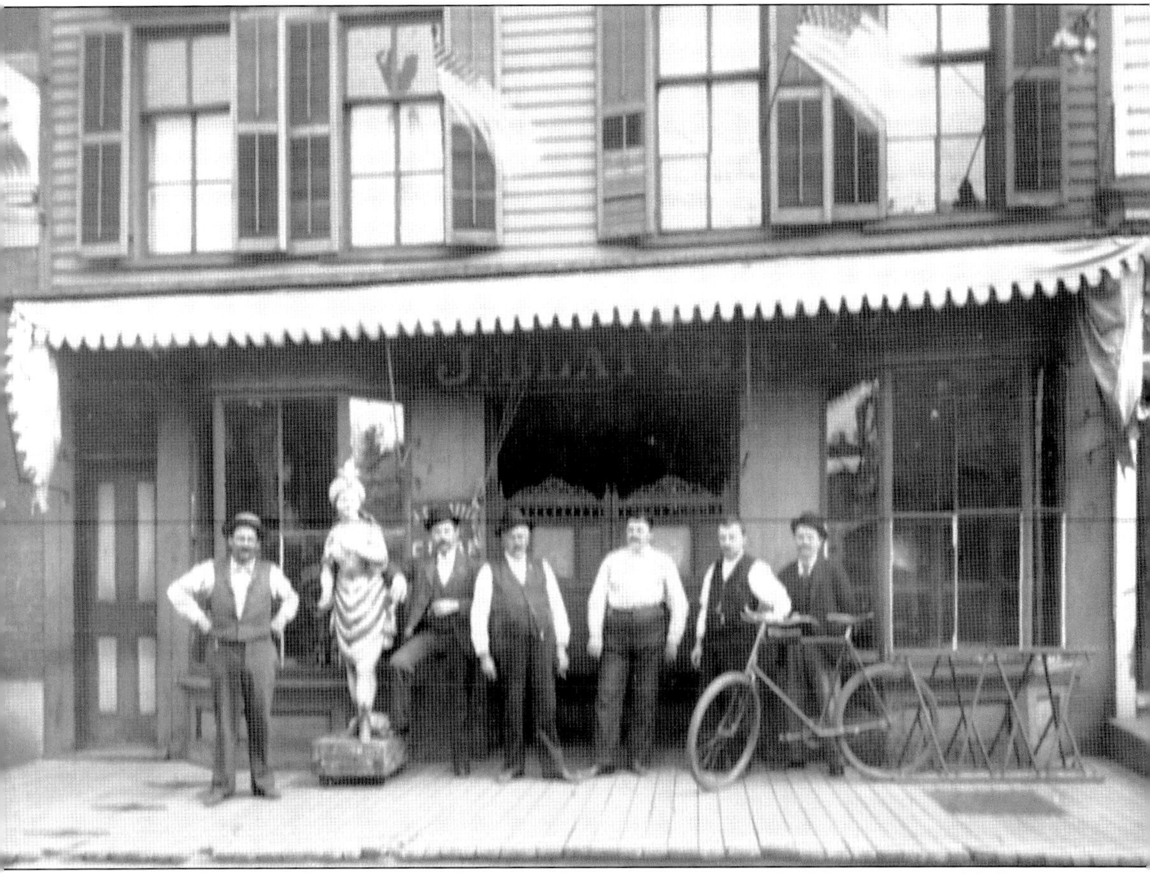

Brothers Henry, and John Blatter (unidentified in photograph) owned a popular cigar establishment located on Lackawanna Avenue in Scranton. Henry was born on May 19, 1846, in New York State and passed away on March 26, 1888, before this photograph was taken. The second floor of their establishment was their hotel called the Blatter House. (Courtesy of Ellen Sayers.)

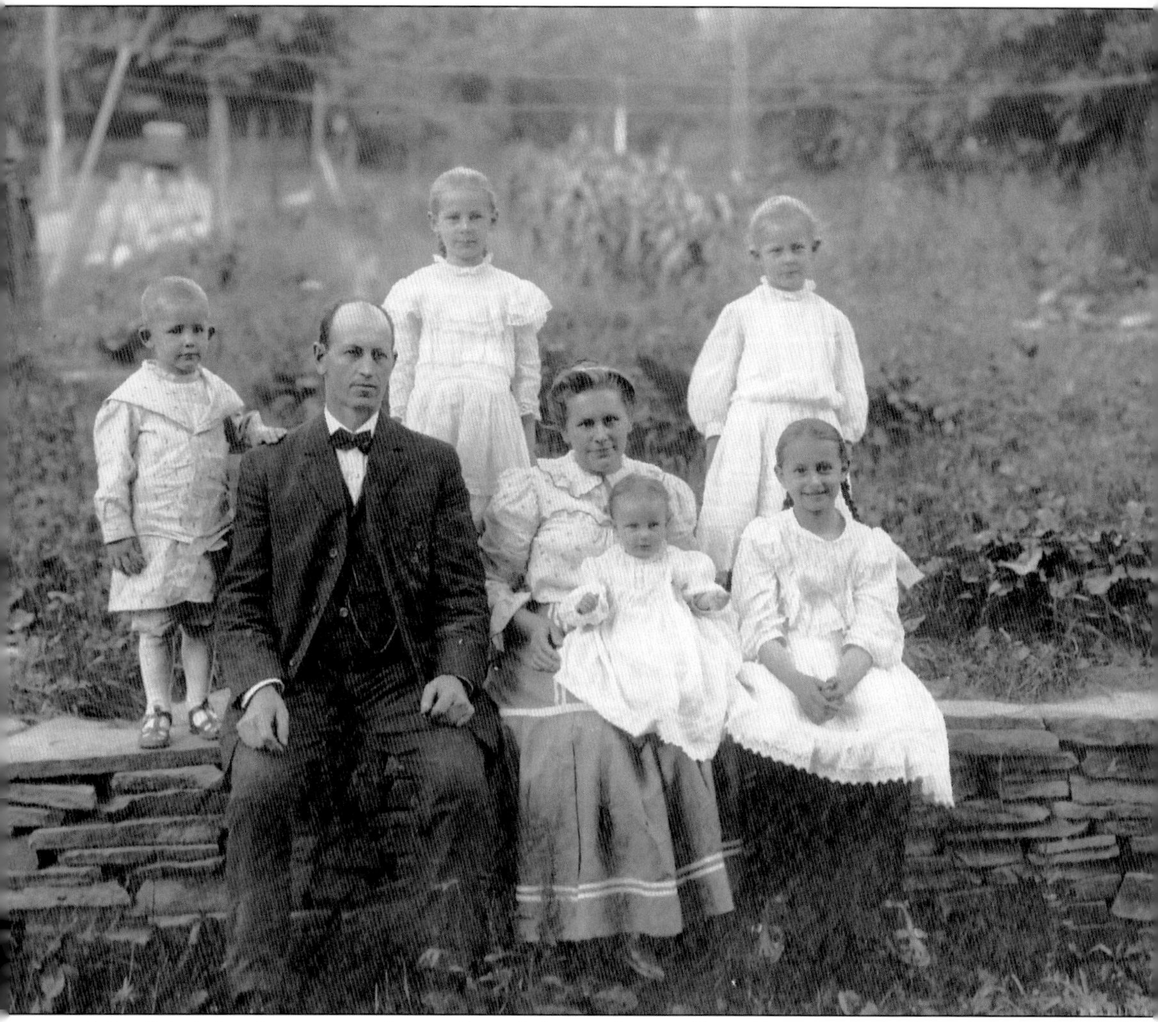

The Kehrli family is pictured here. From left to right are (first row, seated) Andrew Sr., mother Eleanora (holding baby Marie), and Rose; (second row, standing) Andrew, Eleanore, and Louise. (Courtesy of Ellen Sayers.)

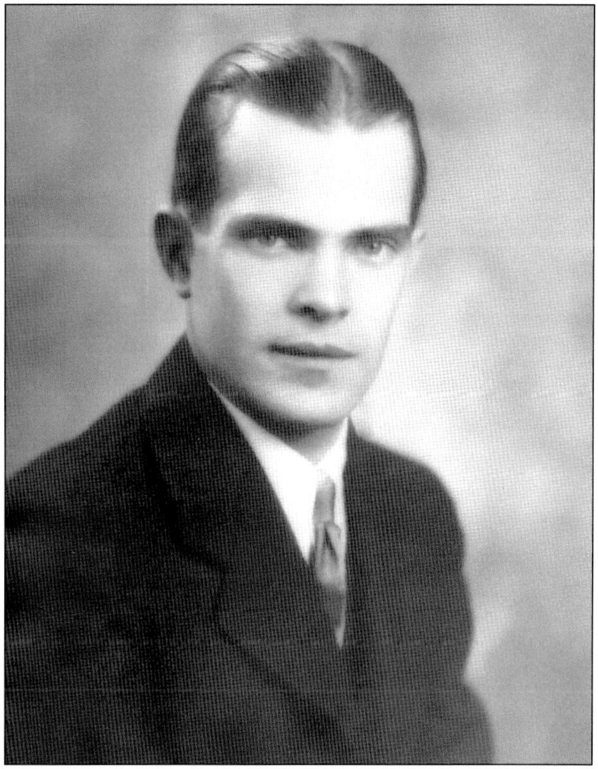

Douglas Sayers (right) married Marie Kehrlie (below), who was born in Factoryville in 1906. She was very active in various organizations, including the Girl Scouts. Douglas died on August 20, 1967. He worked as a civil engineer mainly out of New York City and, at one time, was employed by the government and traveled around the world. (Both, courtesy of Ellen Sayers.)

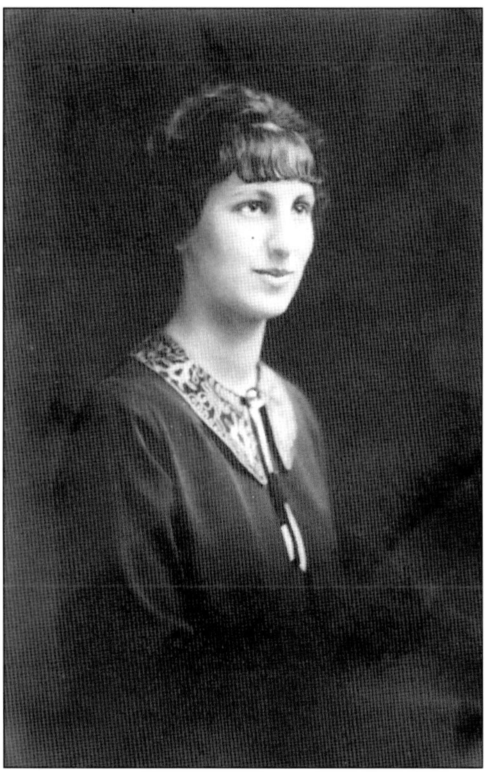

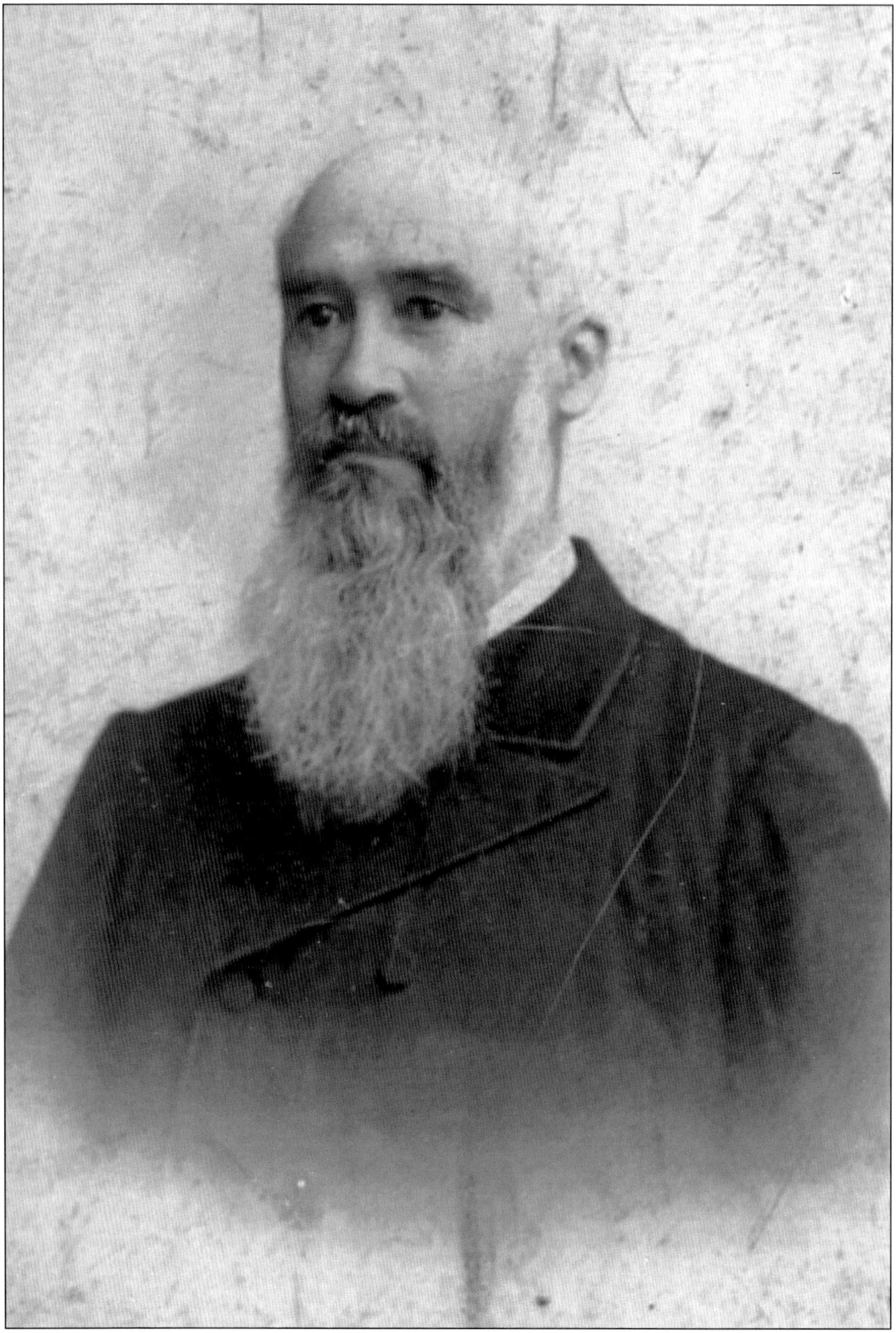

Dr. Jones Memorial Church, which today is the Shiloh Baptist Church, was named for Rev. Rees Saron Jones. (Courtesy of Forest Hill Archives.)

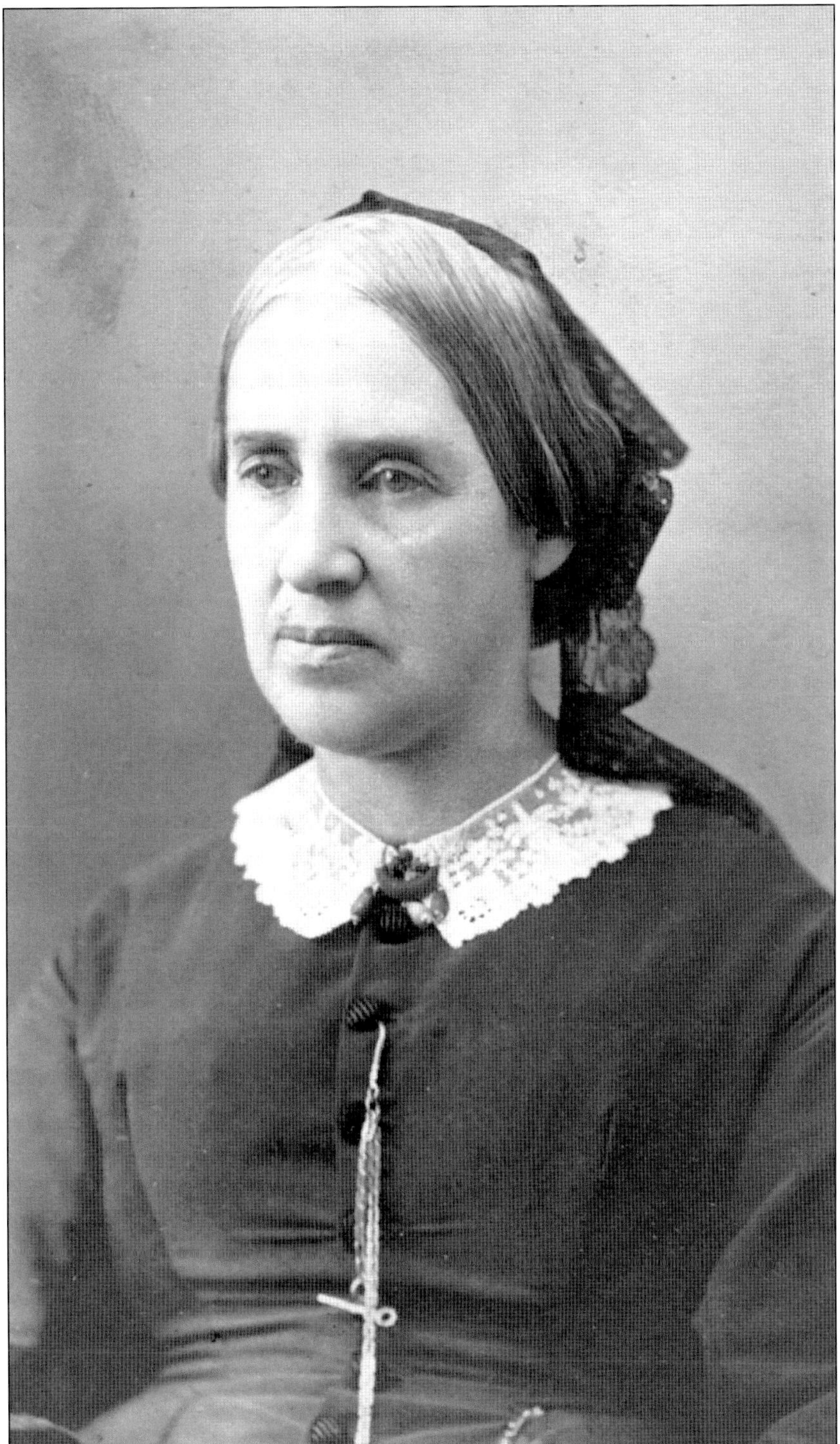

Pictured is Anne Henwood Matthews, born October 29, 1809, in Cornwall, England. She was the second wife of Robert Matthews. Anne raised their children and the children from her husband's first marriage. She died on October 23, 1884. (Courtesy of Roger Matthews.)

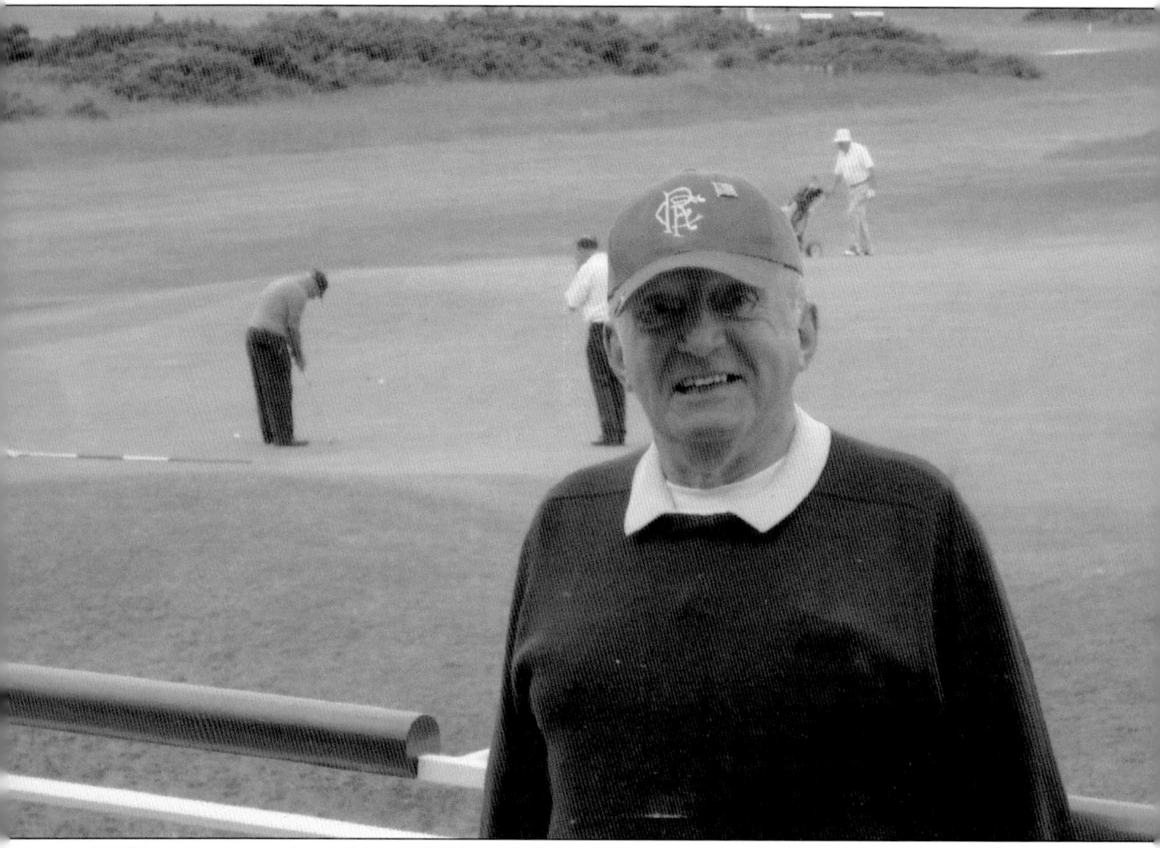

William Fagan was born May 6, 1934, in Scotland. Fagan was in the Army for 30 years. He served in both the Korean and Vietnam Wars and died June 13, 2011. (Courtesy of Louise Fagan.)

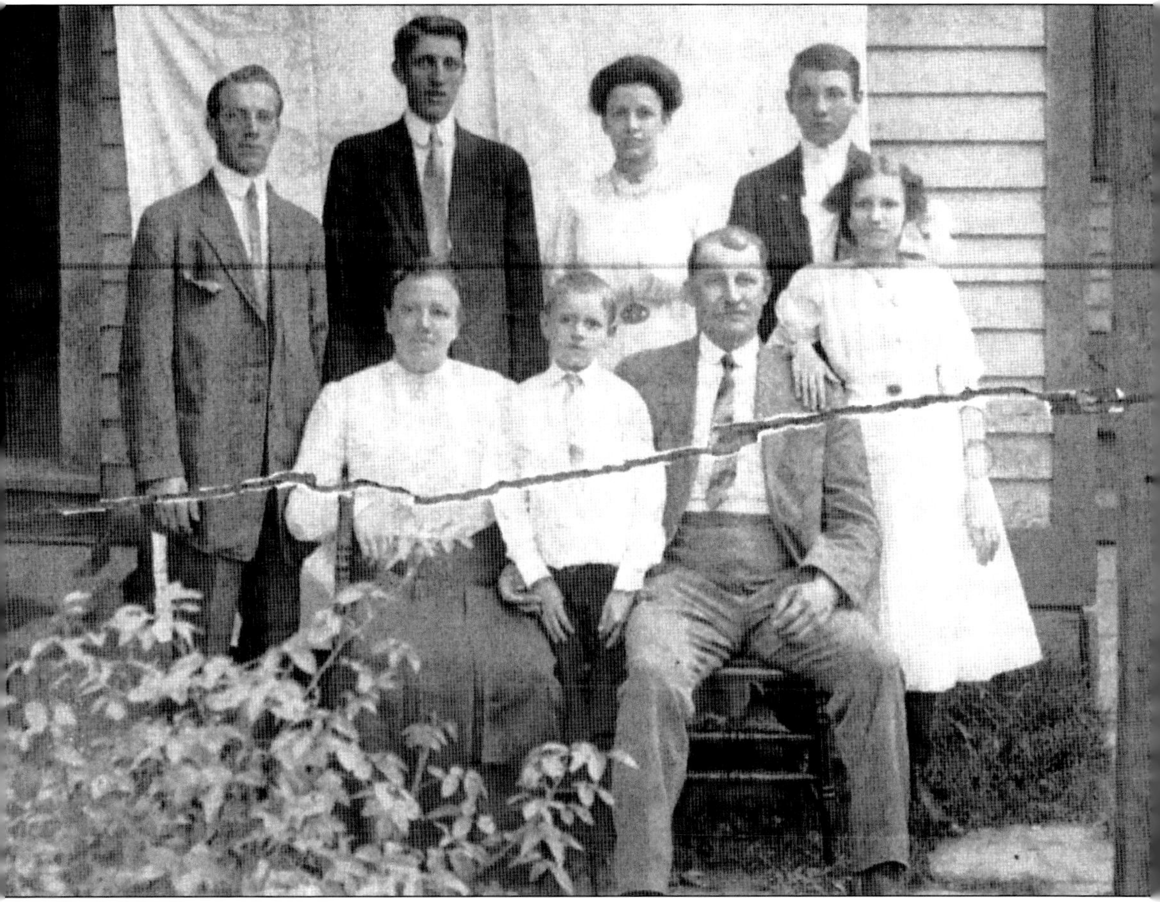

All but one member of the Jobs family are buried in Forest Hill. Pictured from left to right are (first row) Amelia Schmidt Jobs, unidentified, August Jobs Sr., and Theresa Jobs Kaub; (second row) Walter Jobs, Paul Jobs, and two unidentified persons. (Courtesy of Anita Drabor.)

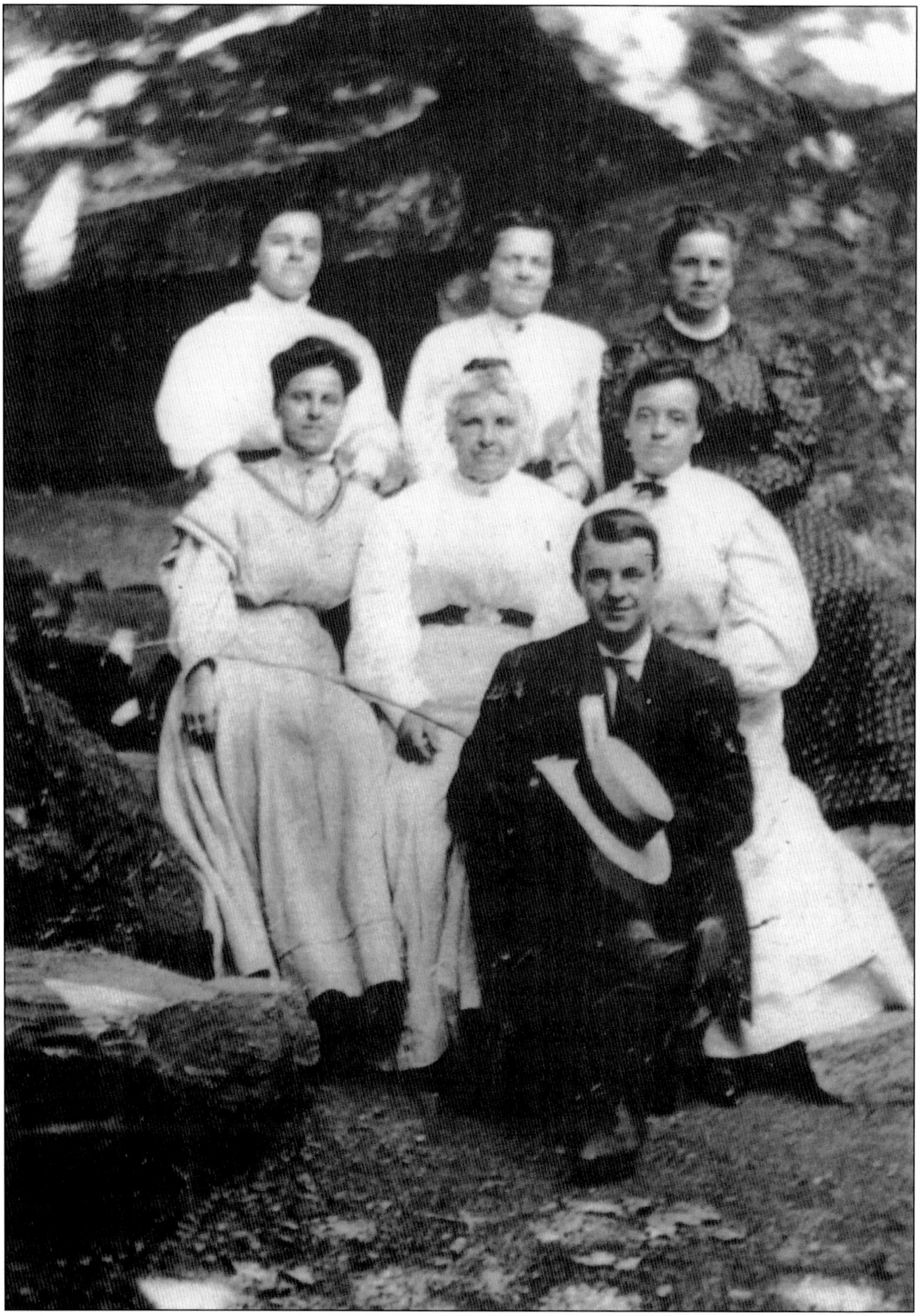

This portrait is of the Walker family, who immigrated to the United States in 1887. Pictured from left to right are (first row, kneeling) Robert Walker; (second row) Robert's sister Emma, his mother Margaret, and sister Margaret; (third row) sisters Elizabeth, Maria, and Sarah. (Courtesy of Sally Morgan.)

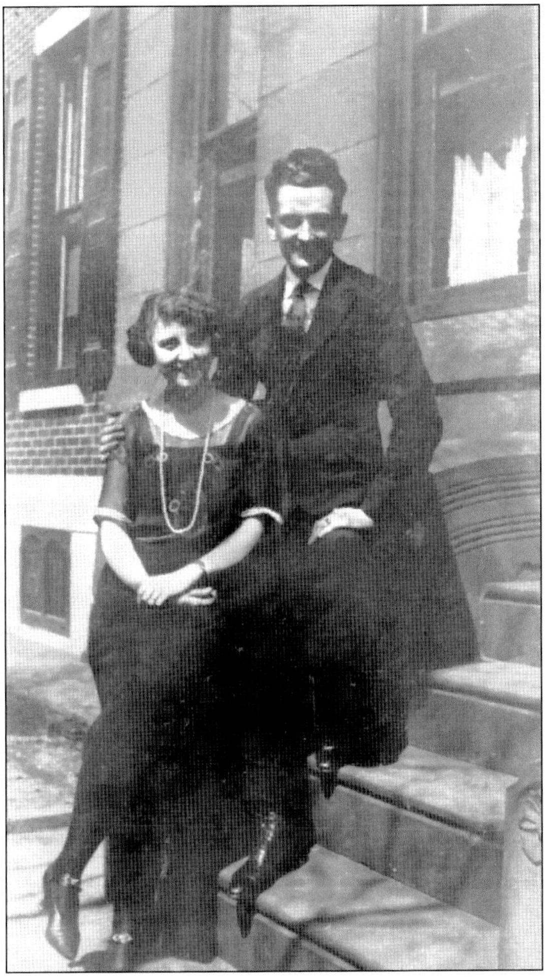 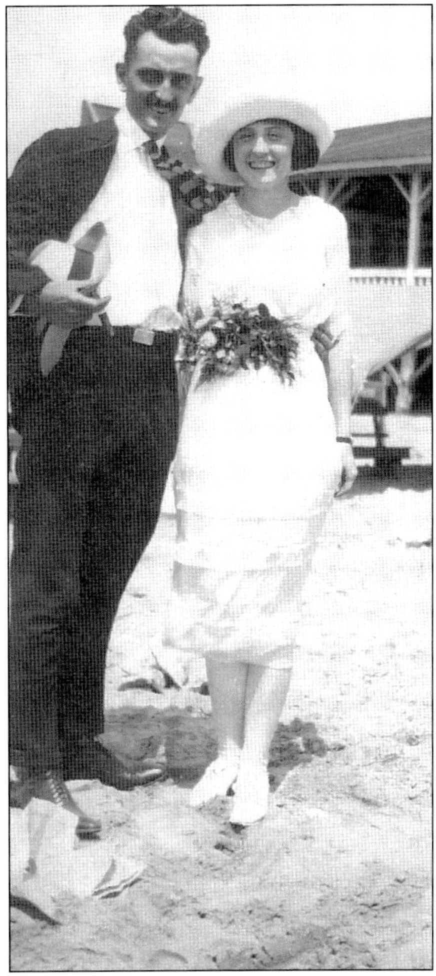

On March 5, 1928, a heinous act sent shockwaves through residents up and down the valley. Russell McGarrah, a 35-year-old former athletic director for Central High School, fatally stabbed his wife, Dorothy Tuckey McGarrah, age 28, two hours after they received the Lord's sacrament in the Asbury Church. Then afterwards, with the 10-inch butcher knife still clutched in his hand, he calmly related the events to Rev. J.W. Nicholson. Upon leaving church, the couple left their only son, Jack, age five, in the care of Russell's sister and then returned to their Green Ridge home. At home, Russell claims he saw a piece of white rope lying on the davenport in the living room. This stirred the thought in him that his wife was planning to strangle him, a thought he had become increasingly obsessed with. According to his confession, the couple sat in the living room and read for a while before Dorothy rose from the couch and started toward the kitchen. Russell followed closely behind, and once there, he grabbed the butcher knife from the drawer and attacked her without so much as an exchange of words. Russell and Dorothy are pictured here during happier times. (Both, courtesy of Dorothy McGarrah.)

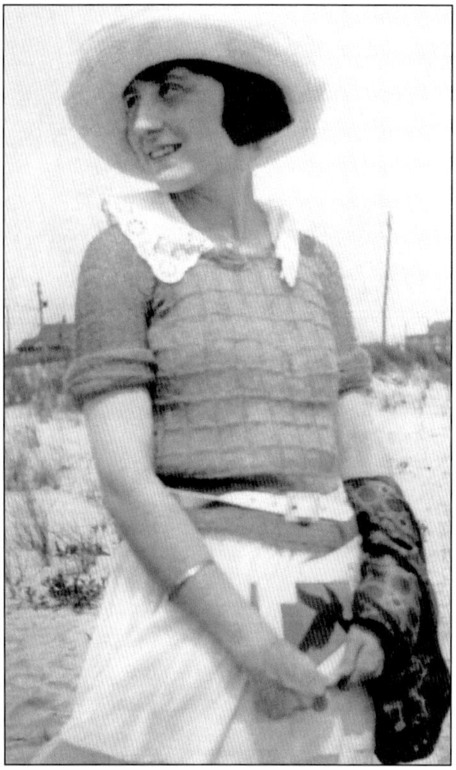

Dorothy Tuckey McGarrah was stabbed 12 times in various places on her body. The deep wound that severed the upper region of her heart caused almost instant death, according to the coroner's report. That Dorothy fought for her life was evident by the fact the tip of one finger had been severed by trying to ward off the knife from striking her. Because Russell believed he "had done what was right," he did not hurry to notify anyone of the crime. Another three hours would pass before he sought out his pastor to make the confession. Upon hearing the horrendous details, Reverend Nicholson advised McGarrah to turn himself into the authorities, which he readily consented to do so. The police found Dorothy's body lying in a pool of blood near the bathtub. They never did discover the "white rope" McGarrah claimed to have seen. Dorothy is pictured at left and below with her son Jack. (Both, courtesy of Dorothy McGarrah.)

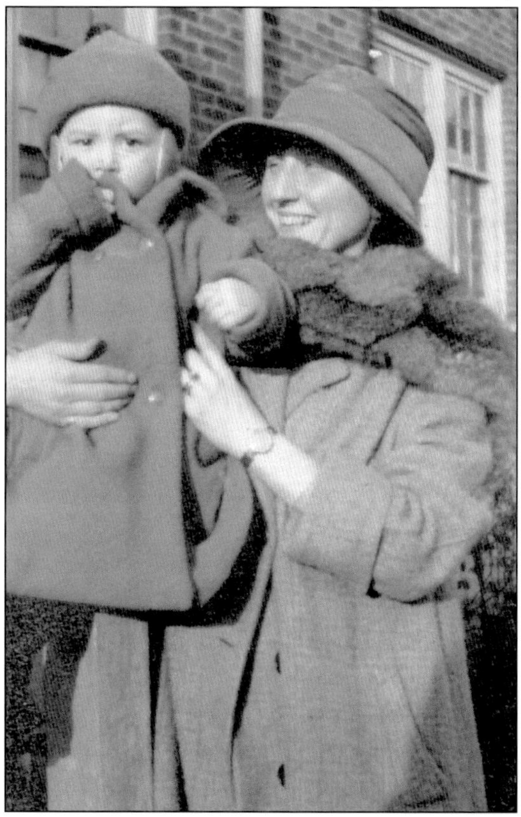

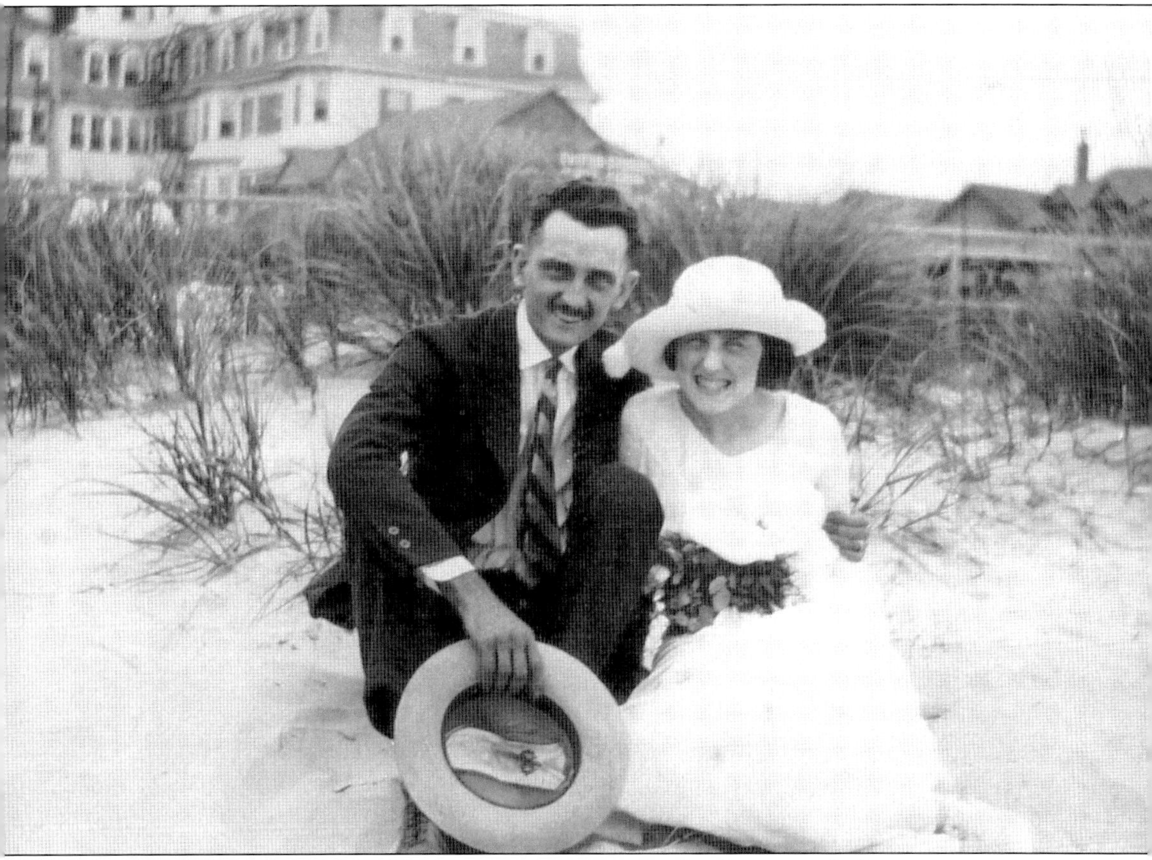

Family, friends, and neighbors felt there was no motive for the slaying, and all were in agreement that the couple's home life was ideal. One explanation was that a year prior, Russell had suffered a nervous breakdown and was forced to stay away from work for quite some time. Many, reportedly, ignored the fact that Russell was never quite the same afterwards. According to news reports in the days following the murder, detective A.J. Reilly said McGarrah expressed no sorrow for his actions; he appeared well rested and was hungry and anxious for a cup of coffee. Upon answering questions, he continued to repeat the words, "I feel I did right. I did what my conscience told me. It was either she or I." Russell was convicted and sent to the Fairview State Hospital for the Criminally Insane, where he died in 1958. (Courtesy of Dorothy McGarrah)

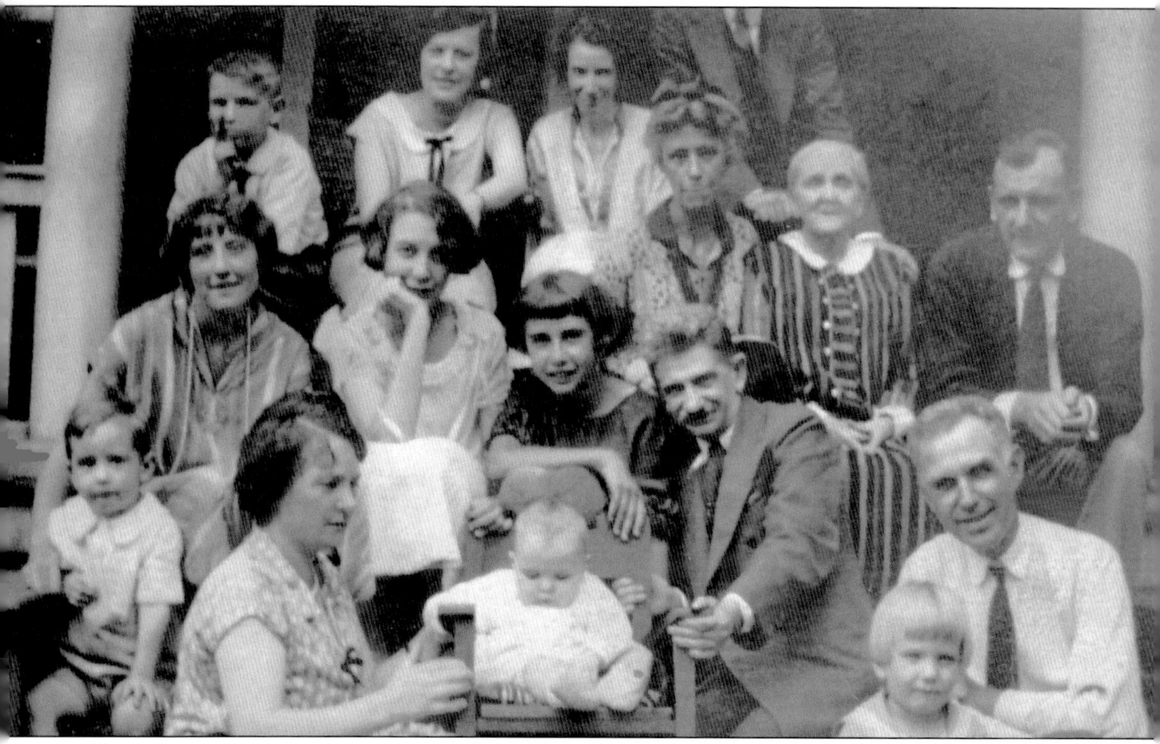

Dorothy and her family are pictured during happier times on Labor Day. Dorothy sits in the second row to the left, with little Jack below her. Next to her, with her chin in her hand, is one of her relative's named Anne Swartz, or as the family called her, "Tudy." Next to Anne, with her arms on the chair, is her sister Katherine, who was known lovingly as "Kit." (Courtesy of Dorothy McGarrah.)

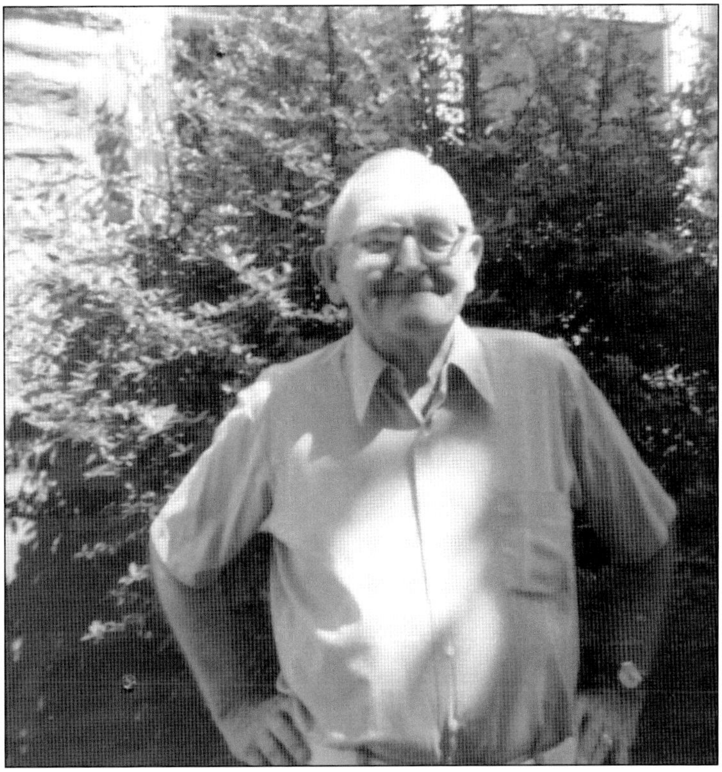

Bob Stroh (right), born July 14, 1919, was a descendant of cemetery founder Elisha Phinney and is buried on the same lot. He was a captain in World War II and worked as a salesman/manager for Coca Cola. Pictured below is his wife, Julia, born February 2, 1918, who was very fond of reading. Bob died on May 16, 1988, and Julia followed on January 2, 2006. (Both, courtesy of Forest Hill Archives.)

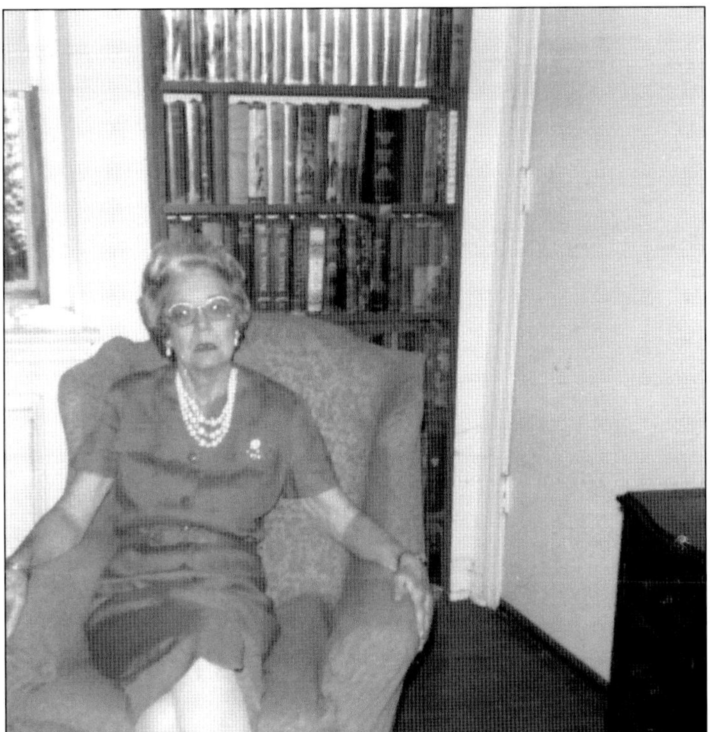

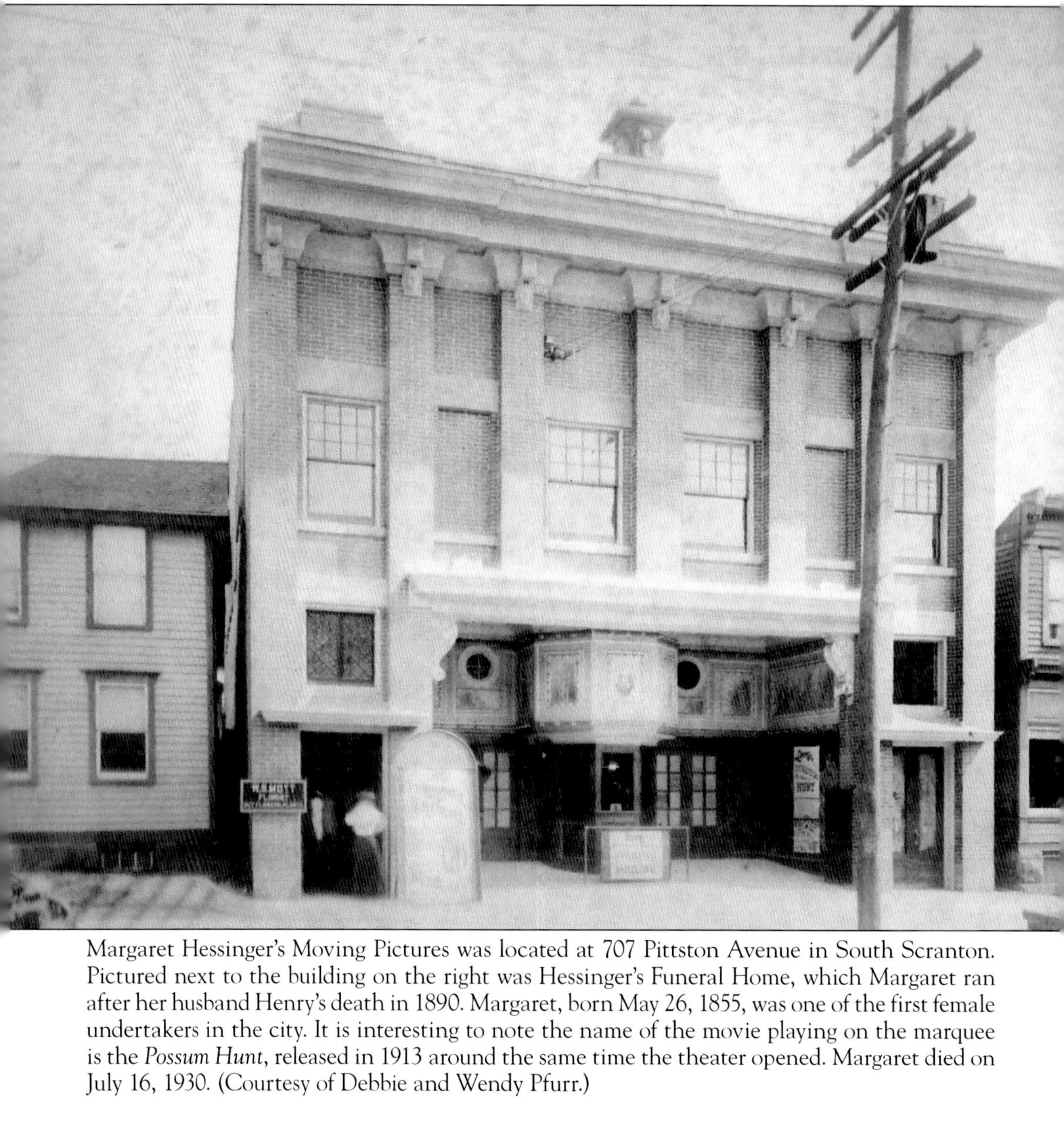

Margaret Hessinger's Moving Pictures was located at 707 Pittston Avenue in South Scranton. Pictured next to the building on the right was Hessinger's Funeral Home, which Margaret ran after her husband Henry's death in 1890. Margaret, born May 26, 1855, was one of the first female undertakers in the city. It is interesting to note the name of the movie playing on the marquee is the *Possum Hunt*, released in 1913 around the same time the theater opened. Margaret died on July 16, 1930. (Courtesy of Debbie and Wendy Pfurr.)

Six

ORGANIZATIONS

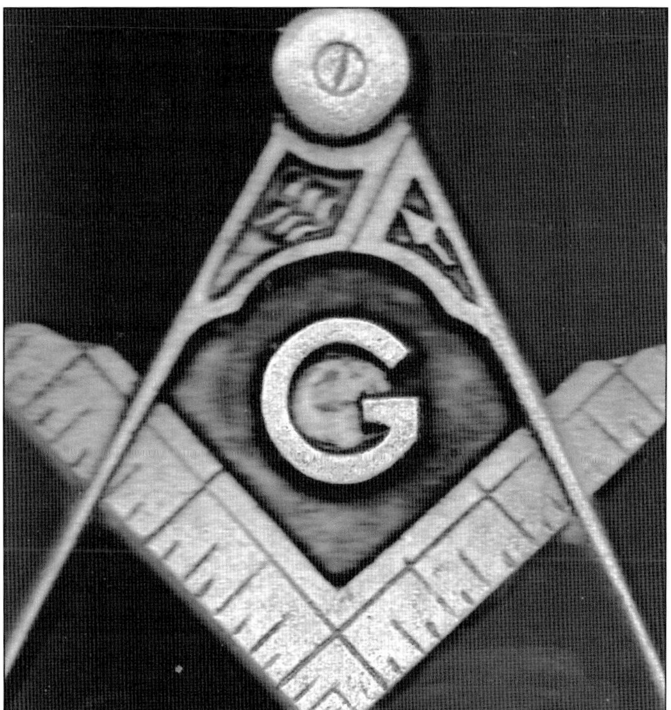

The symbolic flag holders pictured on the following pages represent military and fraternal organizations that the deceased belonged to. These are just a few one may encounter as they tour the Forest Hill Cemetery. Many Freemasons reside at Forest Hill. No one knows for certain the exact date the Masonic fraternity was formed; however, historians believe it arose from the Stonemasons Guild during the Middle Ages. Throughout the centuries, Freemasonry developed into a worldwide fraternity with members that included George Washington, Benjamin Franklin, and Paul Revere, just to name a few. (Courtesy of Forest Hill Archives.)

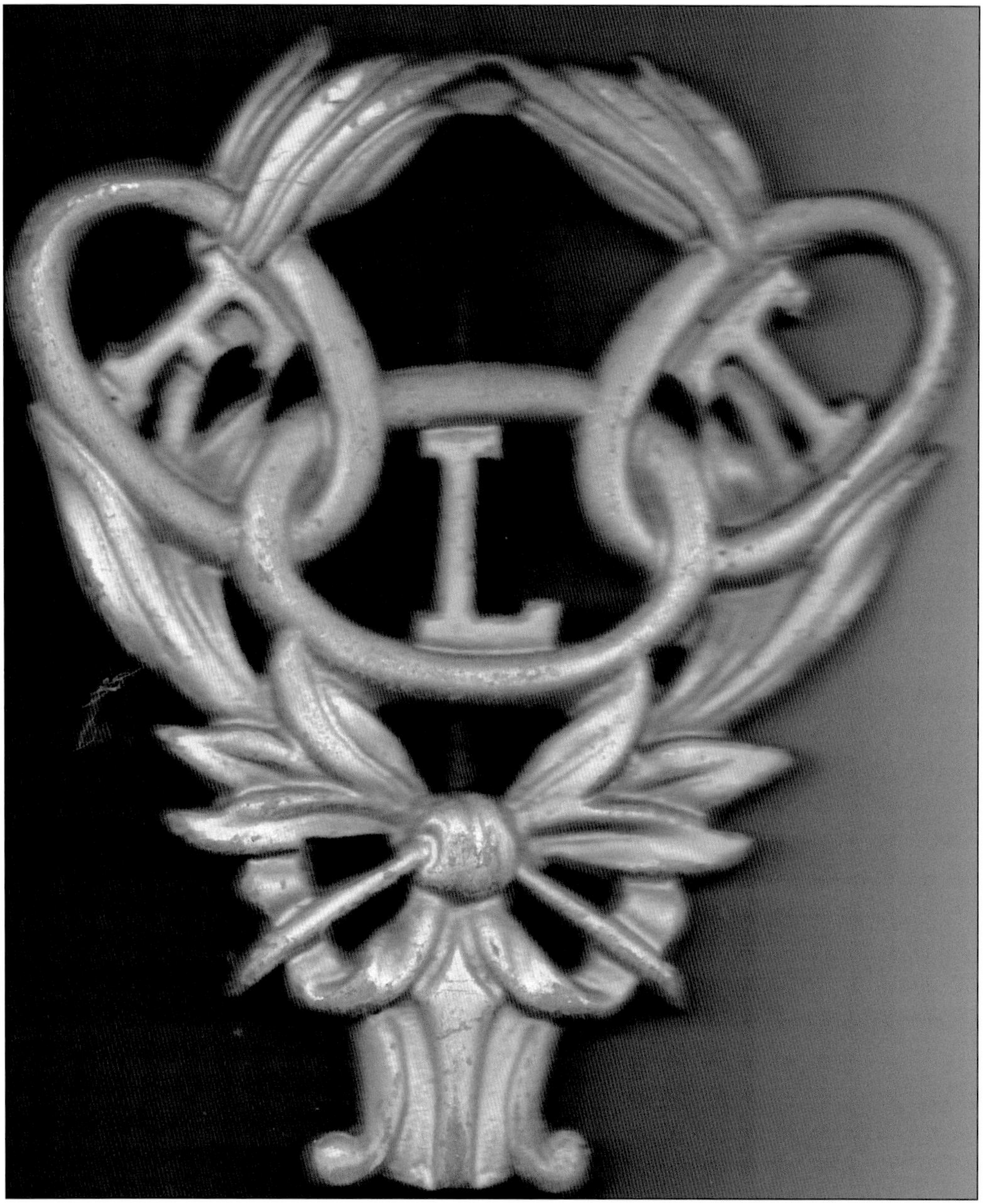

The Independent Order of Odd Fellows is a benevolent fraternal organization derived from the British Odd Fellows service organizations, which came into being during the 1700s. Some say they were called "Odd" because the beginning of the Odd Fellowship in the 18th century was during the time of industrialization, and it was considered odd to find noble values such as benevolence, charity, and fraternalism. The first Odd Fellows Lodge organized in Scranton was Lackawanna Lodge No. 291, instituted on March 16, 1848, in the village then known as Harrison, better known as Slocum Hollow. (Courtesy of Forest Hill Archives.)

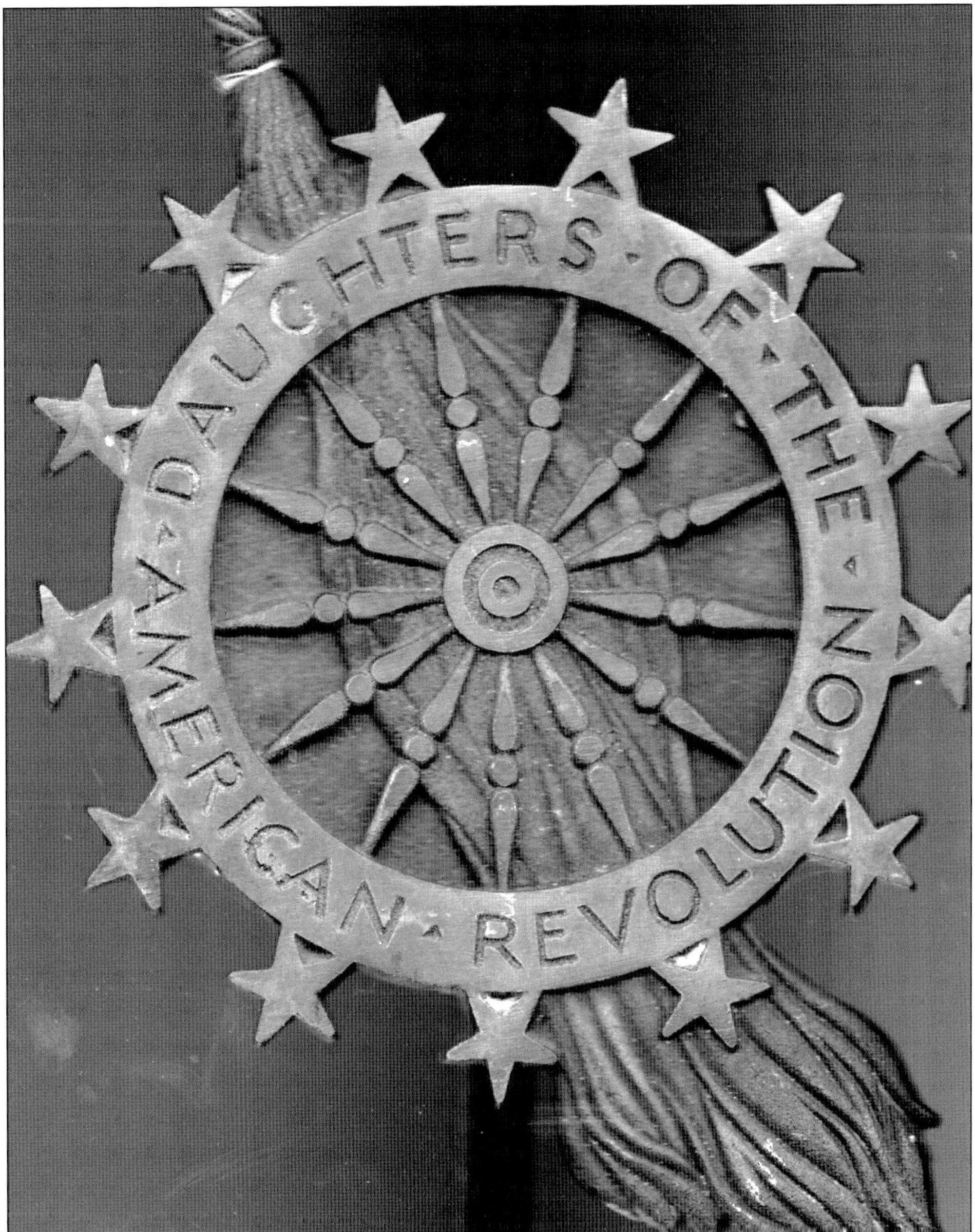

The Daughters of the American Revolution was founded on October 11, 1890, by Mary S. Lockwood, Ellen Walworth, Mary Desha, and Eugenia Washington. At the time, women were excluded from men's organizations that were formed to honor their patriotic ancestors. Based upon their frustration, a group of women formed the Daughters of the American Revolution (DAR) to show their patriotism. (Courtesy of Forest Hill Archives.)

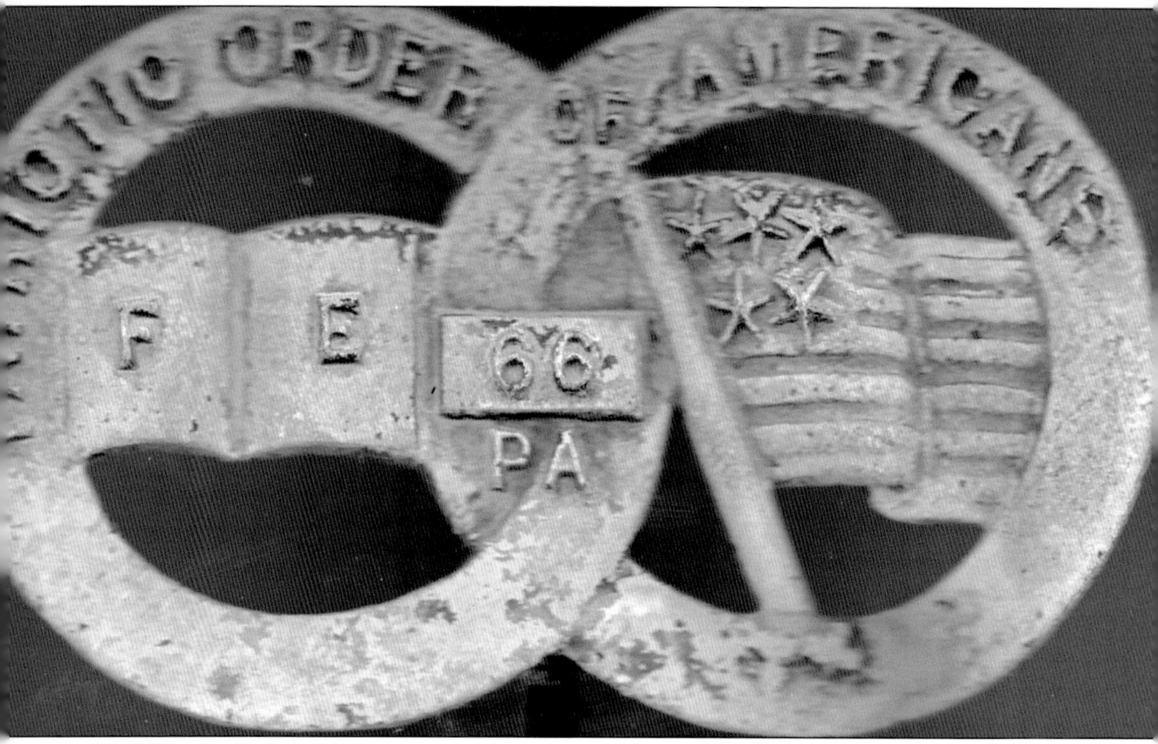

The Patriotic Order of Americans was the ladies' auxiliary of the Patriotic Order Sons of America. It was founded in 1847 to uphold the principles of Americanism and duty to the flag. (Courtesy of Forest Hill Archives.)

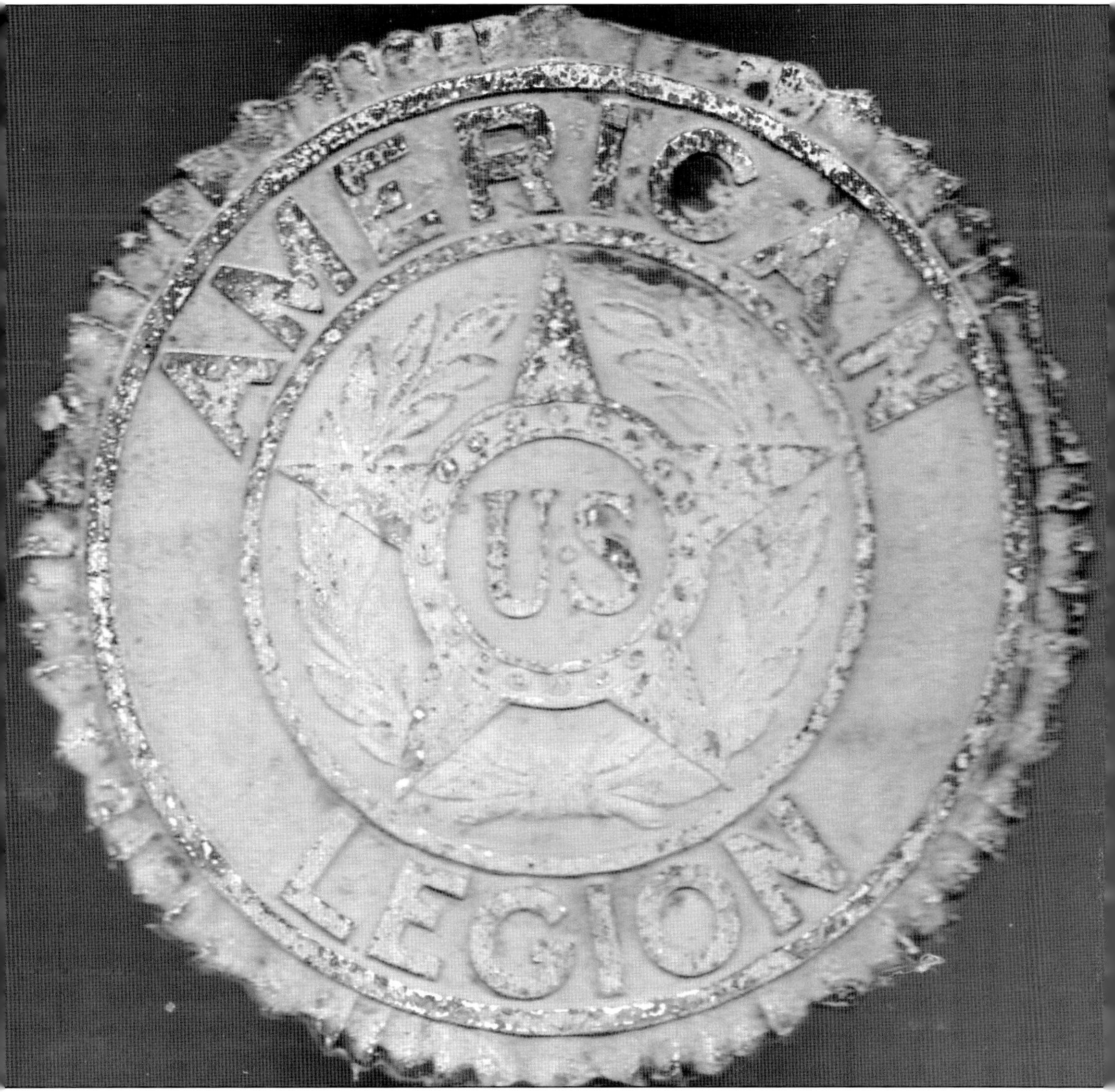

The American Legion was chartered in 1919 by Congress as a patriotic veteran organization. Its founders were Theodore Roosevelt Jr., Franklin D'Olier, and Eric Fisher Wood. (Courtesy of Forest Hill Archives.)

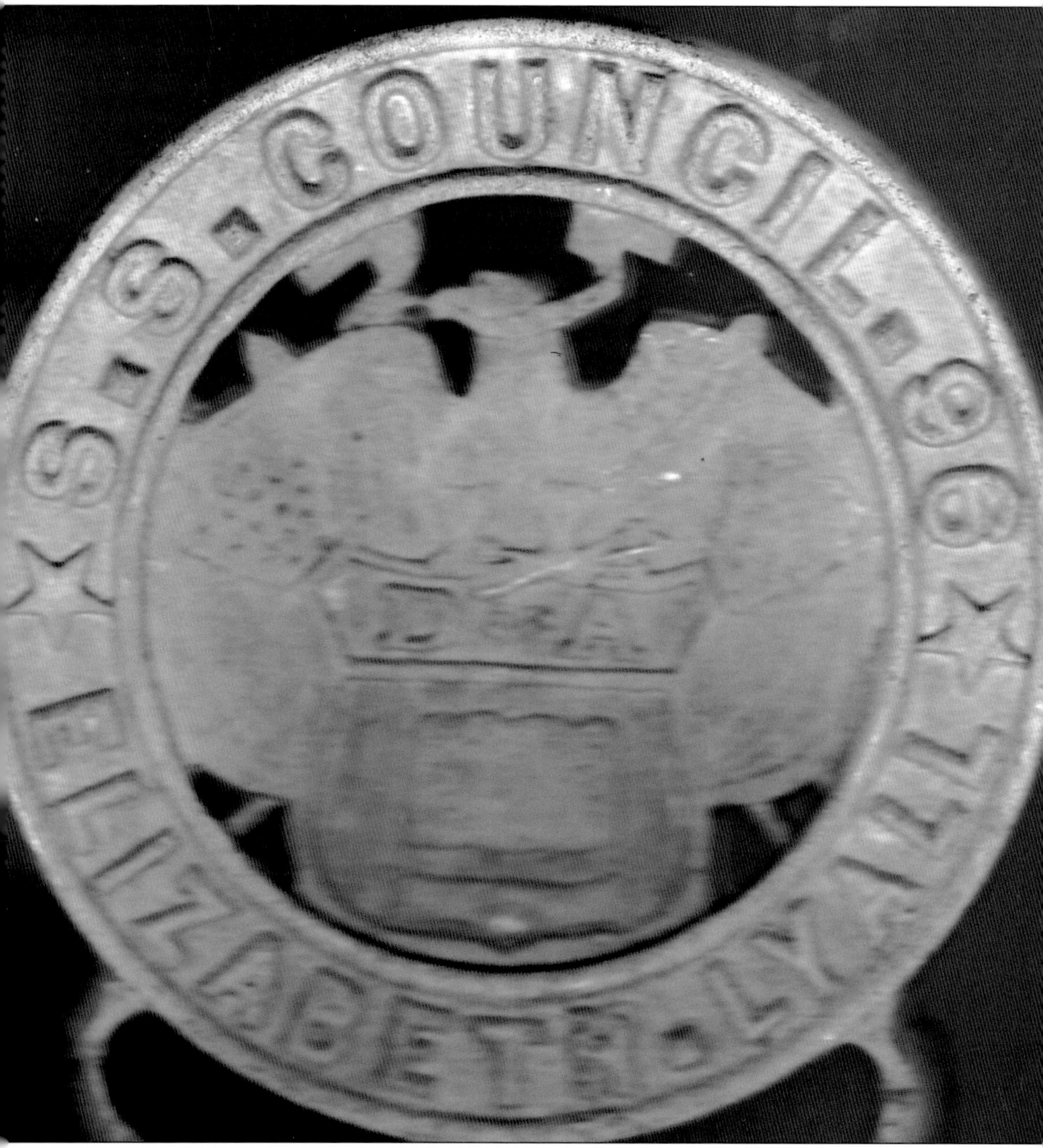

Daughters of America, not to be confused with the Daughters of the American Revolution, was founded in the later part of the 19th century. It is known for being an anti-immigrant movement. (Courtesy of Forest Hill Archives.)

The police department flag holders are used to honor the men and women who served in law enforcement. The mission statement for the Scranton Police Department is "to protect and preserve life and property; to understand and serve the needs of the Scranton Neighborhoods and to improve the quality of life by maintaining order, recognizing and resolving community problems, and apprehending criminals." (Courtesy of Forest Hill Archives.)

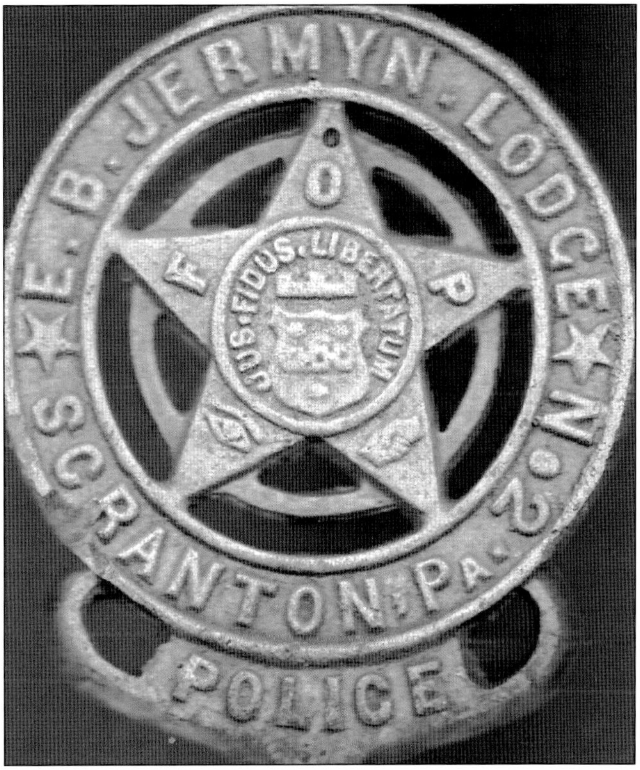

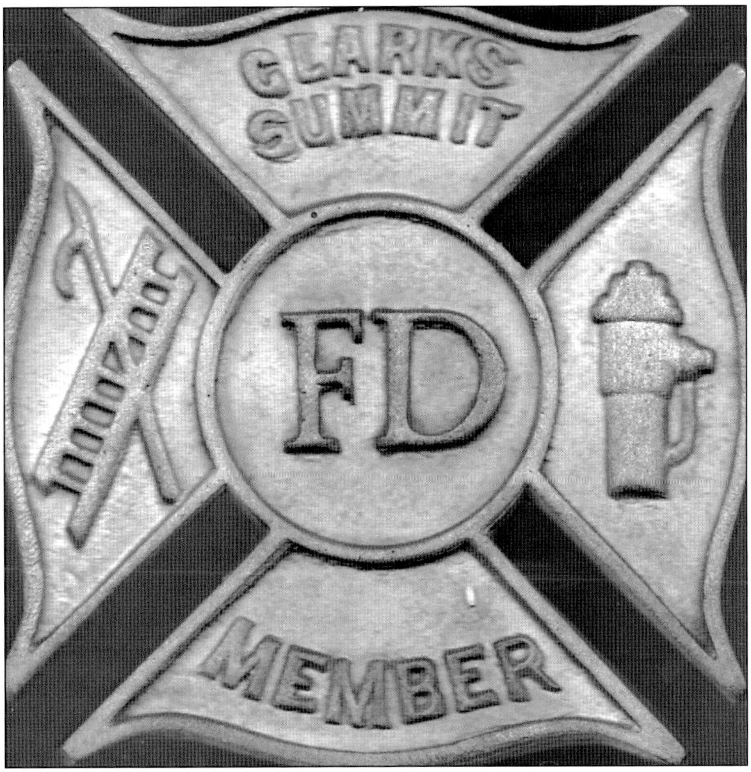

The fire department grave markers honor many of the brave first responders who are buried in Forest Hill Cemetery. Fire Chief Ferber is one of many who have this flag holder on their grave. (Courtesy of Forest Hill Archives.)

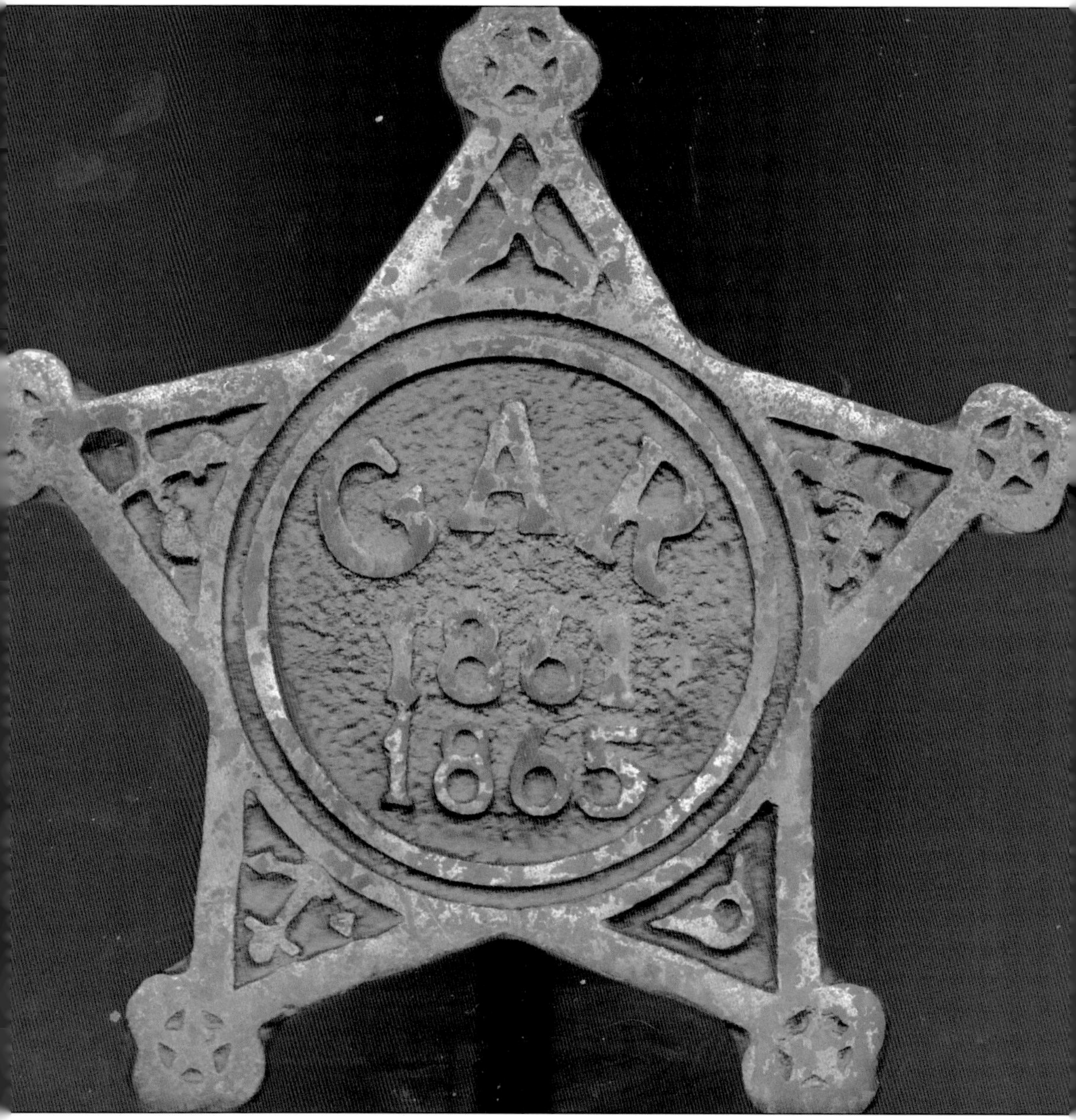

The Grand Army of the Republic flag holders mark the graves of Union soldiers who fought in the Civil War, from 1861 to 1865. Many of the Civil War soldiers buried in the cemetery were members of the Griffin Post No. 139 of the GAR. (Courtesy of Forest Hill Archives.)

There are only two of these markers in Forest Hill for the Confederate US veterans, and they mark the graves of Edward Clarke and John Knoble. (Courtesy of Forest Hill Archives.)

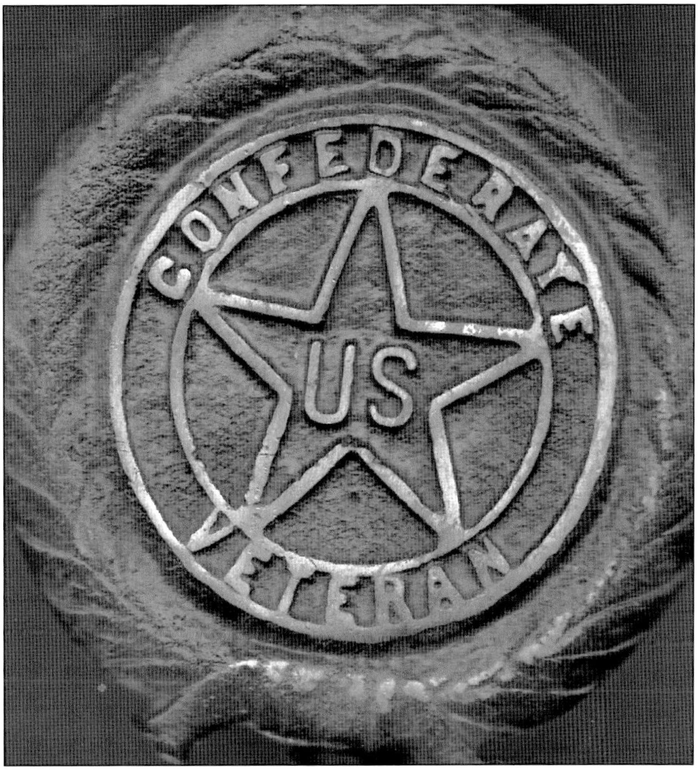

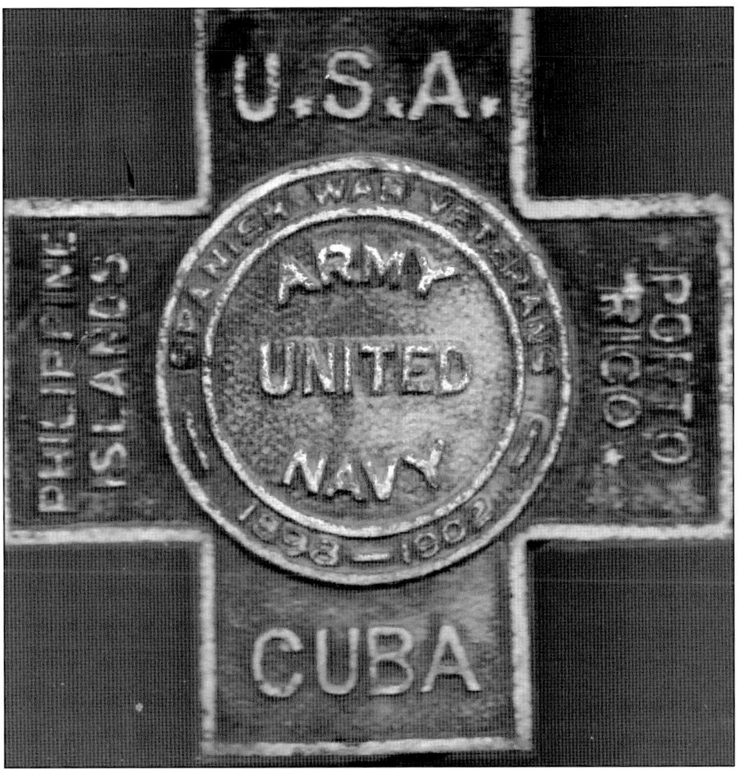

There are an estimated 24 veterans who fought in the Spanish American War buried in Forest Hill. The United States declared war on Spain following the sinking of the battleship *Maine* in 1898. (Courtesy of Forest Hill Archives.)

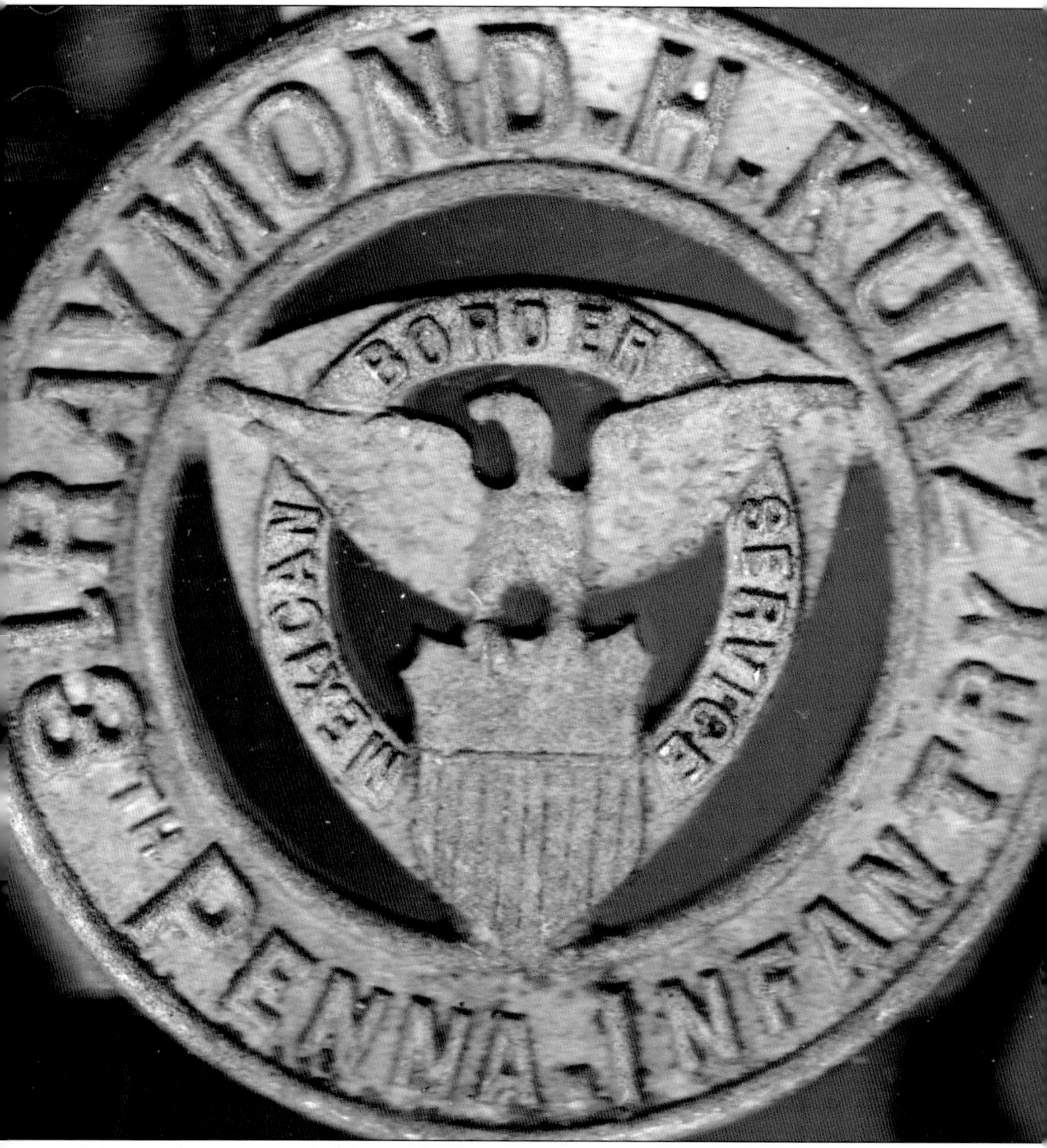

These markers represent the Mexican Border Service prior to World War I. This marks the Raymond H. Kunz grave, 13th Pennsylvania Volunteer Infantry, Scranton. It is very unusual to have the veteran's name on the marker, as seen in the photograph. (Courtesy of Forest Hill Archives.)

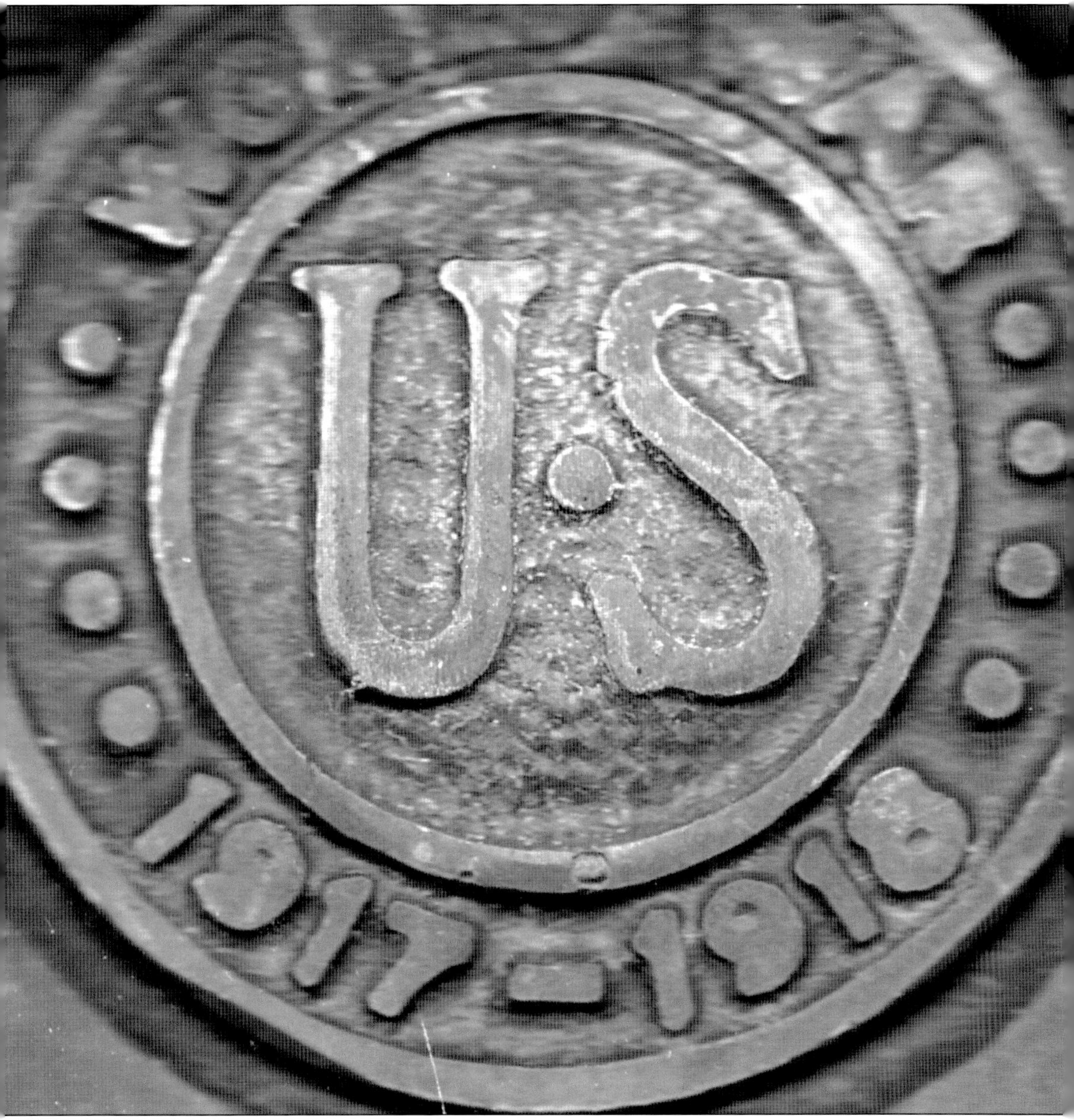

It is interesting to note that the original flag holders for World War I veterans did not have "I" on them, as there were no other wars anticipated at the time. (Courtesy of Forest Hill Archives.)

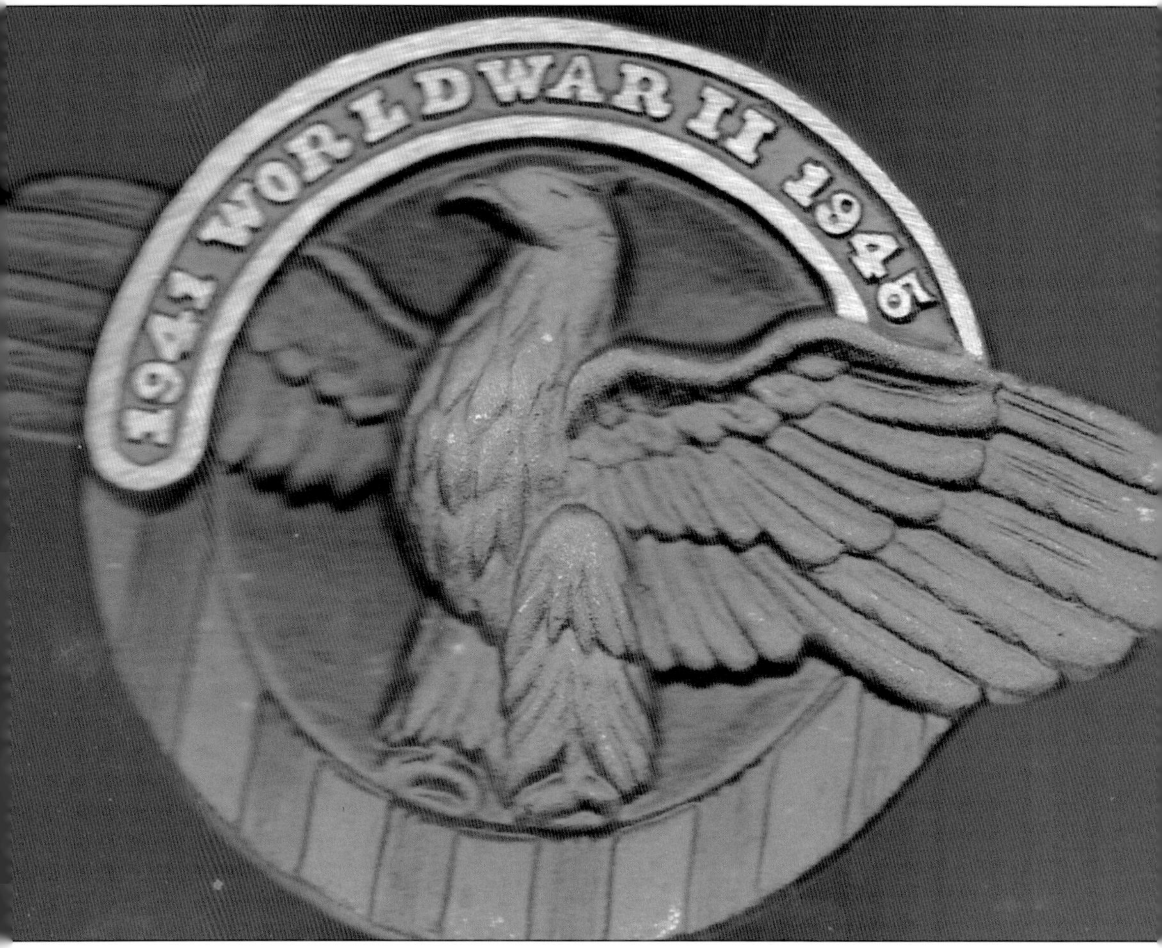

The men and women who served in World War II (1941–1945) will always be memorialized at Forest Hill as "the Greatest Generation." World War II is still considered the deadliest conflict in human history. (Courtesy of Forest Hill Archives.)

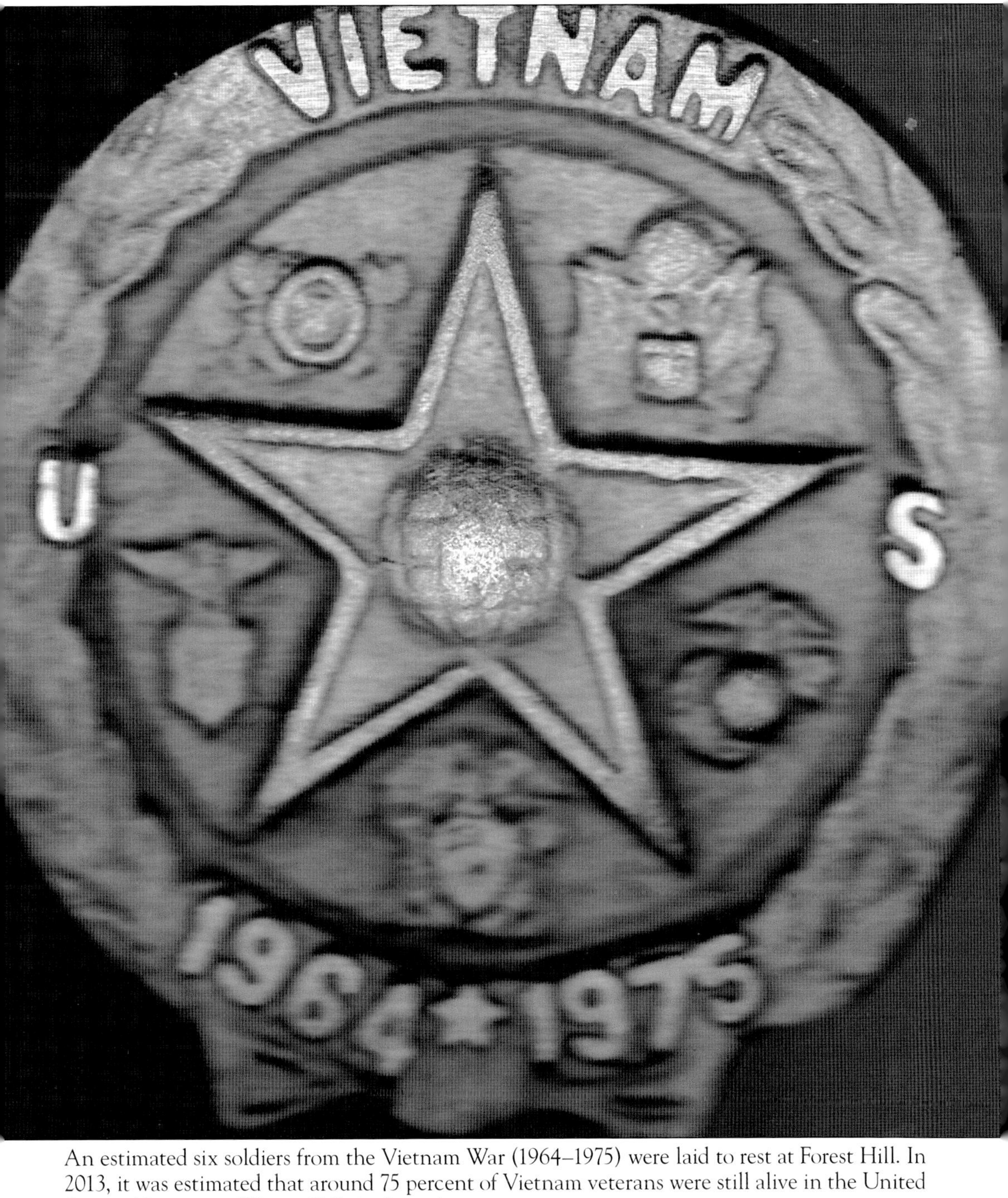

An estimated six soldiers from the Vietnam War (1964–1975) were laid to rest at Forest Hill. In 2013, it was estimated that around 75 percent of Vietnam veterans were still alive in the United States. (Courtesy of Forest Hill Archives.)

Consistent with our mission to preserve history on a local level, this book was printed in South Carolina on American-made paper and manufactured entirely in the United States. Products carrying the accredited Forest Stewardship Council (FSC) label are printed on 100 percent FSC-certified paper.

MADE IN THE USA